Stability, Periodicity, and Related Problems in Fractional-Order Systems

Stability, Periodicity, and Related Problems in Fractional-Order Systems

Editors

Michal Fečkan
Marius-F. Danca

MDPI • Basel • Beijing • Wuhan • Barcelona • Belgrade • Manchester • Tokyo • Cluj • Tianjin

Editors
Michal Fečkan
Comenius University in
Bratislava
Slovak Academy of Sciences
Slovakia

Marius-F. Danca
STAR-UBB Institute
Babes-Bolyai University
Romanian Institute of Science and Technology
Romania

Editorial Office
MDPI
St. Alban-Anlage 66
4052 Basel, Switzerland

This is a reprint of articles from the Special Issue published online in the open access journal *Mathematics* (ISSN 2227-7390) (available at: https://www.mdpi.com/journal/mathematics/special_issues/Stability_Periodicity_and_Related_Problems_in_Fractional_Order_Systems).

For citation purposes, cite each article independently as indicated on the article page online and as indicated below:

LastName, A.A.; LastName, B.B.; LastName, C.C. Article Title. *Journal Name* **Year**, *Volume Number*, Page Range.

ISBN 978-3-0365-4589-9 (Hbk)
ISBN 978-3-0365-4590-5 (PDF)

© 2022 by the authors. Articles in this book are Open Access and distributed under the Creative Commons Attribution (CC BY) license, which allows users to download, copy and build upon published articles, as long as the author and publisher are properly credited, which ensures maximum dissemination and a wider impact of our publications.

The book as a whole is distributed by MDPI under the terms and conditions of the Creative Commons license CC BY-NC-ND.

Contents

About the Editors . . . . **vii**

Michal Fečkan and Marius-F. Danca
Stability, Periodicity, and Related Problems in Fractional-Order Systems
Reprinted from: *Mathematics* **2022**, *10*, 2040, doi:10.3390/math10122040 . . . . **1**

Humaira, Muhammad Sarwar, Thabet Abdeljawad, Nabil Mlaiki
Fixed Point Results via Least Upper Bound Property and Its Applications to Fuzzy Caputo Fractional Volterra–Fredholm Integro-Differential Equations
Reprinted from: *Mathematics* **2021**, *9*, 1969, doi:10.3390/math9161969 . . . . **3**

Marius-F. Danca, Michal Fečkan, Nikolay Kuznetsov and Guanrong Chen
Coupled Discrete Fractional-Order Logistic Maps
Reprinted from: *Mathematics* **2021**, *9*, 2204, doi:10.3390/math9182204 . . . . **21**

Abdulkafi M. Saeed, Mohammed S. Abdo and Mdi Begum Jeelani
Existence and Ulam–Hyers Stability of a Fractional-Order Coupled System in the Frame of Generalized Hilfer Derivatives
Reprinted from: *Mathematics* **2021**, *9*, 2543, doi:10.3390/math9202543 . . . . **35**

Muath Awadalla, Kinda Abuasbeh, Muthaiah Subramanian, Murugesan Manigandan
On a System of ψ- Caputo Hybrid Fractional Differential Equations with Dirichlet Boundary Conditions
Reprinted from: *Mathematics* **2022**, *10*, 1681, doi:10.3390/math10101681 . . . . **53**

Muthaiah Subramanian , Jehad Alzabut, Mohamed I. Abbas, Chatthai Thaiprayoon and Weerawat Sudsutad
Existence of Solutions for Coupled Higher-Order Fractional Integro-Differential Equations with Nonlocal Integral and Multi-Point Boundary Conditions Depending on Lower-Order Fractional Derivatives and Integrals
Reprinted from: *Mathematics* **2022**, *10*, 1823, doi:10.3390/math10111823 . . . . **69**

About the Editors

Michal Fečkan

Michal Fečkan has been a Professor of Mathematics at the Department of Mathematical Analysis and Numerical Mathematics in the Faculty of Mathematics, Physics and Informatics at the Comenius University in Bratislava, Slovak Republic since 2003. He received his master's degree from Comenius University in Bratislava in 1985 and PhD from the Mathematical Institute of Slovak Academy of Sciences in Bratislava, Slovak Republic in 1993. He is interested in nonlinear functional analysis, bifurcation theory, dynamical systems and fractional calculus with applications to mechanics, vibrations and economics. He is a Highly Cited Researcher in Mathematics.

Marius-F. Danca

Marius-F. Danca graduated from Babes-Bolyai University of Cluj-Napoca, Romania, Faculty of Mathematics and Computer Science, and Technical University of Cluj-Napoca, Romania, Faculty of Electronics, Telecommunications and Information Technology. Obtained a PhD in Engineering, Faculty of Automation and Computer Science, Technical University of Cluj-Napoca, Department of Automation and the PhD in Mathematics, Faculty of Mathematics and Computer Science, Babes-Bolyai University. He has more than 90 WOS papers with 1000+ WOS citations (he is a highly cited author in the top 1% of the academic field of Mathematics), WOS IF 20, and he is in the top 100,000 (2%) scientists by citation score (Scopus Data Base 2019, 2020).

Editorial

Stability, Periodicity, and Related Problems in Fractional-Order Systems

Michal Fečkan [1,2] and Marius-F. Danca [3,4,*]

[1] Department of Mathematical Analysis and Numerical Mathematics, Comenius University in Bratislava, 842 48 Bratislava, Slovakia; michal.feckan@fmph.uniba.sk
[2] Mathematical Institute of Slovak Academy of Sciences, Štefánikova 49, 814 73 Bratislava, Slovakia
[3] STAR-UBB Institute, Babes-Bolyai University, 400084 Cluj-Napoca, Romania
[4] Romanian Institute of Science and Technology, 400487 Cluj-Napoca, Romania
* Correspondence: danca@rist.ro

Abstract: This Special Issue aims to collect new perspectives on the trends in both theory and applications of stability of fractional order continuous and discrete systems, analytical and numerical approaches, and any related problems regarding (but not limited to) time-delayed systems and impulsive systems in all fields of science, as well as engineering and multidisciplinary applications.

Keywords: fractional-order system; stability; periodic solution; fractional calculus

MSC: 37N30; 34K37; 26A33

Citation: Fečkan, M.; Danca, M.-F. Stability, Periodicity, and Related Problems in Fractional-Order Systems. *Mathematics* **2022**, *10*, 2040. https://doi.org/10.3390/math10122040

Received: 2 June 2022
Accepted: 7 June 2022
Published: 12 June 2022

Publisher's Note: MDPI stays neutral with regard to jurisdictional claims in published maps and institutional affiliations.

Copyright: © 2022 by the authors. Licensee MDPI, Basel, Switzerland. This article is an open access article distributed under the terms and conditions of the Creative Commons Attribution (CC BY) license (https://creativecommons.org/licenses/by/4.0/).

This paper contains the submissions [1–5] invited to a Special Issue of *Mathematics* on "Stability, Periodicity, and Related Problems in Fractional-Order Systems".

Fractional-order systems (FOSs), which are said to have fractional dynamics, are modeled by differential equations with non-integer derivatives. Integrals and derivatives of fractional orders illustrate objects with power-law nonlocality, power-law long-range dependence (time history), or fractal properties. FOSs are used to study behavior in nonlinear chaotic systems in electrochemistry, biology, viscoelasticity, physics, etc.

The response to our call for this Special Issue resulted in the following statistics for both published and rejected items: 12 total submissions, of which 5 research articles were published (41.66%), and 7 were rejected (58.3%).

The technical topics covered in the five articles published in this book include:

- The existence and uniqueness of solutions for a nonlinear coupled system of Liouville–Caputo-type fractional integrodifferential equations supplemented with non-local discrete and integral boundary conditions [1] for a coupled system of ψ-Caputo hybrid fractional derivatives of the order of $1 < v \leq 2$ subjected to Dirichlet boundary conditions [2].
- A study of a class of a coupled system of fractional integrodifferential equations in the frame of Hilfer fractional derivatives with respect to another function [3].
- A study of a system of coupled discrete fractional-order logistic maps, modeled by Caputo's delta fractional difference in terms of its numerical integration and chaotic dynamics [4].
- An existence theorem for a unique solution to the fuzzy fractional Volterra–Fredholm integrodifferential equations (FCFVFIDEs) to our result involving the Caputo derivative [5].

We found that the paper selections for this book were very inspiring and rewarding. We also thank the editorial staff and reviewers for their efforts and help during the process.

Author Contributions: All authors have read and agreed to the published version of the manuscript.

Funding: M.F. is partially supported by the Slovak Research and Development Agency under the contract No. APVV-18-0308 and by the Slovak Grant Agency VEGA No. 1/0358/20 and No. 2/0127/20.

Conflicts of Interest: The authors declare no conflict of interest.

References

1. Humaira; Sarwar, M.; Abdeljawad, T.; Mlaiki, N. Fixed Point Results via Least Upper Bound Property and Its Applications to Fuzzy Caputo Fractional Volterra–Fredholm Integro-Differential Equations. *Mathematics* **2021**, *9*, 1969. [CrossRef]
2. Danca, M.; Fečkan, M.; Kuznetsov, N.; Chen, G. Coupled Discrete Fractional-Order Logistic Maps. *Mathematics* **2021**, *9*, 2204. [CrossRef]
3. Saeed, A.; Abdo, M.; Jeelani, M. Existence and Ulam–Hyers Stability of a Fractional-Order Coupled System in the Frame of Generalized Hilfer Derivatives. *Mathematics* **2021**, *9*, 2543. [CrossRef]
4. Awadalla, M.; Abuasbeh, K.; Subramanian, M.; Manigandan, M. On a System of ψ-Caputo Hybrid Fractional Differential Equations with Dirichlet Boundary Conditions. *Mathematics* **2022**, *10*, 1681. [CrossRef]
5. Subramanian, M.; Alzabut, J.; Abbas, M.; Thaiprayoon, C.; Sudsutad, W. Existence of Solutions for Coupled Higher-Order Fractional Integro-Differential Equations with Nonlocal Integral and Multi-Point Boundary Conditions Depending on Lower-Order Fractional Derivatives and Integrals. *Mathematics* **2022**, *10*, 1823. [CrossRef]

Article

Fixed Point Results via Least Upper Bound Property and Its Applications to Fuzzy Caputo Fractional Volterra–Fredholm Integro-Differential Equations

Humaira [1], Muhammad Sarwar [1,*], Thabet Abdeljawad [2,*] and Nabil Mlaiki [3]

[1] Department of Mathematics, University of Malakand, Chakdara Dir(L) 18800, Pakistan; humaira.swatpk@gmail.com
[2] Department of Medical Research, China Medical University, Taichung 40402, Taiwan
[3] Department Mathematics and General Sciences, Prince Sultan University, P.O. Box 66833, Riyadh 11586, Saudi Arabia; Nmlaki@psu.edu.sa
* Correspondence: sarwar@uom.edu.pk (M.S.); tabdeljawad@psu.edu.sa (T.A.)

Citation: Humaira; Sarwar, M.; Abdeljawad, T.; Mlaiki, N. Fixed Point Results via Least Upper Bound Property and Its Applications to Fuzzy Caputo Fractional Volterra–Fredholm Integro-Differential Equations. *Mathematics* **2021**, *9*, 1969. https://doi.org/10.3390/math9161969

Academic Editors: Michal Fečkan and Marius-F. Danca

Received: 22 June 2021
Accepted: 6 August 2021
Published: 17 August 2021

Publisher's Note: MDPI stays neutral with regard to jurisdictional claims in published maps and institutional affiliations.

Copyright: © 2021 by the authors. Licensee MDPI, Basel, Switzerland. This article is an open access article distributed under the terms and conditions of the Creative Commons Attribution (CC BY) license (https://creativecommons.org/licenses/by/4.0/).

Abstract: In recent years, complex-valued fuzzy metric spaces (in short CVFMS) were introduced by Shukla et al. (Fixed Point Theory 32 (2018)). This setting is a valuable extension of fuzzy metric spaces with the complex grade of membership function. They also established fixed-point results under contractive condition in the aforementioned spaces and generalized some essential existence results in fixed-point theory. The purpose of this manuscript is to derive some fixed-point results for multivalued mappings enjoying the least upper bound property in CVFMS. Furthermore, we studied the existence theorem for a unique solution to the Fuzzy fractional Volterra–Fredholm integro-differential equations (FCFVFIDEs) as an application to our derived result involving the Caputo derivative.

Keywords: complex-valued fuzzy metric space; fuzzy mappings; fixed-point; cauchy sequence and contractive condition; least upper bound property

MSC: Primary 47H10; Secondary 54H25

1. Introduction

It is a well-known fact that metric fixed-point theory is developed by Banach fixed-point theorem. This result is widely applied in nonlinear functional analysis. Indeed, it is the abstract setting of the successive approximation method to investigate the solution of differential equations. Additionally, the advances made in fixed-point theory are applied to differential equations and integral equations. Specifically, fixed-point theory has applications in nonlinear fractional differential equations.

Mathematical tools such as mathematical logics and mathematical arithmetic etc. are used to modal many natural phenomena. However, it is not easy to obtain the deterministic models of mathematical problems using the above-mentioned tools. Such models also have some vagueness and errors. To obtain or reduce the errors and vagueness, it is essential to introduce another way of modeling and investigating solutions. In 1965, Zadeh introduced the fuzzy sets concept [1]. In recent years, fuzzy sets were applied in many applied branches of science and engineering. This concept has clear advantages over deterministic-stochastic problems. Observing these applications, the mathematical models are converted to fuzzy fields, which form a natural association with between crisp and fuzzy problems, as well as having a natural association between fuzzy fractional and fuzzy non-fractional problems.

Agarwal et al. solved fuzzy fractional differential equations in the sense of the Riemann–Liouville dirivative. Following this, several authors have extended the definitions of generalized gH-differentiability, Caputo derivative and different types of integral equations in fuzzy field. For example Ahmad et al. [2] performed an analysis of fuzzy fractional order Volterra–Fredholm integro-differentials. In [3], the authors studied fuzzy fractional differentail equations under a generalized Caputo derivative. Hoa [4] studied a fuzzy fractional functional integral and differental equations. Moreover, fuzzy fractional functional differential equations under Caputo gH-differentiability were investigated in [5]. Using the Caputo–Katagampola fractional derivative approach, Hoa et al. [6] studied fuzzy fractional differential equations. In 2020, using the concept of kernal ψ-functions, Vu and Hoa [7] investigated the applications of contractive-like mapping principal to fuzzy fractional integral equations. A variety of fuzzy fractional differential and integral equation applications, in different fields of the sciences, such as electrochemistry, physics, economy, chemistry, electromagnetic, viscoelasticity and control theory, are present in the literature—for example, [8–13].

Classically, a fuzzy set is associated with a membership function, which assigns a numerical value ranging between zero and one to each of its elements. In other words, that fuzzy set is the generalization of the traditional set. Ramot et al. proposed complex fuzzy sets, which are characterized by complex valued membership functions [14]. This extension looks like an extension from real numbers to complex numbers. After this, complex fuzzy sets and logics were systematically reviewed by some authors [15]. Nadler introduced the concept of multivalued contraction mappings and obtained the fixed-point results [16]. Heilpern established the idea of fuzzy contractions, which represents the fuzzy generalization of Banach's contraction principle [17]. Continuing this, Weiss and Butnairu also obtained fixed points of fuzzy mappings [18,19]. Kramosil and Michalek established the notion of fuzzy metric space [20]. Grabiec followed the work of Kramosil, Michalek and obtained the fuzzy version of the Banach contraction principle [21]. George and Veeramani modified the setting of fuzzy metric spaces due to Kramosil, and defined the Hausdorff topology of fuzzy metric space [22]. Following this, many authors have studied different fixed-point results in fuzzy metric spaces [23]. Furthermore, there are many extensions of metric space terms, including fuzzy metric spaces.

Very recently, Shukla et al. have initiated a new approach to complex valued fuzzy metric space, viewing it as a generalization of fuzzy matrices by replacing $[0,1]$ for the grade of membership with the complex unit closed interval [24]. They obtained some significant fixed-point results with valid illustrated examples. This work is quite new and interesting, so researchers are interested in generalizing more results in this setting and discussing its applications.

Due to important applications of rational type contractions in complex valued metric spaces, and the the work carried out in [24], using Dass and Gupta's [25] rational type expression, some fixed-point results are established in the context of CVFMS. For the authenticity of the presented results, an example and existence theorem for the solution of fuzzy fractional Volterra–Fredholm integro-differential equation under a generalized fuzzy Caputo derivative is also discussed.

2. Preliminaries

In this section, we present some basic definitions and lemmas of CVFMS and prove some properties for multi-valued mappings in this setting. In This manuscript is labeled

(I)   The set of complex numbers by $\mathfrak{C}$,
(II) $\wp = \{(\lambda, \chi) : 0 \leq \lambda < \infty, 0 \leq \chi < \infty\} \subset \mathfrak{C}$ where $(0,0) = \theta$, $(1,1) = \ell$,
(III) $\daleth = \{(\lambda, \chi) : 0 \leq \lambda \leq 1, 0 \leq \chi \leq 1\}$,
(IV) $\daleth_0 = \{(\lambda, \chi) : 0 \leq \lambda < 1, 0 \leq \chi < 1\}$,
(V) $\daleth^+ = \{(\lambda, \chi) : 0 < \lambda \leq 1, 0 \leq \chi \leq 1\}$,
(VII) $\wp_\theta = \{(\lambda, \chi) : 0 < \lambda < \infty, 0 < \chi < \infty\}$.

Define a partial ordering $\preceq$ on $\mathfrak{C}$ by $c_1 \preceq c_2$ iff $c_2 - c_1 \in \wp$. The relations $c_1 \preceq c_2$ and $c_1 \prec c_2$ indicate that

i. $\text{Re}(c_1) \leq \text{Re}(c_2)$, $\text{Im}(c_1) \leq \text{Im}(c_2)$,
ii. $\text{Re}(c_1) < \text{Re}(c_2)$, $\text{Im}(c_1) < \text{Im}(c_2)$.

For $c, \lambda \in \mathfrak{C}, \lambda \preceq c$ iff $\lambda - c \in \wp_\theta$. Suppose $\mathfrak{G} \subset \mathfrak{C}$. Let the inf $\mathfrak{G}$ exists and it is the lower bound of $\mathfrak{G}$, that is inf $\mathfrak{G} \preceq c \quad \forall c \in \mathfrak{G}$ and $\mathbf{v} \preceq \inf \mathfrak{G}$ for each lower bound $\mathbf{v}$ of $\mathfrak{G}$, then inf $\mathfrak{G}$ is called the greatest lower bound(glb) of $\mathfrak{G}$. In the same fashion, one can define sup $\mathfrak{G}$, the least upper bound(lub) of $\mathfrak{G}$.

Definition 1 ([24]). *A sequence $\{c_b\}$ is monotonic with respect to $\preceq$ if either $c_b \preceq c_{b+1}$ or $c_{b+1} \preceq c_b \ \forall \ q \in \aleph$.*

Definition 2 ([24]). *A binary relation $\diamond : \daleth \times \daleth \to \daleth$ is called a complex valued $\check{t}$-norm if the conditions given below hold:*
1. $\hbar_1 \diamond \hbar_2 = \hbar_2 \diamond \hbar_1$;
2. $\hbar_1 \diamond \hbar_2 \preceq \hbar_3 \diamond \hbar_4$ whenever $\hbar_1 \preceq \hbar_3, \hbar_2 \preceq \hbar_4$;
3. $\hbar_1 \diamond (\hbar_2 \diamond \hbar_3) = (\hbar_1 \diamond \hbar_2) \diamond \hbar_3$;
4. $\hbar \diamond \theta = \theta, \hbar \diamond \ell = \hbar$;

for all $\hbar, \hbar_1, \hbar_2, \hbar_3, \hbar_4 \in \daleth$

Definition 3 ([24]). *If $\mathcal{S}$ is a non-empty set and $\diamond$ is continuous complex-valued $\check{t}$-norm, $\mho$ a complex fuzzy set on $\mathcal{S} \times \mathcal{S} \times \wp_\theta \to \daleth$, observing the following conditions:*
1. $0 \preceq \mho(\hbar, \lambda, \mathbf{r})$;
2. $\mho(\hbar, \lambda, \mathbf{r}) = \ell$ for every $\mathbf{r} \in \wp_\theta$ if and only if $\hbar = \lambda$;
3. $\mho(\hbar, \lambda, \mathbf{r}) = \mho(\lambda, \hbar, \mathbf{r})$;
4. $\mho(\hbar, \lambda, \mathbf{r}) \diamond \mho(\lambda, y, \mathbf{r}') \preceq \mho(\hbar, y, \mathbf{r} + \mathbf{r}')$;
5. $\mho(\hbar, \lambda, \diamond) : \wp_\theta \to \daleth$ is continuous for all $\hbar, \lambda, y \in \mathcal{S}$ and $\mathbf{r}, \mathbf{r}' \in \wp_\theta$.

Then $(\mathcal{S}, \mho, \diamond)$ is known to be a CVFMS. The function $\mho(\hbar, \lambda, \mathbf{r})$ represents the degree of nearness and non-nearness between $\hbar$ and λ with respect to the complex parameter $\mathbf{r}$, respectively.

Example 1. *Let $X = \aleph$(set of natural numbers). Define $\diamond$ by $c' \diamond c'' = (a'a'', b'b'')$ for all $c' = (a', b'), c'' = (a'', b'') \in \daleth$. Define complex fuzzy set $\mho$ as*

$$\mho(\lambda, \chi, \mathbf{r}) = \begin{cases} \dfrac{\lambda}{\chi} \ell & \text{if } \lambda \leq \chi \\ \dfrac{\chi}{\lambda} \ell & \text{if } \chi \leq \lambda, \end{cases}$$

for each $\lambda, \chi \in X, c \in \wp_\theta$. Then $(X, \mho, \diamond)$ is CVFMS.

Definition 4 ([24]). *Let $\mathcal{S}$ be a non-empty set. A complex fuzzy set A is characterized by a mapping defined on $\mathcal{S}$ and ranging closed unit complex interval $\daleth$.*

Definition 5 ([24]). *Suppose $(\mathcal{S}, \mho, \diamond)$ is CVFMS. A sequence $\{\lambda_b\}$ in $\mathcal{S}$ is called a Cauchy sequence if*

$$\lim_{b \to \infty} \inf_{d > b} \mho(\lambda_b, \lambda_d, \mathbf{r}) = \ell \quad \forall \quad \mathbf{r} \in \wp_\theta.$$

The CVFMS $(\mathcal{S}, \mho, \diamond)$ is said to be complete if every Cauchy sequence converges to an element of $\mathcal{S}$.

Definition 6 ([24]). *For assumed $\mathbf{t} \in \daleth_\theta, \mathbf{r} \in \wp_\theta$ and $u_\theta \in \mathcal{S}$, we fixed $B[u_\theta, \mathbf{t}, \mathbf{r}]\{z \in \mathcal{S} : \ell - \mathbf{t} \preceq \mho(u_\theta, z, \mathbf{r})\}$.*

Lemma 1 ([24]). *If $(\mathcal{S}, \mho, \diamond)$ is a CVFMS. If $\mathbf{r}, \mathbf{r}' \in \wp_\theta$ and $\mathbf{r} \preceq \mathbf{r}'$, then $\mho(\lambda, \zeta, \mathbf{r}) \preceq \mho(\lambda, \zeta, \mathbf{r}')$ $\forall \lambda, \zeta \in \mathcal{S}$.*

Lemma 2 ([24]). *Let $(\mathcal{S}, \mho, \diamond)$ be CVFMS. A sequence $\{\lambda_b\}$ in $\mathcal{S}$ converges to $\mathbf{v} \in \mathcal{S}$ iff $\lim_{b \to \infty} \mho(\lambda_b, \mathbf{v}, \mathbf{r}) = \ell$ holds $\forall \ \mathbf{r} \in \wp_\theta$.*

Lemma 3 ([24]). *Let $(\mathcal{S}, \mho, \diamond)$ be CVFMS. If $\mathbf{r}, \mathbf{r}' \in \wp_\theta$ and $\mathbf{r} \preceq \mathbf{r}'$, then $\mho(\lambda, \xi, \mathbf{r}) \preceq \mho(\lambda, \xi, \mathbf{r}') \forall \lambda, \xi \in \mathcal{S}$.*

Lemma 4 ([24]). *Let $(\mathcal{S}, \mho, \diamond)$ be CVFMS. A sequence $\{\lambda_q\}$ in $\mathcal{S}$ converges to $\mathbf{v} \in \mathcal{S}$ iff $\lim_{q \to \infty} \mho(\lambda_q, \mathbf{v}, \mathbf{r}) = \ell$ holds $\forall\, t \in \wp_\theta$.*

Remark 1 ([24]). *Suppose $\lambda_b \in \wp\ \forall\, b \in \aleph$ and $\preceq$ are in partial order, then:*
(a) *If the sequence $\{\lambda_b\}$ is monotonic and there exists $\gamma, \eta \in \wp$ with $\gamma \preceq \lambda_b \preceq \eta, \forall\, b \in \aleph$, then there exists $\lambda \in \wp$ such that $\lim_{b \to \infty} \lambda_b = \lambda$.*
(b) *Although the partial ordering $\preceq$ is not a linear order on $\mathfrak{C}$, the pair $(\mathfrak{C}, \preceq)$ is a lattice.*
(c) *If $\mathcal{S} \subset \mathfrak{C}$, then $\inf \mathcal{S}$ and $\sup \mathcal{S}$ both exist for $\gamma, \eta \in \mathfrak{C}$ with $\gamma \preceq s \preceq \eta\ \forall\, s \in \mathcal{S}$.*

Remark 2 ([24]). *Let $\lambda_b, \lambda'_b, \hbar \in \wp, \forall\, b \in \aleph$, then*
(a) *If $\lambda_b \preceq \lambda'_b \preceq \ell\ \forall\, b \in \aleph$ and $\lim_{b \to \infty} \lambda_b = \ell$, then $\lim_{b \to \infty} \lambda'_b = \ell$.*
(b) *If $\lambda_b \preceq \hbar\ \forall\, b \in \aleph$ and $\lim_{b \to \infty} \lambda_b = \lambda$, then $\lambda \preceq \mathbf{w}$.*
(c) *If $\hbar \preceq \lambda_b\ \forall\, b \in \aleph$ and $\lim_{b \to \infty} \lambda_b = \lambda$, then $\mathbf{w} \preceq \lambda$.*

A relatively important notion in complex fuzzy set theory is σ-level set. Let A be a complex fuzzy set in $\mathcal{S}$. Then, the function values of A(λ) are said to be the grade of membership of $\lambda \in$ A. The collection of all those elements in $\mathcal{S}$ belonging to A have at least a degree $\sigma \in \daleth^+$, which is called the σ-level set and denoted by $[A]_\sigma$. That is,

$$[A]_\sigma = \{\lambda : A(\lambda) \succeq \sigma\} \quad \text{if} \quad \sigma \in \daleth = [A_\sigma^-, A_\sigma^+].$$

Please note that the σ-level representation of fuzzy valued function T is expressed by $T_\sigma(t) = [T_\sigma^-(t), A_\sigma^+(t)], \sigma \in [0,1]$.

Definition 7. *Let $T : \mathcal{S} \to \mathfrak{F}(\mathcal{S})$ be a fuzzy mapping. An element $\mathbf{u} \in \mathcal{S}$ is known to be a fuzzy fixed point of T if there exists an $\sigma \in \daleth^+$ such that $\mathbf{u} \in [T\mathbf{u}]_\sigma$, where $\mathfrak{F}(\mathcal{S})$ is a collection of complex fuzzy sets.*

Let $(\mathcal{S}, \mho, \diamond)$ be a CVFMS. We denote the family of all nonempty, closed and bounded subsets of a complex valued fuzzy metric space by CB$(\mathcal{S})$. From now on we denote for $\bar{w} \in \mathcal{S}$, for $\mathbf{r} \in \wp_\theta, c \in \mathcal{S}$ and $\mathfrak{G} \in$ CB$(\mathcal{S})$:

$$s(\bar{w}, \mathbf{r}) = \{(\bar{z}, \mathbf{r}) \in \daleth : (\bar{z}, \mathbf{r}) \preceq (\bar{w}, \mathbf{r})\}$$

and

$$s(c, \mathfrak{G}, \mathbf{r}) = \bigcup_{d \in \mathfrak{G}} s(\mho(c, d, \mathbf{r})) = \bigcup_{d \in \mathfrak{G}} \{\bar{z} \in \mathcal{S} : \bar{z} \preceq \mho(c, d, \mathbf{r})\}$$

For C, $\mathfrak{G} \in$ CB$(\mathcal{S})$, we denote

$$s(C, \mathfrak{G}, \mathbf{r}) = \left(\bigcap_{c \in C} s(\mho(c, \mathfrak{G}, \mathbf{r})) \right) \bigcap \left(\bigcap_{d \in \mathfrak{G}} s(\mho(d, C, \mathbf{r})) \right)$$

Let T be a multivalued mapping from $\mathcal{S}$ into CB$(\mathcal{S})$, for $z \in \mathcal{S}$ and $\mathcal{A} \in$ CB$(\mathcal{S})$, we define

$$\mathcal{W}_z(\mathcal{A}, \mathbf{r}) = \{\mho(z, a, \mathbf{r}) : a \in \mathcal{A}\}.$$

Thus for $z, w \in \mathcal{S}$

$$\mathcal{W}_z(Tw, \mathbf{r}) = \{\mho(z, u, \mathbf{r}) : u \in Tw\}.$$

Definition 8. *In a $(\mathcal{S}, \mho, \diamond)$ CVFMS a subset K of $\mathcal{S}$ is said to be bounded from above if there exists some $\mathbf{w} \in \mathcal{S}$, such that $k \preceq \mathbf{w}$ for all $k \in \mathcal{S}$.*

Definition 9. In a CVFMS, a multivalued mapping $\mathcal{T} : \mathcal{S} \to 2^\wp$ is said to be bounded from above if and only if, for each $z \in \mathcal{S}$, there exists $x_z \in \wp$, such that

$$w \preceq x_z$$

for all $w \in \mathcal{T}z$.

Definition 10. A fuzzy mapping $F : \mathcal{S} \to \mathfrak{F}(\mathcal{S})$ is supposed to have an upper bound property on $(\mathcal{S}, \mho, \diamond)$, if, for any $z \in \mathcal{S}$ related with some $\sigma \in \daleth$, the multivalued mapping $\mathcal{T} : \mathcal{S} \to 2^\wp$ defined by

$$\mathcal{T}_z(w) = \mathcal{W}_z([Fw]_\sigma)$$

is bounded from above, i.e., for $z, w \in \mathcal{S}$ there is an element $l_z([Fw]_\sigma) \in \wp$ with

$$v \preceq l_z([Fw]_\sigma)$$

for each $v \in \mathcal{W}_z([Fw]_\sigma)$, where $l_z([Fw]_\sigma)$ is known as the upper bound of F.

Lemma 5. Let $(\mathcal{S}, \mho, \diamond)$ be CVFMS.
(i) Let $(a, f), (b, f) \in \wp$. If $(a, f) \preceq (b, f)$ then $s(a, r) \subseteq s(b, r)$
(ii) Let $(a, f) \in \wp, \mathfrak{P}, \mathfrak{G} \in CB(\mathcal{S})$ and $c \in \mathfrak{P}$. If $(a, f) \in s(\mathfrak{P}, \mathfrak{G}, r)$ then $a \in s(c, \mathfrak{G}, r)$ for all $c \in \mathfrak{P}$ or $a \in s(\mathfrak{P}, d, r)$ for all $d \in \mathfrak{G}$.

Proof.
(i) Let $(\mathcal{S}, \mho, \diamond)$ be a CVFMS. Suppose $(x, f) \in s(a, r)$ then $(x, f) \preceq (a, f)$. But $(a, f) \preceq (b,, f)$, therefore $(x, f) \preceq (b, f)$. Consequently $(x, f) \in s(b, r)$. Hence $s(a, r) \subseteq s(b, r)$.
(ii) Suppose $c \in \mathfrak{P}$ and $(a, f) \in s(\mathfrak{P}, \mathfrak{G}, r)$

$$(a, f) \in \left(\bigcap_{c \in \mathfrak{P}} s(c, \mathfrak{G}, r)\right) \bigcap \left(\bigcap_{d \in \mathfrak{G}} s(d, \mathfrak{P}, r)\right),$$

yields that

$$(a, f) \in \left(\bigcap_{c \in \mathfrak{P}} s(c, \mathfrak{G}, r)\right) \text{ and } (a, f) \in \left(\bigcap_{d \in \mathfrak{G}} s(d, \mathfrak{P}, r)\right).$$

Since $(a, f) \in \bigcap_{c \in \mathfrak{P}} s(c, \mathfrak{G}, r)$ implies that $(a, f) \in s(c, \mathfrak{G}, r)$ for all $c \in \mathfrak{P}$. Similarly $b \in s(d, \mathfrak{P}, r)$ for all $d \in \mathfrak{G}$. □

Remark 3. Let $(\mathcal{S}, \mho, \diamond)$ be CVFMS. If $\daleth = [0, 1]$, then $(\mathcal{S}, \mho, \diamond)$ is a fuzzy metric space. Moreover, for $\mathfrak{P}, \mathfrak{G} \in CB(\mathcal{S})$, then $H(\mathfrak{P}, \mathfrak{G}, r) = \sup s(\mathfrak{P}, \mathfrak{G}, r)$ is the Hausdorff distance induced by $\mho$.

Definition 11. Let $(\mathcal{S}, \mho, \diamond)$ be CVFMS and let G be fuzzy mappings from $\mathcal{S}$ into $\mathfrak{F}(\mathcal{S})$. A point $\lambda \in G$ is called a fuzzy fixed point of G if $\lambda \in [G\lambda]_\sigma$, for some $\sigma \in \daleth$.

Definition 12. Let $(\mathcal{S}, \mho, \diamond)$ be CVFMS and the fuzzy mapping $U : \mathcal{S} \to \mathfrak{F}(\mathcal{S})$ satisfies the least upper bound property (lub) on $(\mathcal{S}, \mho, \diamond)$, if for any $\hbar \in \mathcal{S}$ and $\sigma \in (0, 1]$, the least upper bound (lub) of $\hbar_\omega([U\chi]_\sigma, r)$ exists in $\mathfrak{C}$ for all $\hbar, \chi \in \mathcal{S}$ and $r \in \wp_\theta$. If $\mho(\hbar, [Uy]_\sigma, \diamond)$ be the lub of $\hbar_\omega([U\chi]_\sigma, r)$. Then,

$$\mho(\hbar, [U\chi]_\sigma, r) = \sup\{\mho(\hbar, u, r) : u \in [U\chi]_\sigma, r\}.$$

Definition 13. *The generalized Hukuhara difference of two fuzzy numbers* $u, v \in \mathfrak{F}(\mathcal{S})$ *is defined as follows*

$$u \ominus_{gH} v = w \Leftrightarrow \begin{cases} (i) u = v + w \\ or\ (ii) v = u + (-1)w. \end{cases}$$

Definition 14 ([2]). *The generalized Hukuhara derivative of a fuzzy-valued function* $T : (a, b) \to \mathfrak{F}(\mathcal{S})$ *at t_0 is defined as*

$$T'_{gH}(t_0) = \lim_{h \to 0} \frac{T(t_0 + \delta) \ominus_{gH} T(t_0)}{\delta},$$

if $(T)'_{gH}(t_0) \to \mathfrak{F}(\mathcal{S})$, *we say that* T *is generalized Hukuhara differentiable (gH-differentiable) at t_0.*

Additionally, we say that T is $[(i) - gH]$-differentiable at t_0 if

$$(T'_{gH})_\sigma(t_0) = [(T_\sigma^-)'(t_0), (T_\sigma^+)'(t_0)], \quad 0 \le \sigma \le 1,$$

and that f is $[(ii) - gH]$-differentiable at t_0 if

$$(T'_{gH})_\sigma(t_0) = [(T_\sigma^+)'(t_0), (T_\sigma^-)'(t_0)], \quad 0 \le \sigma \le 1.$$

Definition 15. *Consider* $f : [a, b] \to \mathbb{R}$, *fractional derivative of* $f(t)$ *in the Caputo sense is defined as*

$$(D_*^q f)(t) = (I^{m-q} D^m f)(t) = \frac{1}{\Gamma(m-q)} \int_a^t (t-s)^{(q-m-1)} f^{(m)}(s) ds \quad m - 1 < q \le m, m \in \mathbb{N}, t > a$$

where D stands for classic derivative.

We denote $C^F[a, b]$ as the space of all continuous fuzzy-valued functions on $[a, b]$. Additionally, we denote the space of all Lebesgue integrable fuzzy-valued functions on the bounded interval $[a, b] \subset \mathbb{R}$ by $L^F[a, b]$.

Definition 16. *Let* $f' \in C^F[a,b] \cap L^F[a,b]$. *The fractional generalized Hukuhara Caputo derivative of fuzzy-valued function f is defined as follows:*

$$(_{gH}D_*^q f)(t) = I_a^{1-q}(f'_{gH})(t) = \frac{1}{\Gamma(1-q)} \int_a^t \frac{(f'_{gH})(s) ds}{(t-s)^q}, \quad a < s < t, \ 0 < q < 1.$$

Additionally, we say that f is $^{cf}[(i) - gH]$-differentiable at t_0 if

$$(_{gH}D_*^q f)_\sigma(t_0) = [(D_*^q f_\sigma^-)(t_0), (D_*^q f_\sigma^+)(t_0)], \quad 0 \le \sigma \le 1,$$

and that f is $^{cf}[(ii) - gH]$-differentiable at t_0 if

$$(_{gH}D_*^q f)_\sigma(t_0) = [(D_*^q f_\sigma^+)(t_0), (D_*^q f_\sigma^-)(t_0)], \quad 0 \le \sigma \le 1.$$

3. Main Results

Theorem 1. *Let* $(\mathcal{S}, \mho, \diamond)$ *CVFMS such that, for any sequence* $\{r_n\}$ *in* $\wp_\theta$ *with* $\lim_{n \to \infty} r_n = \infty$, *we have*

$$\lim_{r \to \infty} \mho(w, z, r_n) = \ell, \quad \text{for all} \ \ w, z \in \mathcal{S}, q + e = \mathfrak{z} \in (0,1) \ \text{and} \ r > 0.$$

Assume that there exists some $\sigma \in (0,1]$, such that, for each $z \in \mathcal{S}$, such that $[F\mathbf{w}]_\sigma$ is a nonempty compact subset of $\mathcal{S}$. Let $F : \mathcal{S} \to \mathfrak{F}(\mathcal{S})$ be a fuzzy mapping with the least upper bound property, such that

$$\frac{[1+\mho(z,[Fz]_\sigma,\mathbf{qr})]\mho(\mathbf{w},[F\mathbf{w}]_\sigma,\mathbf{er})}{1+\mho(\mathbf{w},z,\mathbf{r})}+\mho(z,\mathbf{w},\mathbf{r}) \in s([F\mathbf{w}]_\sigma,[Fz]_\sigma,\mathfrak{z}\mathbf{r}). \tag{1}$$

Then F has a unique σ-fuzzy fixed point.

Proof. Let c_0 be any arbitrary point in $\mathcal{S}$. Define a sequence $\{c_n\}$ in $\mathcal{S}$ by

$$c_n \in [Fc_{n-1}]_\sigma \quad \text{for all} \quad n \in \{1,2\cdots\}.$$

First of all, we have to show that $\{c_n\}$ is a Cauchy sequence. For this, we define

$$\Lambda_b = \{\mho(c_n,c_m,\mathbf{r}) : m > n\} \subseteq \daleth,$$

for $n \in \{1,2\cdots\}$ and fixed $\mathbf{r} \in \wp_\theta$. Since $\theta \prec (c_n,c_m,\mathbf{r}) \preceq \ell$ for all $b \in \{1,2\cdots\}$. Using Remark 1, we obtain that, for all $b \in 1,2\cdots$, the infimum, $\inf \Lambda_b = \varrho_b$ (say) exists. For $\mathbf{r} \in \wp_\theta, n,m \in \aleph$ with $m > n$, from (1) by setting $z = c_n$ and $\mathbf{w} = c_m$, we obtain

$$\frac{[1+\mho(c_n,[Fc_n]_\sigma,\mathbf{qr})]\mho(c_m,[Fc_m]_\sigma,\mathbf{er})}{1+\mho(c_m,c_n,\mathbf{r})}+\mho(c_n,c_m,\mathbf{r}) \in s([Fc_n]_\sigma,[Fc_m]_\sigma,\mathfrak{z}\mathbf{r}).$$

Using Lemma 5 (ii), we obtain

$$\frac{[1+\mho(c_n,[Fc_n]_\sigma,\mathbf{qr})]\mho(c_m,[Fc_m]_\sigma,\mathbf{er})}{1+\mho(c_m,c_n,\mathbf{r})}+\mho(c_n,c_m,\mathbf{r}) \in s(c_{n+1},[Fc_m]_\sigma,\mathfrak{z}\mathbf{r}).$$

Since $[Fc_m]_\sigma$ is nonempty subset of $\mathcal{S}$, there exists some $c_{m+1} \in [Fc_m]_\sigma$ such that

$$\frac{[1+\mho(c_n,[Fc_n]_\sigma,\mathbf{qr})]\mho(c_m,[Fc_m]_\sigma,\mathbf{er})}{1+\mho(c_m,c_n,\mathbf{r})}+\mho(c_n,c_m,\mathbf{r}) \in s(\mho(c_{n+1},c_{m+1},\mathfrak{z}\mathbf{r})).$$

Using Definition 12, we obtain

$$\mho(c_{n+1},c_{m+1},\mathfrak{z}\mathbf{r}) \succeq \frac{[1+\mho(c_n,[Fc_n]_\sigma,\mathbf{qr})]\mho(c_m,[Fc_m]_\sigma,\mathbf{er})}{1+\mho(c_m,c_n,\mathbf{r})}+\mho(c_n,c_m,\mathbf{r}).$$

Applying the least upper bound property of F

$$\mho(c_{n+1},c_{m+1},\mathfrak{z}\mathbf{r}) \succeq \frac{[1+\mho(c_n,c_{n+1},\mathbf{qr})]\mho(c_m,c_{m+1},\mathbf{er})}{1+\mho(c_m,c_n,\mathbf{rq})}+\mho(c_n,c_m,\mathbf{r})$$
$$\succeq \mho(c_n,c_m,\mathbf{r}).$$

Utilizing Lemma 3, this yields

$$\mho(c_{n+1},c_{m+1},\mathbf{r}) \succeq \mho(c_n,c_m,\frac{\mathbf{r}}{\mathfrak{z}}) \succeq \mho(c_n,c_m,\mathbf{r}), \tag{2}$$

which implies that

$$\mho(c_n,c_m,\mathbf{r}) \preceq \mho(c_{n+1},c_{m+1},\mathbf{r}) \quad \text{for all} \quad n,m \in \aleph \quad \text{with} \quad m > n.$$

Therefore, by definition, we have

$$\theta \preceq \varrho_n \preceq \varrho_{n+1} \preceq \ell. \tag{3}$$

Thus, $\{\varrho_n\}$ is a monotonic sequence in $\wp$, and by the use of Remark 1 and (3), there exists $\ell_a \in \wp$, such that
$$\lim_{n \to \infty} \varrho_n = \ell_a. \tag{4}$$

Again, from (2), we have, for $c \in \wp$,
$$\varrho_{n+1} = \inf_{m>n} \mho(c_{n+1}, c_{m+1}, r) \succeq \inf_{m>n} \mho(c_n, c_m, \frac{r}{3}).$$

Similarly, for $c \in \wp_\theta$, we obtain
$$\mho(c_{n+1}, c_{m+1}, r) \succeq \mho(c_n, c_m, \frac{r}{3})$$
$$\succeq \mho(Fc_{n-1}, Fc_{m-1}, \frac{r}{3})$$
$$\succeq \mho(c_{n-1}, c_{m-1}, \frac{r}{3^2}) = \mho(Fc_{n-2}, Fc_{m-2}, \frac{r}{3^2})$$
$$\succeq \mho(c_{n-2}, c_{m-2}, \frac{r}{3^3}) \succeq \cdots \succeq \mho(c_0, c_{m-n}, \frac{r}{3^{n+1}}),$$

hence, for all $c \in \wp_\theta$,
$$\varrho_{n+1} = \inf_{m>n} \mho(c_{n+1}, c_{m+1}, r) \succeq \inf_{m>n} \mho(c_0, c_{m-n}, \frac{r}{3^{n+1}}) \succeq \inf_{w \in \mathcal{S}} \mho(c_0, w, \frac{r}{3^{n+1}}).$$

Since $\lim_{n \to \infty} \frac{r}{3^{n+1}} = \infty$, using (4) and from hypothesis, we have
$$\ell_a \succeq \inf_{w \in \mathcal{S}} \mho(c_0, w, \frac{r}{3^{n+1}}) = \ell. \tag{5}$$

From (4) and (5), we obtain
$$\lim_{n \to \infty} \varrho_n = \ell.$$

Hence, $\{c_n\}$ is a Cauchy sequence in $\mathcal{S}$. Since $\mathcal{S}$ is complete and from Lemma 4, there exists $x \in \mathcal{S}$ such that
$$\lim_{n \to \infty} \mho(c_n, x, r) = \ell \quad \text{for all} \quad c \in \wp_\theta. \tag{6}$$

Considering (1), for any $c \in \wp_\theta$, we obtain
$$\frac{[1 + \mho(c_n, [Fc_n]_\sigma, qr)]\mho(x, [Fx]_\sigma, er)}{1 + \mho(x, c_n, r)} + \mho(c_n, x, r) \in s([Fc_n]_\sigma, [Fx]_\sigma, 3r).$$

Using Lemma 5 (ii), we obtain
$$\frac{[1 + \mho(c_n, [Fc_n]_\sigma, qr)]\mho(x, [Fx]_\sigma, er)}{1 + \mho(x, c_n, r)} + \mho(c_n, x, r) \in s(c_{n+1}, [Fx]_\sigma, r).$$

By definition, we obtain
$$\mho(c_{n+1}, [Fx]_\sigma, 3r) \succeq \frac{[1 + \mho(c_n, [Fc_n]_\sigma, qr)]\mho(x, [Fx]_\sigma, er)}{1 + \mho(x, c_n, r)} + \mho(c_n, x, r).$$

Applying the least upper bound property of F
$$\mho(c_{n+1}, [Fx]_\sigma, 3r) \succeq \frac{[1 + \mho(c_n, c_{n+1}, qr)]\mho(x, x_n, er)}{1 + \mho(x, c_n, r)} + \mho(c_n, x, r)$$
$$\succeq \mho(c_n, x, r). \tag{7}$$

From the definition and using (7), we obtain

$$\eth(x, [Fx]_\sigma, r) \succeq \eth(x, c_{n+1}, \frac{r}{2}) * \eth(c_{n+1}, [Fx]_\sigma, \frac{r}{2})$$
$$\succeq \eth(x, c_{n+1}, \frac{r}{2}) * \eth(c_n, x, \frac{r}{2\mathfrak{z}}).$$

Taking $\lim_{n\to\infty}$, and using (6) and Remark 2, we can see that

$$\eth(x, [Fx]_\sigma, r) = \ell \quad \text{for all} \quad r \in \wp_\theta.$$

i.e., $x \in [Fx]_\sigma$. Let x_1 be another fixed point of F, and there exists $r \in \wp_\theta$ such that $\eth(x, x_1, r) \neq \ell$ then it yields from (1) that

$$\frac{[1+\eth(x, [Fx]_\sigma, \mathfrak{q}r)]\eth(x_1, [Fx_1]_\sigma, \mathfrak{e}r)}{1+\eth(x_1, x, r)} + \eth(x, x_1, r) \in s([Fx]_\sigma, [Fx_1]_\sigma, \mathfrak{z}r).$$

Using Lemma 5 (ii), we get

$$\frac{[1+\eth(x, [Fx]_\sigma, \mathfrak{q}r)]\eth(x_1, [Fx_1]_\sigma, \mathfrak{e}r)}{1+\eth(x_1, x, r)} + \eth(x, x_1, r) \in s(x, [Fx_1]_\sigma, \mathfrak{z}r).$$

Since $[Fx_1]_\sigma$ is nonempty subset of $\mathcal{S}$, there exists some $x_1 \in [Fx_1]_\sigma$ such that

$$\frac{[1+\eth(x, [Fx]_\sigma, \mathfrak{q}r)]\eth(x_1, [Fx_1]_\sigma, \mathfrak{e}r)}{1+\eth(x_1, x, r)} + \eth(x, x_1, r) \in s(\eth(x, x_1, \mathfrak{z}r)).$$

Using Definition 12, we obtain

$$\eth(x, x_1, \mathfrak{z}r) \succeq \frac{[1+\eth(x, [Fx]_\sigma, \mathfrak{q}r)]\eth(x_1, [Fx_1]_\sigma, \mathfrak{e}r)}{1+\eth(x_1, x, r)} + \eth(x, x_1, r).$$

Applying the least upper bound property of F

$$\eth(x, x_1, \mathfrak{z}r) \succeq \frac{[1+\eth(x, x, \mathfrak{q}r)]\eth(x_1, x_1, \mathfrak{e}r)}{1+\eth(x_1, x, r)} + \eth(x, x_1, r)$$
$$\succeq \eth(x, x_1, r).$$

On simplification, we get

$$\eth(x, x_1, r) \succeq \eth(x, x_1, \frac{r}{\mathfrak{z}}) \succeq \eth(x, x_1, \frac{r}{\mathfrak{z}^2}) \succeq \cdots \succeq \eth(x, x_1, \frac{r}{\mathfrak{z}^n}).$$

Using $\lim_{n\to\infty} \frac{r}{\mathfrak{z}^n} = \infty$ and $\eth(x, x_1, \frac{r}{\mathfrak{z}^n}) \succeq \inf_{w\in\mathcal{S}} \eth(x, x_1, \frac{r}{\mathfrak{z}^n})$. From this we get $\eth(x, x_1, r) \succeq \ell$, which is a contradiction. Thus, $\eth(x, x_1, r) = \ell$, for all $r \in \wp_\theta$. i.e., $x = x_1$, which follows the uniqueness. $\square$

In the succeeding theorem, we use Definition 6 to demonstrate the existence of fixed-point for a mapping enjoying a restricted condition.

Theorem 2. *Let* $(\mathcal{S}, \eth, \diamond)$ *CVFMS and* $F : \mathcal{S} \to \mathfrak{F}(\mathcal{S})$ *be a fuzzy mapping where the least upper bound property enjoys:*
(1) *There exists* $u_\theta \in \mathcal{S}$ *and* $r \in \daleth_\theta$ *with* $\ell - \mathbf{t} \preceq \eth(u_\theta, F[u_\theta]_\sigma, r)$ *for all* $r \in \wp_\theta$.
(2)
$$\frac{[1+\eth(z, [Fz]_\sigma, \mathfrak{q}r)]\eth(w, [Fw]_\sigma, \mathfrak{e}r)}{1+\eth(w, z, r)} + \eth(z, w, r) \in s([Fw]_\sigma, [Fz]_\sigma, \mathfrak{z}r). \quad (8)$$

for all $z, \mathbf{w} \in B[u_\theta, F u_\theta, \mathbf{r}]$ and for each $z \in \mathcal{S}$, there exist some $\sigma \in (0, 1]$, such that $[F\mathbf{w}]_\sigma$ be a nonempty closed and bounded subset of $\mathcal{S}$, while $\mathbf{q} + \mathbf{e} = \mathfrak{z} \in [0, 1)$. Then, F has a unique σ-fuzzy fixed point in $B[u_\theta, u_\theta, \mathbf{r}]$.

Proof. To prove this, it is enough to show that $B[u_\theta, \mathbf{t}, \mathbf{r}]$ is complete and $[Fz]_\sigma \in B[u_\theta, \mathbf{t}, \mathbf{r}]$ for all $z \in B[u_\theta, F u_\theta, \mathbf{r}]$.

Let $\{c_n\}$ be a Cauchy sequence in $B[u_\theta, \mathbf{t}, \mathbf{r}]$. Thus, from the completeness of the ground set $\mathcal{S}$ and Lemma 4, there is an $\nu \in \mathcal{S}$ with

$$\lim_{n \to \infty} \mho(c_n, \nu, \mathbf{r}) = \ell \quad \text{for all} \quad \mathbf{r} \in \wp_\theta,$$

at this instant, for all $m, n \aleph$,

$$\mho(u_\theta, \nu, \mathbf{r} + \frac{\mathbf{r}}{m}) \succeq \mho(u_\theta, \nu, \mathbf{r}) * \mho(u_\theta, \nu, \frac{\mathbf{r}}{m}).$$

Since $c_n \in B[u_\theta, \mathbf{c}, \mathbf{r}]$, and $\lim_{n \to \infty} \mho(u_\theta, \nu, \mathbf{r}) = \ell$, so, by utilizing Remark 2 and using the properties of t-norm, we obtain

$$\mho(u_\theta, \nu, \mathbf{r} + \frac{\mathbf{r}}{m}) \succeq (\ell - \mathbf{c}) \diamond \ell = \ell - \mathbf{c}.$$

Setting a limit such that $m \to \infty$ and using Remark 2, we have $\mho(u_\theta, \nu, \mathbf{r}) \succeq \ell - \mathbf{c}$. Consequently, $\nu \in B[u_\theta, \mathbf{t}, \mathbf{r}]$.

For each $z \in B[u_\theta, \mathbf{c}, \mathbf{r}]$, it can be seen (8) that

$$\frac{[1 + \mho(u_\theta, [F u_\theta]_\sigma, \mathbf{rq})] \mho(z, [Fz]_\sigma, \mathbf{re})}{1 + \mho(z, u_\theta, \mathbf{r})} + \mho(u_\theta, z, \mathbf{r}) \in s([F u_\theta]_\sigma, [Fz]_\sigma, \mathfrak{z}\mathbf{r}).$$

By Definition, we obtain

$$\mho([F u_\theta]_\sigma, [Fz]_\sigma, \mathfrak{z}\mathbf{r}) \succeq \frac{[1 + \mho(u_\theta, [F u_\theta]_\sigma, \mathbf{rq})] \mho(z, [Fz]_\sigma, \mathbf{re})}{1 + \mho(z, u_\theta, \mathbf{r})} + \mho(u_\theta, z, \mathbf{r})$$
$$\succeq \mho(u_\theta, z, \mathbf{r}).$$

This yields

$$\mho(u_\theta, [Fz]_\sigma, \mathbf{r} + \frac{\mathbf{r}}{m}) \succeq \mho(u_\theta, F u_\theta, \frac{\mathbf{r}}{m}) \diamond \mho(F u_\theta, [Fz]_\sigma, \mathbf{r})$$
$$\succeq (\ell - \mathbf{t}) \diamond \mho(u_\theta, z, \frac{\mathbf{r}}{3})$$
$$\succeq (\ell - \mathbf{t}) \diamond \mho(u_\theta, z, \frac{\mathbf{r}}{3^2}) \succeq \cdots \succeq (\ell - \mathbf{t}) \diamond \mho(u_\theta, z, \frac{\mathbf{r}}{3^n}),$$

for all $n \in \aleph$. Using $\lim_{n \to} \frac{\mathbf{r}}{3^n}$ and $\mho(u_\theta, z, \frac{\mathbf{r}}{3^n}) \succeq \inf_{y \in \mathcal{S}} \mho(u_\theta, z, \frac{\mathbf{r}}{3^n})$. It yields from above inequality

$$\mho(u_\theta, [Fz]_\sigma, \mathbf{r} + \frac{\mathbf{r}}{m}) \succeq (\ell - \mathbf{t}) \diamond \ell$$
$$\succeq (\ell - \mathbf{t})$$

Taking $\lim_{m \to \infty}$ and utilizing Remark 2, we have

$$\mho(u_\theta, [Fz]_\sigma, \mathbf{r}) \succeq (\ell - \mathbf{t})$$

Thus, $[Fz] \in B[u_\theta, \mathbf{t}, \mathbf{r}]$. □

In Theorem 1 the contractive condition (1) for F can be replaced by the following, analogous proof:

Corollary 1.

$$\frac{[1+\eth(z,[Fz]_\sigma,q(r)r)]\eth(w,[Fw]_\sigma,e(r)r)}{1+\eth(w,z,r)} + \eth(z,w,r) \in s([Fw]_\sigma,[Fz]_\sigma,\mathfrak{z}(r)r),$$

for each $z,w \in \wp_\theta$. Where $q,e,\mathfrak{z} : \wp_\theta \to (0,1)$.

By setting $\eth(z,w,r) = \theta$ in Theorem 1, we get the following corollary.

Corollary 2. Let $(\mathcal{S}, \eth, *)$ be a complete complex valued fuzzy metric space, such that, for any sequence $\{r_n\}$ in $\wp_\theta$ with $\lim_{n\to\infty} r_n = \infty$, we have

$$\lim_{r\to\infty} M(w,z,r_n) = \ell, \text{ for all } w,z \in \mathcal{S}, q \in (0,1) \text{ and } r > 0.$$

Assume that there exists some $\sigma \in (0,1]$, such that, for each $z \in \mathcal{S}$ such that $[Fw]_\sigma$ is a nonempty compact subset of $\mathcal{S}$ for all $w \in \mathcal{S}$. Let $F : \mathcal{S} \to \mathfrak{F}(\mathcal{S})$ be a fuzzy mapping with least upper bound property, such that

$$[1+\eth(z,[Fz]_\sigma,qr)]\eth(w,[Fw]_\sigma,er) \in s([Fw]_\sigma,[Fz]_\sigma,\mathfrak{z}r),$$

where $q + e = \mathfrak{z} < 1$ Then, F has a unique σ-fuzzy fixed point.

By setting $\eth(w,[Fw]_\sigma,er) = \theta$ in Theorem 1, we get the following corollary.

Corollary 3. Let $(\mathcal{S}, \eth, \diamond)$ be a complete complex valued fuzzy metric space such that, for any sequence, $\{r_n\}$ in $\wp_\theta$ with $\lim_{n\to\infty} r_n = \infty$, we have

$$\lim_{r\to\infty} M(w,z,r_n) = \ell, \text{ for all } w,z \in \mathcal{S}, q \in (0,1) \text{ and } r > 0.$$

Assume that there exists some $\sigma \in (0,1]$, such that, for each $z \in \mathcal{S}$ such that $[Fw]_\sigma$ is a nonempty compact subset of $\mathcal{S}$ for all $w \in \mathcal{S}$. Let $F : \mathcal{S} \to \mathfrak{F}(\mathcal{S})$ be a fuzzy mapping with the least upper bound property, such that

$$\eth(z,w,r) \in s([Fw]_\sigma,[Fz]_\sigma,\mathfrak{z}r),$$

where $\mathfrak{z} < 1$. Then F has a unique σ-fuzzy fixed point.

The task of Theorem 1, can also be obtained for self mapping while relaxing the least upper bound property, with analogous proof:

Corollary 4. Let $(\mathcal{S}, \eth, \diamond)$ CVFMS such that, for any sequence, $\{r_n\}$ in $\wp_\theta$ with $\lim_{n\to\infty} r_n = \infty$, we have

$$\lim_{r\to\infty} \eth(w,z,r_n) = \ell, \text{ for all } w,z \in \mathcal{S}, q + e = \mathfrak{z} \in (0,1) \text{ and } r > 0.$$

Let $F : \mathcal{S} \to \mathcal{S}$ enjoy

$$\eth(Fw,Fz,\mathfrak{z}r) \succeq \frac{[1+\eth(z,Fz,qr)]\eth(w,Fw,er)}{1+\eth(w,z,r)} + \eth(z,w,r).$$

Then, F has a unique σ-fuzzy fixed point.

Remark 4. To obtain a unique fixed-point in the the above Corollary, it is sufficient that, to some extent, sequence $\{c_n\} \in \wp_\theta$ such that $\lim_{n\to\infty}$, we get $\lim_{n\to\infty} \mho(z, w, c_n) = \ell \ \forall \ z, w\mathcal{S}$. This state is obtained from the suppositions of Corollary 4 as, for any sequence, $\{c_n\} = \infty$ also for each $z, w \in \mathcal{S}$.

$$\lim_{n\to\infty} \mho(z, w, c_n) \geq \lim_{n\to\infty} \inf_{v\mathcal{S}} \mho(z, v, c_n) = \ell.$$

By the use of the above remark, and the rest of the proof of Corollary 4, we can use a more general statement for our main theorem, as follows.

Corollary 5. Let $(\mathcal{S}, \mho, \diamond)$ be CVFMS. Suppose for any sequence $\{c_n\} \in \wp_\theta$ such that $\lim_{n\to\infty} = \infty$, we obtained $\lim_{n\to\infty} \mho(z, w, c_n) = \ell \ \forall \ z, w\mathcal{S}$. Moreover, let for any sequence in $\wp_\theta$ there exists $c_0 \in \mathcal{S}$ with $\lim_{n\to\infty} = \infty$, we obtained

$$\lim_{n\to\infty} \inf_{y \Xi_{c_0}} \mho(c_0, y, c_n) = \ell, \tag{9}$$

where Ξ_{c_0} represents the collection of F−iterates of c_0. If $F : \mathcal{S} \to \mathcal{S}$ with:

$$\mho(Fw, Fz, \mathfrak{z}r) \succeq \frac{[1 + \mho(z, Fz, qr)]\mho(w, Fw, er)}{1 + \mho(w, z, r)} + \mho(z, w, r),$$

where $q + e = \mathfrak{z} \in [0, 1)$. Then F has a unique σ-fuzzy fixed point in $\mathcal{S}$.

Proof. Define a sequence $\{c_n\}$ as $c_n = Fc_{n-1}$, for all $n \in \aleph$. Thanks to (9), which guarantee that $\{c_n\}$ is a Cauchy sequence, as for $r \in \wp_\theta$,

$$\varrho_{n+1} = \inf_{m>n} \mho(c_n + 1, c_m + 1, r) \succeq \inf_{m>n} \mho(c_0, c_m + 1, \frac{r}{\mathfrak{z}^{n+1}})$$

$$= \inf_{m>n} \mho(c_0, F^{m-n}c_0, \frac{r}{\mathfrak{z}^{n+1}}) = \inf_{y \in \Xi_{c_0} > n} \mho(c_0, yc_0, \frac{r}{\mathfrak{z}^{n+1}}).$$

Thus

$$\lim_{n\to\infty} \varrho_{n+1} \succeq \lim_{n\to\infty} \inf_{y \in \Xi_{c_0} > n} \mho(c_0, yc_0, \frac{r}{\mathfrak{z}^{n+1}}) = \ell.$$

The proof is in the same fashion of Theorem 1. □

Corollary 6. Let $(\mathcal{S}, \mho, \diamond)$ be CVFMS such that, for any sequence $\{r_n\}$ in $\wp_\theta$ with $\lim_{n\to\infty} r_n = \infty$, we have

$$\lim_{r\to\infty} M(w, z, r_n) = \ell, \text{ for all } w, z \in \mathcal{S}, q \in (0, 1) \text{ and } r > 0.$$

Suppose $L : \mathcal{S} \to CB(\mathcal{S})$ be a multivalued mapping with least upper bound property, such that

$$\frac{[1 + \mho(z, Lz, qr)]\mho(w, Lw, er)}{1 + \mho(w, z, r)} + \mho(z, w, r) \in s(Lw, Lz, \mathfrak{z}r). \tag{10}$$

Then, L has a unique fixed point.

Proof. Consider the fuzzy mapping $F : \mathcal{S} \to \mathfrak{F}(\mathcal{S})$ defined by

$$F(x)(t) = \begin{cases} \sigma & \text{if } t \in Lx \\ \theta & \text{if } t \notin Lx, \end{cases}$$

where $\sigma \in \daleth^+$. Then,

$$[Fx]_\sigma = \{t : F(x)(t) \geq \sigma\} = Lx.$$

Thus, Theorem 1 can be applied to obtain a fixed point, i.e., there exists $v \in \mathcal{S}$ such that $v \in Fv$. □

Example 2. *Let* $\daleth_\mathbb{R} = [0,1]$ *and* $\mathcal{S} = \daleth_\mathbb{R} \times 0 \cup 0 \times \daleth_\mathbb{R}$. *Let* $\diamond$ *be defined by*

$$c_1 \diamond c_2 = (\max\{a' + a'' - 1, 0\}, \max\{b' + b'' - 1, 0\}),$$

for all $c_1 = (a', b'), c_2 = (a'', b'') \in \daleth$. *Define* $D : \mathcal{S} \times \mathcal{S} \to \mathfrak{C}$ *by*

$$D((z,0),(w,0)) = |z-w|(2,1), D((0,z),(0,w)) = |z-w|(1, \tfrac{3}{5})$$

and

$$D((z,0),(0,w)) = D((0,w),(z,0)) = (2z+w, z + \tfrac{3}{5}w).$$

Clearly, $(\mathcal{S}, D)$ *is a complex valued metric space. Let* $\mho_D$ *be defined by*

$$\mho_D(u, v, c_1) = \ell - \frac{5D(u,v)}{18 + 5ab} \quad \textit{for all} \quad u, v \in \mathcal{S}, c_1 = (a,b) \in \wp_\theta.$$

Then, $(\mathcal{S}, \mho_D, \diamond)$ *is a complete CVFMS. Let* $\sigma \in (0,1]$ *and* $G : \mathcal{S} \to \mathfrak{F}(\mathcal{S})$ *be a fuzzy mapping defined by:*

$$G(\theta)(t) = \begin{cases} \ell & \textit{if } t = \theta \\ \tfrac{1}{2}\ell & \textit{if } \theta < t \leq \tfrac{w}{50} \\ \theta & \textit{if } \tfrac{w}{50} < t \leq \ell, \end{cases}$$

if $(w, 0) \neq \theta$,

$$G(w)(t) = \begin{cases} \sigma & \textit{if } \theta \leq t \leq \tfrac{w}{75} \\ \tfrac{\sigma}{3} & \textit{if } \tfrac{w}{75} < t \leq \tfrac{w}{10} \\ \tfrac{\sigma}{4} & \textit{if } \tfrac{w}{10} < t \leq \ell, \end{cases}$$

Then, for $w = \theta$, $[G\theta]_\ell = \{\theta\}$ *and* $\forall \ w, z \neq \theta$, $[Gw]_\sigma = [\theta, \tfrac{w}{75}]$. *Thus,*

$$\mathcal{W}_w([Gw]_\sigma, c_1) = \{\mho_D(z, p, r) : p \in [\theta, \tfrac{w}{75}]\}.$$

Let $\mho_D(z, [Gw]_\sigma, r)$ *be the least upper bound of* $\mathcal{W}_w([Gw]_\sigma, r)$. *Moreover, if* $\omega_{wz} \in \daleth$ *such that*

$$\omega_{wz} = \ell - \frac{5D([Gw]_\sigma, [Gz]_\sigma)}{18 + 5ab},$$

then,

$$s\big(\mho_D([Gw]_\sigma, [Gz]_\sigma, 3r)\big) = \{\omega \in \daleth : \omega_{yw} \succeq \omega\}.$$

Consider

$$\begin{aligned}
\omega_{wz} &= \ell - \frac{5D([Gw]_\sigma, [Gz]_\sigma)}{18 + 5ab} \\
&= \ell - \frac{5|\tfrac{w}{75} - \tfrac{z}{75}|}{18 + 5ab} \\
&\succeq \ell - \frac{5|w - z|}{18 + 5ab} \\
&= \ell - \frac{5D(w, z)}{18 + 5ab} \\
&= \mho_D(w, z, r)
\end{aligned}$$

Therefore, we have
$$\mathcal{U}_D(z, \mathbf{w}, \mathbf{r}) \in s([F\mathbf{w}]_\sigma, [Fz]_\sigma, 3\mathbf{r}).$$

Hence, all conditions of Corollary 3 are satisfied by G; therefore, there exists $(0,0) \in \mathcal{S}$, such that $(0,0) \in [G(0,0)]_\sigma$.

4. Applications Fuzzy Caputo Fractional Volterra–Fredholm Integro-Differential Equations

Consider initial value problem

$$\begin{cases} (_{gH}D_*^{fl}u)t = f(t, u(t), \mathcal{K}u(t), \mathcal{H}u(t)), t \in \mathbf{J} = [t_0, T] \\ u(t_0) = u_0 \in \mathbb{R}_\mathcal{F}, \end{cases} \quad (11)$$

where $0 < \gamma < 1$ is a real number and $_{gH}D_*^{fl}$ denote the Caputo fractional generalized derivative of order γ, $f : \mathbf{J} \times \mathbb{R}_\mathcal{F} \times \mathbb{R}_\mathcal{F} \times \mathbb{R}_\mathcal{F} \to \mathbb{R}_\mathcal{F}$ is continuous in t, which satisfies some assumptions that will be specified later, and

$$\mathcal{K}u(t) = \int_{t_0}^t \mathcal{K}(t, ru(r))dr, \quad \mathcal{H}u(t) = \int_{t_0}^T \mathcal{H}(t, ru(r))dr, \quad (12)$$

This problem is equivalent to the integral equation

$$u(t) = u_0 + \frac{1}{\Gamma(\gamma)} \int_{t_0}^t (t-r)^{\gamma-1} f(r, u(r), \mathcal{K}u(r), \mathcal{H}u(r))dr, \quad (13)$$

where u is a fuzzy valued $^{cf}[(i) - gH]$-differentiable on $\mathbf{J}$.

For a detailed study of problem (11), we recommend that the readers look at [8].

To study our results for the existence of a fixed point, we define the integral operator $\mathcal{T}$ as

$$\mathcal{T}u(t) = u_0 + \frac{1}{\Gamma(\gamma)} \int_{t_0}^t (t-r)^{\gamma-1} f(r, u(r), \mathcal{K}u(r), \mathcal{H}u(r))dr. \quad (14)$$

For the sake of simplicity, we mentioned $\frac{1}{\Gamma(\gamma)} \int_t^{t_0} (t-r)^{\gamma-1} f(r, u(r), \mathcal{K}u(r), \mathcal{H}u(r))dr = \mathcal{F}_u$ Now, we study the existence and uniqueness of solutions to problem (11). To proceed, we use the following hypotheses:

Hypothesis 1 (H1). $f : \mathbf{J} \times \mathbb{R}_\mathcal{F} \times \mathbb{R}_\mathcal{F} \times \mathbb{R}_\mathcal{F} \to \mathbb{R}_\mathcal{F}$ is continuous such that

$$\mathcal{H}_{(\mathcal{T}u\mathcal{T}v)}(t) \succeq \frac{(1 + \mathcal{A}_{(uv)}(t))\mathcal{B}_{(uv)}(t)}{1 + \mathcal{G}_{(uv)}(t)} + \mathcal{G}_{(uv)}(t), \quad (15)$$

where

$$\mathcal{H}_{(\mathcal{T}u\mathcal{T}v)}(t) = \frac{c}{c + \|\mathcal{F}_u - \mathcal{F}_v\|_\infty} \ell$$

$$\mathcal{A}_{(uv)}(t) = \frac{c}{\|u - u_0 + \mathcal{F}_u\|_\infty} \ell$$

$$\mathcal{B}_{(uv)}(t) = \frac{c}{\|v - v_0 + \mathcal{F}_v\|_\infty} \ell$$

$$\mathcal{G}_{(uv)}(t) = \frac{c}{\|u - v\|_\infty} \ell$$

Then, the initial value problem (11) has only one solution.

Proof. Consider $\mathcal{S} = ([0, T], \mathbb{R}_\mathcal{F})$ with the metric

$$\mathcal{D}(\hat{x}, \hat{y}) = \max_{t_0 \leq t \leq T} (\hat{x}\|t) - \hat{y}(t)\|_\infty.$$

Let $\mho : S \times S \times \wp_\theta \to \daleth$ defined by

$$\mho(\hat{x}, \hat{y}, c) = \frac{c}{c + \mathcal{D}(\hat{x}, \hat{y})} \ell$$

for $c = (a, b) \in \wp_\theta$. It is obvious that $(S, \mho, *)$ is CVFMS. Consider (14), define the integral operator $\mathcal{T} : S \to S$. For $\hat{x}, \hat{y} \in S$, we have

$$[\mathcal{T}\hat{x}]_\sigma = \{u \in [t, t_0] : u(j) = u_0 + \mathcal{F}_u \succeq \sigma, j \in [t, T], \mathcal{T}\hat{x}(u) \succeq \sigma\},$$

$$\begin{cases} \mho(u, v, c) = \dfrac{c}{c + \max_{t_0 \leq t} \|u - v\|_\infty} \ell \\ \mho(u, [\mathcal{T}u]_\sigma, qc) = \dfrac{c}{c + \max_{t_0 \leq t} \|u - u_0 + \mathcal{F}_u\|_\infty} \ell \\ \mho(v, [\mathcal{T}v]_\sigma, ec) = \dfrac{c}{c + \max_{t_0 \leq t} \|v - v_0 + \mathcal{F}_v\|_\infty} \ell \\ \mho([\mathcal{T}u]_\sigma, [\mathcal{T}v]_\sigma, 3c) = \dfrac{3c}{3c + \max_{t_0 \leq t} \|u_0 + \mathcal{F}_u - v_0 + \mathcal{F}_v\|_\infty} \ell \end{cases} \tag{16}$$

From assumption (15), we obtain, for each $t \in [t, t_0]$

$$\mathcal{H}_{(\mathcal{T}u\mathcal{T}v)}(t) \succeq \frac{(1 + \mathcal{A}_{(uv)}(t))\mathcal{B}_{(uv)}(t)}{1 + \mathcal{G}_{(uv)}(t)} + \mathcal{G}_{(uv)}(t)$$

$$= \frac{(1 + \frac{c}{\|u-u_0+\mathcal{F}_u\|_\infty}\ell)\frac{c}{\|v-v_0+\mathcal{F}_v\|_\infty}\ell}{1 + \frac{c}{\|u-v\|_\infty}\ell} + \frac{c}{\|u-v\|_\infty}\ell$$

$$\succeq \frac{(1 + \frac{c}{c+\max_{t_0 \leq t}\|u-u_0+\mathcal{F}_u\|_\infty}\ell)\frac{c}{c+\max_{t_0 \leq t}\|v-v_0+\mathcal{F}_v\|_\infty}\ell}{1 + \frac{c}{c+\max_{t_0 \leq t}\|u-v\|_\infty}\ell} + \frac{c}{c + \max_{t_0 \leq t}\|u-v\|_\infty}\ell.$$

This yields

$$\frac{3c}{3c + \max_{t_0 \leq t}\|\mathcal{F}_u - \mathcal{F}_v\|_\infty}\ell \succeq \frac{(1 + \frac{c}{c+\max_{t_0 \leq t}\|u-u_0+\mathcal{F}_u\|_\infty}\ell)\frac{c}{c+\max_{t_0 \leq t}\|v-v_0+\mathcal{F}_v\|_\infty}\ell}{1 + \frac{c}{c+\max_{t_0 \leq t}\|u-v\|_\infty}\ell}$$

$$+ \frac{c}{c + \max_{t_0 \leq t}\|u-v\|_\infty}\ell.$$

By using (16), we get

$$\mho([\mathcal{T}u]_\sigma, [\mathcal{T}v]_\sigma, 3c) \succeq \left(\frac{\mho(u, [\mathcal{T}u]_\sigma, c)\mho(v, [\mathcal{T}v]_\sigma, c)}{1 + \mho(u, v, c)} + \mho(u, v, c) \right).$$

Thus, all conditions of Theorem 1 hold. Therefore, there exists only one fixed point of $\mathcal{T}$ in S, and so there exists a unique solution to the system (11). □

5. Discussion and Conclusions

In many situations, classical models fail to describe the features of natural phenomena such as the dynamics of viscoelastic materials such as polymers, the atmospheric diffusion of pollution, and signal transmissions through strong magnetic fields. In such situations, fuzzy concepts are the best solution. This concept has the ability to model difficult uncertainties with ease. In our research work, we considered a complex fuzzy set in fuzzy metric spaces, which is more general than classical fuzzy metric fixed-point theory. We obtained complex fuzzy versions of rational type contractions via the least upper bound property in the new approach (complex valued fuzzy metric spaces). We also discussed its applications in multivalued mappings. Then, we proposed an existence theorem for a unique solution to fractional Volterra–Fredholm integro-differential equations under generalized fuzzy

Caputo Hukuhara differentiability using the technique of a fixed point. As an application, we provided an illustrative example, which shows the applicability and validity of the approach we used in this article.

Our results will open doors for researchers working on rational type contraction in complex valued fuzzy spaces. The studied results and their applications can be extended to functional, differential and integral equations via numerical experiment.

Author Contributions: Conceptualization, writing—original draft preparation, writing—review and editing, supervision, investigation, H. and M.S.; methodology, formal analysis, funding acquisition, visualization T.A. and N.M. All authors have read and agreed to the published version of the manuscript.

Funding: This research received no external funding.

Institutional Review Board Statement: Not applicable.

Informed Consent Statement: Not applicable.

Data Availability Statement: Not applicable.

Acknowledgments: We are very grateful to the editor and unbiased arbitrator for his/her prudent interpretation and proposition which refined the excellency of this manuscript. The last two authors would like to thank Prince Sultan University for funding this work through the research lab TAS.

Conflicts of Interest: The authors declare no conflict of interest.

References

1. Zadeh, L.A. Fuzzy sets. *Inf. Control.* **1965**, *8*, 338–353. [CrossRef]
2. Ahmad, N.; Ullah, A.; Ullah, A.; Ahmad, S.; Shah, K.; Amtiaz, A. On analysis of the fuzzy fractional order Volterra-Fredholm integro-differential equation. *Alex. Eng. J.* **2021**, *60*, 1827–1838. [CrossRef]
3. Allahviranloo, T.; Armand, A.; Gouyandeh, Z. Fuzzy fractional differential equations under generalized fuzzy Caputo derivative. *J. Intell. Fuzzy Syst.* **2014**, *26*, 1481–1490. [CrossRef]
4. Hoa, N.V. Fuzzy fractional functional integral and differential equations. *Fuzzy Sets Syst.* **2015**, *280*, 58–90. [CrossRef]
5. Hoa, N.V. Fuzzy fractional functional differential equations under Caputo gH-differentiability. *Commun. Nonlinear Sci. Numer. Simul.* **2015**, *22*, 1134–1157. [CrossRef]
6. Hoa, N.V.; Vu, H.; Duc, T.M. Fuzzy fractional differential equations under Caputo–Katugampola fractional derivative approach. *Fuzzy Sets Syst.* **2019**, *375*, 70–99. [CrossRef]
7. Vu, H.; Hoa, N.V. Applications of contractive-like mapping principles to fuzzy fractional integral equations with the kernel ψ-functions. *Soft Comput.* **2020**, *24*, 18841–18855. [CrossRef]
8. Allahviranloo, T.; Armand, A.; Gouyandeh, Z.; Ghadiri, H. Existence and uniqueness of solutions for fuzzy fractional Volterra-Fredholm integro-differential equations. *J. Fuzzy Set Valued Anal.* **2013**, *2013*, 1–9. [CrossRef]
9. Alkan, S.; Hatipolglu, V. Approximate solution of Volterra-Fredholm integro-differential equations of fractional oreder. *Tablisi Math. J.* **2017**, *10*, 1–13. [CrossRef]
10. Hamoud, A.D.; Ghadle, K.P. The reliable modified of Laplace Adomian decomposition method to solve nonlinear interval Volterra-Fredholm integral equations. *Korean J. Math.* **2017**, *3*, 323–334. [CrossRef]
11. Hamoud, A.D.; Ghadle, K.P. The combined modified of Laplace with Adomian decomposition method for solving the nonlinear Volterra-Fredholm integro-differential equations. *J. Korean Soc. Ind. Appl. Math.* **2017**, *21*, 17–28. [CrossRef]
12. Ma, X.; Haung, C. Numerical solution of fractional integro-differential equations by hybrid collection method. *Appl. Math. Comput.* **2013**, *12*, 6750–6760. [CrossRef]
13. Mital, R.; Nigam, R. Solution of fractional integro-differential equations by Adomian decompusition method. *Int. J. Appl. Math. Mech.* **2008**, *2*, 87–94. [CrossRef]
14. Ramot, D.; Milo, F.; Friedman, M.; Kandel, A. Complex fuzzy sets. *IEEE Trans. Fuzzy Syst.* **2002**, *2*, 171–186. [CrossRef]
15. Yazdanbakhsh, O.; Dick, S. A systematic review of complex fuzzy sets and logic. *Fuzzy Sets Syst.* **2018**, *338*, 1–22. [CrossRef]
16. Nadler, S.B. Multivalued contraction mappings. *Pac. J. Appl. Math.* **1969**, *30*, 475–488.
17. Heilpern, S. Fuzzy fixed point theorems. *J. Math. Anal.* **1981**, *83*, 566–569.
18. Butnariu, D. Fixed points for fuzzy mappings. *Fuzzy Sets Syst.* **1982**, *7*, 191–207.
19. Weiss, M.D. Fixed points, separation and induced topologies for fuzzy sets. *J. Math. Anal. Appl.* **1975**, *1*, 142–150.
20. Kramosil, I.; Michalek, J. Fuzzy metric and statistical metric spaces. *Kybernetica* **1975**, *11*, 336–344. [CrossRef]
21. Garbiec, M. Fixed points in fuzzy metric spaces. *Fuzzy Sets Syst.* **1988**, *27*, 385–399. [CrossRef]
22. George, A.; Veeramani, P. On some results in fuzzy metric spaces. *Fuzzy Sets Syst.* **1994**, *64*, 395–399. [CrossRef]

23. Dosenović, T.; Rakić, D.; Carić, B.; Radenović, S. Multivalued generalizations of fixed point results in fuzzy metric spaces. *Nonliner Anal. Model. Control* **2016**, *2*, 211–222. [CrossRef]
24. Shukla, S.; Rodríguez-López, R.; Abbas, M. Fixed point results for contractive mappings in complex valued fuzzy metric spaces. *Fixed Point Theory* **2018**, *19*, 751–774. [CrossRef]
25. Dass, B.K.; Gupta, S. An extension of Banach contraction principle through rational expression. *Indian J. Pure Appl. Math.* **1975**, *6*, 1455–1458. [CrossRef]

Article

Coupled Discrete Fractional-Order Logistic Maps

Marius-F. Danca [1,*], Michal Fečkan [2,3,*], Nikolay Kuznetsov [4,5] and Guanrong Chen [6]

1 Romanian Institute of Science and Technology, 400504 Cluj-Napoca, Romania
2 Faculty of Mathematics, Physics and Informatics, Comenius University in Bratislava, 84215 Bratislava, Slovakia
3 Mathematical Institute, Slovak Academy of Sciences, 84104 Bratislava, Slovakia
4 Mathematics and Mechanics Faculty, Saint-Petersburg State University, 199034 Saint Petersburg, Russia; nkuznetsov239@gmail.com
5 Department of Mathematical Information Technology, University of Jyväskylä, 40014 Jyväskylä, Finland
6 Department of Electronic Engineering, City University of Hong Kong, Hong Kong, China; eegchen@cityu.edu.hk
* Correspondence: danca@rist.ro (M.-F.D.); michal.feckan@gmail.com or Michal.Feckan@fmph.uniba.sk (M.F.)

Abstract: This paper studies a system of coupled discrete fractional-order logistic maps, modeled by Caputo's delta fractional difference, regarding its numerical integration and chaotic dynamics. Some interesting new dynamical properties and unusual phenomena from this coupled chaotic-map system are revealed. Moreover, the coexistence of attractors, a necessary ingredient of the existence of hidden attractors, is proved and analyzed.

Keywords: discrete fractional-order system; caputo delta fractional difference; fractional-order difference equation; stability; hidden attractor

Citation: Danca, M.-F.; Fečkan, M.; Kuznetsov, N.; Chen, G. Coupled Discrete Fractional-Order Logistic Maps. *Mathematics* **2021**, *9*, 2204. https://doi.org/10.3390/math9182204

Academic Editor: José A. Tenreiro Machado

Received: 11 August 2021
Accepted: 6 September 2021
Published: 8 September 2021

Publisher's Note: MDPI stays neutral with regard to jurisdictional claims in published maps and institutional affiliations.

Copyright: © 2021 by the authors. Licensee MDPI, Basel, Switzerland. This article is an open access article distributed under the terms and conditions of the Creative Commons Attribution (CC BY) license (https://creativecommons.org/licenses/by/4.0/).

1. Introduction

Nonlinear phenomena are difficult to describe by models analysis based only on smoothness; thereby, fractional calculus has been used to model many such processes for which the standard integer-order derivatives cannot be applied adequately. The generalization of the concept of derivatives of non-integer values dates back to the beginning of the theory of differential calculus, while the rapid development of the theory of fractional calculus started from the work of Euler, Liouville, Riemann, Letnikov, and so on [1,2]. In the past, new results of fractional modeling and applications were reported every year. The fractional derivatives and integrals are useful in engineering and mathematics, being helpful for scientists and researchers working with real-life applications (see, e.g., [3,4]).

It is well-known that the classical derivative of a continuous-time periodic function is a periodic function with the same period. However, with respect to derivatives of fractional order, this is not necessarily the case [5–12]. The non-periodicity of solutions in fractional-order (FO) systems was first discovered by engineers (see, e.g., [7]), and then proved by mathematicians (see, e.g., [5,12]). Generally, FO systems have no non-constant periodic solutions by their nature (verified, e.g., using Laplace or Z transformations). Nevertheless, both continuous and discrete FO systems may have asymptotic periodic solutions. However, just like continuous FO systems, the periodicity of solutions in discrete FO systems is a delicate issue [10,13–17]. As a consequence, all reported results based on the "periodicity" of continuous- or discrete-time autonomous FO systems became questionable.

In this paper, orbits apparently indicating some regular behavior will be called "periodic-like" orbits. Recall that for some values of the bifurcation parameter of the integral-order (IO) logistic map, unstable periodic orbits (UPOs) will emerge, leading to chaos. For FO logistic maps, this will be referred to as "chaotic-like" behavior. In [18], these kinds of periodic-like orbits are called "numerically periodic orbits". It is also well-known that in the theory of dynamical systems, every emerging abrupt period-doubling phenomenon is considered as bifurcation. Therefore, in this paper, the term *bifurcation* or *bifurcation diagram* is understood in the above sense of a periodic-like phenomenon.

On the other hand, from a computational point of view, based on the complexity or simplicity in finding a basin of attraction in the phase space, it is natural to consider the following classification of attractors: self-excited attractors, which can be revealed numerically by integrating the systems with initial conditions within small neighborhoods of unstable equilibria, and hidden attractors, which have the basins of attraction not connected with any equilibria [19–23]. Examples of hidden attractors in continuous-time FO systems exist in some classical systems, such as the Rabinovich-Fabrikant system [24–26], Hopfield neuronal system [27], economic system [28], hyperchaotic discontinuous system [29], and so on [30].

In a numerical approach, the need for previous history in numerical integration requires a trade-off between the calculation time and the approximation precision. This is a basic principle for some classical numerical methods for fractional differential equations (FDEs), such as the Adams-Bashforth-Moulton method [31], for which a tutorial can be found in [32]. Finally, it should also be noted that the mathematical theory of FDEs is still quite limited today, although the subject has been studied since 1956 [33].

With all the above motivations and background, the present paper is devoted to studying a system of discrete coupled FO logistic maps, with respect to its numerical bifurcation analysis and hidden attractor search, which reveals some very interesting new dynamical properties and unusual phenomena.

This paper will also discuss the stability of discrete FO equations, where [34–36] can be referred to for more details.

2. A Model of Coupled FO Logistic Maps

In [37], the bistability of some "aggregates" of logistic maps with excitation-type coupling is studied. One such model is composed by two *functional units*, a neuron or a group of neurons (voxels), as a discrete nonlinear oscillator with two possible states: active (meaning one type of activity) or not (meaning other type of activity). A reasonable modality to take the most elemental local nonlinearity is, for instance, the logistic evolution:

$$x(n+1) = p(3y(n)+1)x(n)(1-x(n)),$$
$$y(n+1) = p(-3x(n)+4)y(n)(1-y(n)), \ n \in \mathbb{N}. \quad (1)$$

The first equation with the coupled functional units (1) refers to excitation coupling, while the second equation, to inhibition coupling. These kinds of models are proposed in [37] to mimic the waking-sleeping bistability and even multistability found in brain systems (see [37] for details).

In this paper, the Fractional Order (FO) variant of the system (1) is considered.

To obtain the FO form, let $N_a = \{a, a+1, a+2, \ldots\}$. Then, for $q > 0$ and $q \notin \mathbb{N}$, the q-th Caputo-like discrete fractional difference of a function $u : N_a \to \mathbb{R}$ is defined as [38,39]

$$\Delta_a^q u(t) = \Delta_a^{-(n-q)} \Delta^n u(t) = \frac{1}{\Gamma(n-q)} \sum_{s=a}^{t-(n-q)} (t-s-1)^{(n-q-1)} \Delta^n u(s), \quad (2)$$

for $t \in N_{a+n-q}$ and $n = [q]+1$. In (4), Δ^n is the n-th order forward difference operator,

$$\Delta^n u(s) = \sum_{k=0}^{n} \binom{n}{k} (-1)^{n-k} u(s+k)$$

and Δ_a^{-q} represents the fractional sum of order q of u, namely,

$$\Delta_a^{-q} u(t) = \frac{1}{\Gamma(q)} \sum_{s=a}^{t-q} (t-s-1)^{(q-1)} u(s), \ t \in \mathbb{N}_{a+q} \quad (3)$$

with the falling factorial $t^{(q)}$ in the following form:

$$t^{(q)} = \frac{\Gamma(t+1)}{\Gamma(t-q+1)}.$$

Note that the fractional operator Δ_a^{-q} maps functions defined on $\mathbb{N}_a$ to functions on $\mathbb{N}_{a+q}$.

For the case considered in this paper, $q \in (0,1)$, when $n=1$, $\Delta u(s) = u(s+1) - u(s)$, and Caputo's fractional difference, denoted hereafter Δ_*^q, becomes

$$\Delta_*^q u(t) = \frac{1}{\Gamma(1-q)} \sum_{s=a}^{t-(1-q)} (t-s-1)^{(-q)} \Delta u(s). \tag{4}$$

Assuming the starting point of the fractional sum (3), $a = 0$, one can consider the following discrete autonomous Initial Value Problem (IVP) of FO (the non-autonomous case can be found in [40,41]):

$$\Delta_*^q u(t) = f(u(t+q-1)), \ t \in \mathbb{N}_{1-q}, \ u(0) = u_0, \tag{5}$$

for $q \in (0,1)$ and f is a continuous map.

The solution of the IVP (5) is given by [40,41]

$$u(t) = u_0 + \frac{1}{\Gamma(q)} \sum_{s=1-q}^{t-q} (t-s-1)^{(q-1)} f(u(s+q-1)). \tag{6}$$

A convenient iterative form of the integral (6) is [35]

$$u(n) = u(0) + \frac{1}{\Gamma(q)} \sum_{i=1}^{n} \frac{\Gamma(n-i+q)}{\Gamma(n-i+1)} f(u(i-1)), \ u(0) = u_0, \ n \in \mathbb{N}, n > 0. \tag{7}$$

Now, one can introduce the FO variant of the system (1) modeled by the Caputo delta fractional difference equation:

$$\begin{aligned}
\Delta_*^q x(t) &= p(3y(t+q-1)+1)x(t+q-1)(1-x(t+q-1)), \\
\Delta_*^q y(t) &= p(-3x(t+q-1)+4)y(t+q-1)(1-y(t+q-1)), \\
t &\in \mathbb{N}_{1-q}, \ x(0) = x_0, \ y(0) = y_0,
\end{aligned} \tag{8}$$

where $p \in \mathbb{R}$ is a parameter. In this case,

$$f(u) := f(x,y) = \begin{pmatrix} p(3y+1)x(1-x) \\ p(-3x+4)y(1-y) \end{pmatrix}, \tag{9}$$

and the integral (7) has the following form, which will be used to integrate and simulate the system dynamics later:

$$\begin{aligned}
x(n) &= x(0) + \frac{1}{\Gamma(q)} \sum_{i=1}^{n} \frac{\Gamma(n-i+q)}{\Gamma(n-i+1)} p(3y(i-1)+1)x(i-1)(1-x(i-1)), \\
y(n) &= y(0) + \frac{1}{\Gamma(q)} \sum_{i=1}^{n} \frac{\Gamma(n-i+q)}{\Gamma(n-i+1)} p(-3x(i-1)+4)y(i-1)(1-y(i-1)), \\
n &\in \mathbb{N}, \ n > 0, \ x(0) = x_0, \ y(0) = y_0.
\end{aligned} \tag{10}$$

3. Bounds and Global Dynamics

The theory of orbits for discrete FO systems is technically rather sophisticated in general and is still under development. Additionally, finding either bounds of solutions or qualitative properties of global dynamics are difficult tasks.

Nevertheless, from the expressions (10), one can see that $x(n)$ and $y(n)$ are polynomials of p, that is,

$$x(n) = \sum_{j=0}^{k(n)} a_{nj}(x(0), y(0)) p^j$$
$$y(n) = \sum_{j=0}^{k(n)} b_{nj}(x(0), y(0)) p^j, \tag{11}$$

where the coefficients $a_{nj}(x(0), y(0))$, $b_{nj}(x(0), y(0))$ are polynomials of $x(0), y(0)$.

From (10), the degree k of polynomials (11) is

$$k(0) = 0, \quad k(n) = 3k(n-1) + 1, \ n \geq 1,$$

so

$$k(n) = \frac{3^n - 1}{2}.$$

The formulas $a_{nj}(x(0), y(0))$ and $b_{nj}(x(0), y(0))$ are difficult to find explicitly for general n, but nevertheless, one can find that

$$a_{n0}(x(0), y(0)) = x(0), \quad b_{n0}(x(0), y(0)) = y(0),$$

$$a_{n1}(x(0), y(0)) = \frac{(3y(0) + 1)x(0)(1 - x(0))}{\Gamma(q)} \sum_{i=1}^{n} \frac{\Gamma(n - i + q)}{\Gamma(n - i + 1)},$$

$$b_{n1}(x(0), y(0)) = \frac{(-3x(0) + 4)y(0)(1 - y(0))}{\Gamma(q)} \sum_{i=1}^{n} \frac{\Gamma(n - i + q)}{\Gamma(n - i + 1)}.$$

Using [42] (Proposition 1), one obtains the following result.

Theorem 1. *The following limits hold:*

$$\lim_{n \to \infty} \frac{a_{n1}(x(0), y(0))}{n^q} = \frac{(3y(0) + 1)x(0)(1 - x(0))}{\Gamma(q + 1)},$$

$$\lim_{n \to \infty} \frac{b_{n1}(x(0), y(0))}{n^q} = \frac{(-3x(0) + 4)y(0)(1 - y(0))}{\Gamma(q + 1)}.$$

Consequently, the first-order approximations of (11) diverges to ∞ as $n \to \infty$, except at the equilibria, where $f(u(0)) = 0$.

Concerning global dynamics, the following result holds (for the dynamical behavior of discrete-time linear FO systems, see [43]).

Theorem 2. *There is no orbit $\{(x(n), y(n))\}_{n=1}^{\infty}$ of (8) such that*

$$(x(n), y(n)) \in S, \quad \forall n \geq n_0, \tag{12}$$

for some $n_0 \in \mathbb{N}$, where S is one of the following subsets of $\mathbb{R}^2$:

$$\left\{ x \geq 1 + \delta, \ y \geq -\frac{1}{3} + \delta \right\}, \quad \left\{ x \leq -\delta, \ y \leq -\frac{1}{3} - \delta \right\},$$
$$\left\{ x \leq \frac{4}{3} + \delta, \ y \geq 1 + \delta \right\}, \quad \left\{ x \geq \frac{4}{3} + \delta, \ y \leq -\delta \right\}, \tag{13}$$

with $\delta > 0$.

Proof.

(1) If $S = \{x \geq 1 + \delta, y \geq -\frac{1}{3} + \delta\}$ and (12) holds, then (7) implies that

$$\begin{aligned}x(n) &= x(0) + \frac{p}{\Gamma(q)} \sum_{i=1}^{n_0} \frac{\Gamma(n-i+q)}{\Gamma(n-i+1)} (3y(i-1)+1)x(i-1)(1-x(i-1))\\ &\quad + \frac{p}{\Gamma(q)} \sum_{i=n_0+1}^{n} \frac{\Gamma(n-i+q)}{\Gamma(n-i+1)} (3y(i-1)+1)x(i-1)(1-x(i-1))\\ &\leq x(0) + \frac{p}{\Gamma(q)} \sum_{i=1}^{n_0} (3y(i-1)+1)x(i-1)(1-x(i-1))\\ &\quad - 3\delta^2(1+\delta)\frac{p}{\Gamma(q)} \sum_{i=n_0+1}^{n} \frac{\Gamma(n-i+q)}{\Gamma(n-i+1)},\end{aligned} \quad (14)$$

for $n \geq n_0 + 1$. By applying [42] (Proposition 1), (15) gives $\lim_{n \to \infty} x(n) = -\infty$, which contradicts $x(n) \geq 1 + \delta$ for $n \geq n_0$. The proof is completed for the first subset of (13).

(2) If $S = \{x \leq -\delta, y \leq -\frac{1}{3} - \delta\}$ and (12) holds, then (7) implies that

$$\begin{aligned}x(n) &\geq x(0) + \frac{p}{\Gamma(q)} \sum_{i=1}^{n_0} (3y(i-1)+1)x(i-1)(1-x(i-1))\\ &\quad + 3\delta^2(1+\delta)\frac{p}{\Gamma(q)} \sum_{i=n_0+1}^{n} \frac{\Gamma(n-i+q)}{\Gamma(n-i+1)},\end{aligned} \quad (15)$$

for $n \geq n_0 + 1$. By applying [42] (Proposition 1), (15) gives $\lim_{n \to \infty} x(n) = \infty$, which contradicts $x(n) \leq -\delta$ for $n \geq n_0$. The proof is completed for the second subset of (13).

(3) If $S = \{x \leq \frac{4}{3} - \delta, y \geq 1 + \delta\}$ and (12) holds, then (7) implies that

$$\begin{aligned}y(n) &\leq y(0) + \frac{p}{\Gamma(q)} \sum_{i=1}^{n_0} (-3x(i-1)+4)y(i-1)(1-y(i-1))\\ &\quad - 3\delta^2(1+\delta)\frac{p}{\Gamma(q)} \sum_{i=n_0+1}^{n} \frac{\Gamma(n-i+q)}{\Gamma(n-i+1)},\end{aligned} \quad (16)$$

for $n \geq n_0 + 1$. By applying [42] (Proposition 1), (16) gives $\lim_{n \to \infty} y(n) = -\infty$, which contradicts $y(n) \geq 1 + \delta$ for $n \geq n_0$. The proof is completed for the third subset of (13).

(4) If $S = \{x \geq \frac{4}{3} + \delta, y \leq -\delta\}$ and (12) holds, then (7) implies that

$$\begin{aligned}y(n) &\geq y(0) + \frac{p}{\Gamma(q)} \sum_{i=1}^{n_0} (-3x(i-1)+4)y(i-1)(1-y(i-1))\\ &\quad + 3\delta^2(1+\delta)\frac{p}{\Gamma(q)} \sum_{i=n_0+1}^{n} \frac{\Gamma(n-i+q)}{\Gamma(n-i+1)},\end{aligned} \quad (17)$$

for $n \geq n_0 + 1$. By applying [42] (Proposition 1), (17) gives $\lim_{n \to \infty} y(n) = \infty$, which contradicts $y(n) \geq -\delta$ for $n \geq n_0$. The proof is completed for the fourth subset of (13). The whole proof is thus completed. □

Remark 1. *Theorem 2 asserts the non-existence of an attractor of (8) within any subsets shown in (13).*

4. Non-Existence of Hidden Attractors

To numerically find hidden attractors, it is necessary to determine the stability of the system equilibria.

Proposition 1. *The equilibria of system (8) are*

$$E_1 = \left(\frac{4}{3}, -\frac{1}{3}\right), \quad E_2 = (0,0), \quad E_3 = (1,0), \quad E_4 = (0,1), \quad E_5 = (1,1). \tag{18}$$

Proof. For $0 < q < 1$, by using the explicit form of $f(u)$ given by (9), the equilibrium means that $u(n) = u(0)$ for all $n \geq 1$. This is equivalent to the equation $f(u(0)) = 0$. By (9), the equation $f(u(0)) = 0$ becomes:

$$(3y(0) + 1)x(0)(1 - x(0)) = 0, \tag{19}$$

$$(-3x(0) + 4)y(0)(1 - y(0)) = 0, \tag{20}$$

with solutions (18). □

The Jacobian of the function (9)

$$J(x,y) = p\begin{pmatrix} (3y+1)(1-2x) & 3x(1-x) \\ -3y(1-y) & (4-3x)(1-2y) \end{pmatrix}, \tag{21}$$

evaluated at equilibria E_i, $i = 1, 2, \ldots, 5$, gives the spectrum of eigenvalues σ as shown in Table 1.

Table 1. Spectrum σ of eigenvalues of J evaluated at equilibria E_i, $i = 1, 2, \ldots, 5$.

E	$\sigma(J)$
E_1	$(-\frac{4p}{3}\imath, \frac{4p}{3}\imath)$
E_2	$(p, 4p)$
E_3	$(-p, p)$
E_4	$(-4p, 4p)$
E_5	$(-4p, -p)$

The stability of the linearized FO system implies the stability of the nonlinear FO system (8), which conforms to [44] (Theorem 1.4). The system (8) is asymptotically stable if all the eigenvalues belong to the following set S^q:

$$S^q = \left\{ z \in \mathbb{C} : |z| < \left(2\cos\frac{|\lambda| - \pi}{2-q}\right)^q \text{ and } |\lambda| > \frac{q\pi}{2} \right\},$$

where λ denotes the argument of the eigenvalue.

Obviously, if there exist eigenvalues not belonging to S^q, then the system is unstable.

Theorem 3. *The system (8) is unstable for all $q \in (0,1)$ and p.*

Proof. Consider E_1, for which the arguments of eigenvalues $\{e_1, e_2\}$ are $\lambda_{1,2} = \pm\frac{\pi}{2}$ and $|z| = p\frac{4}{3}$. For both eigenvalues $\{e_1, e_2\}$, the first inequality in S^q becomes (see the first column in Table 2)

$$p < \frac{3}{4}\left(2\cos\frac{|\lambda| - \pi}{2-q}\right)^q = 2^{q-2}3\cos^q\frac{\pi}{2(2-q)}.$$

The second inequality in S^q is verified for both arguments $\lambda_{1,2}$.

For E_5, $\lambda_{1,2} = -\pi$, and the first inequality reads

$$4p < \left(2\cos\frac{0}{2-q}\right)^q = 2^q,$$

which is the result in the last column of Table 2. The second inequality is verified for all $q \in (0, 1)$.

Because for equilibria $E_{2,3,4}$, one argument is zero, the second inequality is not verified, so the eigenvalues do not belong to S^q, $e \notin S^q$. Therefore, $E_{2,3,4}$ are unstable and the system is unstable for all $q \in (0, 1)$ and p (the second column in Table 2). □

Table 2. Stability of equilibria E_i, $i = 1, 2, \ldots, 5$.

E_1	$E_{2,3,4}$	E_5
stable for $p < 3 \times 2^{q-2} \cos^q \frac{\pi}{2(2-q)}$	Unstable for all p and $q \in (0, 1)$	stable for $p < 2^{q-2}$

In the following simulations, unless otherwise mentioned, 3500 iterations were performed for all examples, and the last 600 points are plotted.

The stability regions in the plane (q, p) for equilibria $E_{1,5}$ are plotted in Figure 1a,b. The region where all equilibria are unstable is shown in Figure 1c (light brawn). Figure 1d,e presents orbits starting from initial conditions near equilibria E_1 and E_5. The spiral orbit of E_1 corresponds to complex eigenvalues of the system at this equilibrium, while the orbit of E_5 corresponds to real eigenvalues.

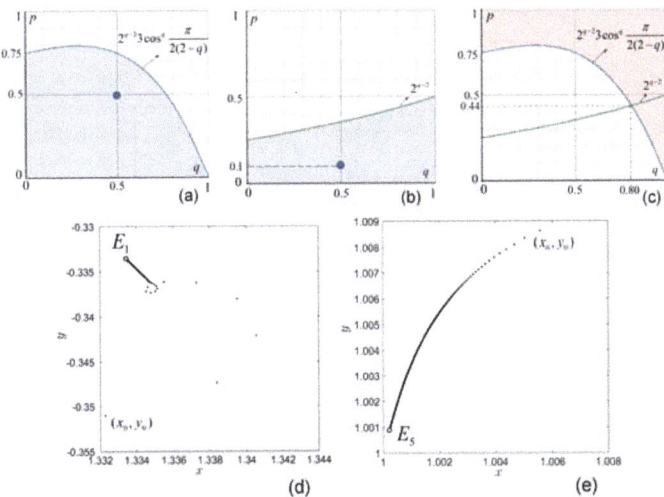

Figure 1. Stability regions of equilibria. (a) Stability region of E_1 (grey plot); (b) Stability region of E_5 (grey plot); (c) Instability region of all equilibria (light red plot); (d) Phase plot of a representative orbit from the point within the stability region of E_1, with $p = 0.5$ and $q = 0.5$ (Figure 1a) from initial condition close to E_1; (e) phase plot of a representative orbit from a point within the stability region of E_1, with $p = 0.1$ and $q = 0.5$ (Figure 1b) from initial condition close to E_5.

It is observed that, sometimes, possible system dynamics are richer than what can be revealed through examining bifurcation diagrams (BDs). As experienced, the BDs are suggestive and they show what parameter values the system can take on, and therefore helps to identify potential hidden attractors coexisting with other attractors. Consider, for example, the BDs of the component x vs. parameter q for fixed $p = 0.55$ with initial condition $(x_0, y_0) = (0.1, 0.3)$ (Figure 2a), and for $q = 0.4$ vs. parameter $p \in (0.3, 0.6)$ (the largest range of p for $q = 0.4$) (Figure 2b). As expected, Figure 2 reveals the influence of the IO logistic map. However, there are some significant differences, which will be illustrated and discussed next.

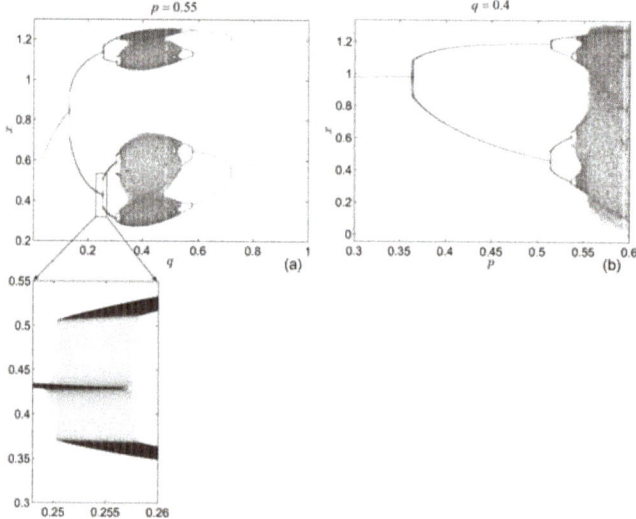

Figure 2. (a) The BD for $p = 0.55$ vs. q obtained for $(x_0, y_0) = (0.1, 0.3)$; (b) the BD and for $q = 0.4$ vs. $p \in (0.3, 0.6)$ for $(x_0, y_0) = (0.1, 0.3)$.

The first interesting phenomenon observed is related to the apparent "bifurcation points" (see the zoomed in rectangular region in Figure 2a). This "explosion" takes place for a relatively large range of q values, which was also found from some other discrete FO systems (e.g., [45,46]).

Note that this system cannot be numerically characterized in some regions of the (p, q)-space. There exist some values of p and q for which the orbits are unbounded for whatever initial conditions (x_0, y_0), as shown by the BD in Figure 2b, where for $q = 0.4$, the upper bound of the range of p values could only be chosen to be $p = 0.6$ (see also Theorem 2).

Now, consider the BDs with respect to $q \in [0.1, 0.5]$ and $p = 0.4$, for two different initial conditions $(0.1, 0.3)$ (blue) and $(0.5, 0.5)$ (red) (Figure 3a), and with respect to $p \in [0.3, 0.5]$ and $q = 0.295$, for initial conditions $(0.1, 0.3)$ (blue) and $(0.9, 0.6)$ (red) (Figure 3b).

Within the BD with respect to q, we denote the bifurcation sets of points corresponding to a single initial condition (Poincaré vertical slices through BD) as bifurcative sets (BSs). For better visualization, within the BD in Figure 3a, the BS corresponding to $(0.1, 0.3)$ is colored blue, while the BD corresponding to $(0.5, 0.5)$ is colored red. Similarly, the BD with respect to p, shown in Figure 3b, is composed of two BSs. To each point on the p- or q-axis, there is a vertical line of points, colored red or blue on the corresponding BS.

The dotted line in Figure 3a indicates a chosen representative case, with $q = 0.28$ for $p = 0.55$. Two different attractors can be seen in the two red and blue BSs: a four-period-like attractor (red bullets numbered 1, 2, 3, and 4; see also Figure 4a, where the light red lines indicate the way in which the points 1, 2, 3, 4 are visited) and a two-band, chaotic-like attractor (dark blue tick lines; see also Figure 4b). The zoomed region around the point 1 (Figure 4c) shows the last 600 points, which reveals the slow convergence of this orbit towards a regular-like state. The schematic arrows marked on the time series in Figure 4d indicate the order in which the points 1, 2, 3, and 4 are visited by the orbit.

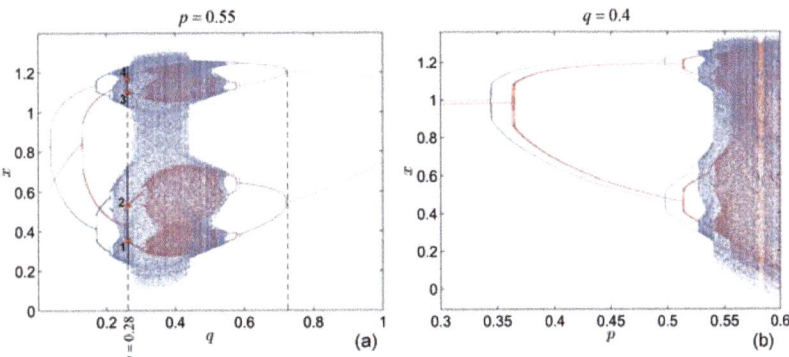

Figure 3. (**a**) The BD for $p = 0.55$ vs. q with two BSs: one obtained for $(x_0, y_0) = (0.1, 0.3)$, in Figure 2a (red plot), and one for a second initial condition $(x_0, y_0) = (0.5, 0.5)$ (blue plot); (**b**) the BD for $q = 0.4$ vs. $p \in (0.3, 0.6)$ with two BSs: one for $(x_0, y_0) = (0.1, 0.3)$, in Figure 2b (red plot), and a new one for $(x_0, y_0) = (0.9, 0.6)$ (blue plot). Dotted line in the BD in Figure 2b indicates the existence of two different attractors: a four-periodic-like orbit (red bullets) and a two-period chaotic band orbit (dark blue segments).

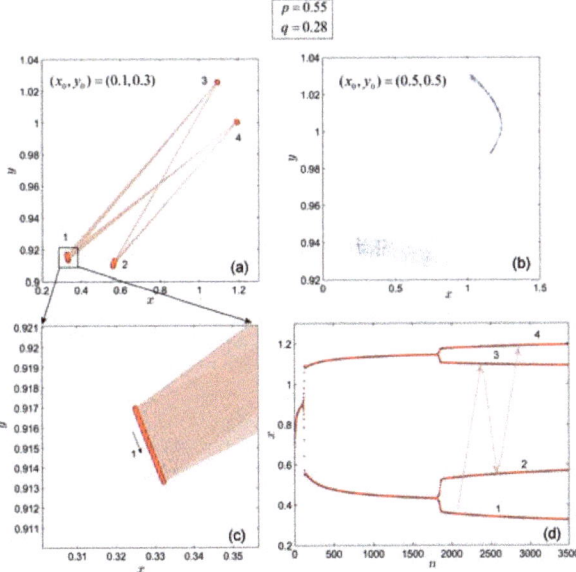

Figure 4. Two attractors for $p = 0.55$ and $q = 0.28$: (**a**) The four-periodic-like attractor for $(x_0, y_0) = (0.1, 0.3)$; (**b**) the two-period chaotic-like attractor for $(x_0, y_0) = (0.5, 0.5)$; (**c**) zoomed region around the point 1 of the periodic-like orbit underlines the slow convergence of the orbit; (**d**) time series of the periodic-like orbit.

From experience, this "coexistence" of attractors or "multistability" suggests the possible existence of hidden attractor(s). However, instead of the two initial conditions $(0.1, 0.3)$ (red BS) and $(0.5, 0.5)$ (blue BS) (Figure 5a), if one considers three initial conditions $(0.1, 0.3)$ (red BS), $(0.5, 0.5)$ (blue BS) and $(0.01, 0.7)$ (green plot) (Figure 5b), then one can see that there exist three BSs, which allow to find three possibly different attractors (see dotted lines I, II, and III within the three attractors) and this phenomenon seems to continue indefinitely.

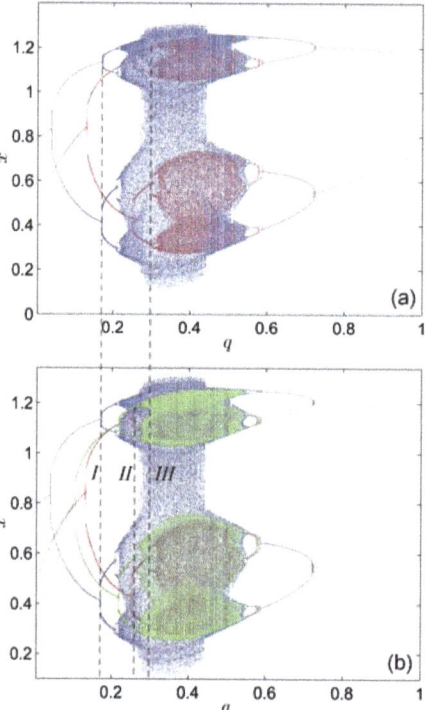

Figure 5. The BDs of system (8) for $p = 0.55$. (**a**) Initial conditions $(0.1, 0.3)$ (red BS) and $(0.5, 0.5)$ (blue BS); (**b**) Initial conditions $(0.1, 0.3)$ (red BS), $(0.5, 0.5)$ (blue BS) and $(0.01, 0.7)$ (green plot).

To verify the influence of the maximum number of iterations on this phenomenon, consider two BDs generated with the above same three initial conditions, but with different numbers of iterations, 3500 and 5000 (Figure 6a,b), respectively. The iteration number affects the shape of BSs only slightly (compare the green two-period chaotic bands generated after 3500 iterations in Figure 6a and the one-period chaotic band in Figure 6b generated after 5000 iterations). However, the existence of different BSs is not affected by the maximum number of iterations.

To this end, one can conclude that the BSs are non-invariant with respect to the initial conditions and, in fact, their positions change significantly with initial conditions in the fractional order space. Similarly, this happens also in the parameter space. While in the parameter space, the non-invariance is evident for all parameter values p, in the fractional order space, this property is conceived only for small values of q (once q grows over $q \approx 0.75$, the phenomenon vanishes, see the right vertical dotted line in Figure 3a).

The above-described numerical simulations on the complex dynamics of system (8) are summarized as follows.

Proposition 2. *The BDs of the FO system (8), obtained with the discretization (7), presents non-invariance with respect to the initial conditions in both the fractional order space and the parameter space.*

Remark 2. *Some interesting observations are worth highlighting.*

(i) *The shapes of BSs approximately preserve the shapes for different initial conditions, but move along the p-axis.*

(ii) This delay-like phenomenon with respect to the initial conditions (the BSs seem to move "forward" or "backward" on the BDs (see the dotted lines I, II, and III in Figure 5, as the initial conditions are changing) was already found in a continuous-time FO system [47], where the "delay" was observed with respect to the integration step-size of the numerical method used.

(iii) It is interesting to compare the above results with the case of the Feigenbaum attractor of the IO logistic map $x(n+1) = px(n)(1-x(n))$, for the limiting value $p_\infty = 3.569946\ldots$ [48], which, however, is not an attracting set and for which there is no sensitive dependence on initial conditions.

By summarizing the investigation in this work, it is concluded that, because of the mentioned dependence on initial conditions, it is impossible to find hidden attractors in the FO system (8) by numerically searching the paths of system orbits by testing initial conditions within neighborhoods of equilibria.

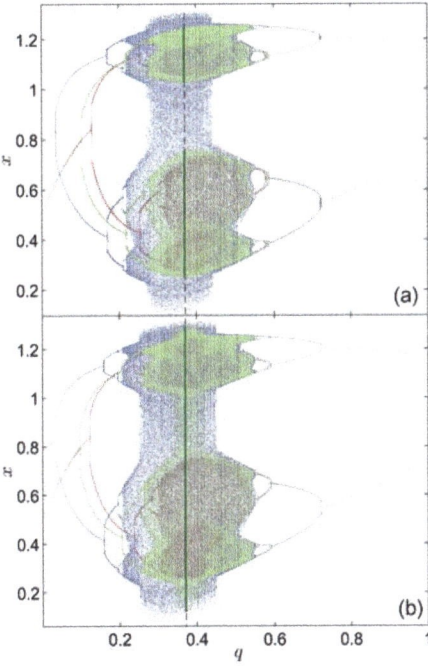

Figure 6. The BDs of system (8) for $p = 0.55$, obtained with the same three different initial conditions but with different maximum iteration numbers: (**a**) 3500 iterations; (**b**) 5000 iterations.

5. Discussion

In this paper, the system of coupled logistic maps modeled by Caputo's delta fractional difference was studied, both analytically and numerically. The system boundedness and global dynamics were analyzed in detail. Extensive numerical simulations were performed on the system dynamics, revealing the impossibility of finding hidden attractors by numerically testing the orbits starting from initial conditions within neighborhoods of equilibria. The main reason appears to be that, at least for the considered system, the BSs forming the BDs for small values of q (about $q < 0.75$) are different for different initial conditions; thereby, the existence of hidden attractors cannot be realized numerically, as typical for continuous integer-order systems. It seems that the coexistence of attractors as necessary for the existence of hidden attractors cannot be well-defined for such a discrete fractional-order system, perhaps also for other discrete fractional-order systems. In general, the phenomenon of "coexistence of attractors" for discrete fractional-order systems needs further investigation.

A possible future research direction is to consider k-periodic problems given by the condition $u(k) = u(0)$ for $k \geq 1$, regarding the existence, uniqueness, and bifurcation of solutions, similarly to the periodic boundary value problem $x(0) = x(T)$ for functional differential equations [49–51].

Author Contributions: Conceptualization, M.-F.D.; methodology, M.-F.D.; software, M.-F.D.; validation, M.F., N.K. and G.C.; formal analysis, M.-F.D. and M.F.; investigation, M.F. and M.-F.D.; writing—original draft preparation, M.-F.D.; writing—review and editing, M.-F.D. and G.C.; visualization, M.F., G.C. and N.K.; supervision, M.-F.D., M.F., G.C. and N.K. All authors have read and agreed to the published version of the manuscript.

Funding: This research was funded by the Russian Science Foundation 19-41-02002 and St. Petersburg, State University and the Slovak Research and Development Agency under the contract No. APVV-18-0308.

Institutional Review Board Statement: Not applicable.

Informed Consent Statement: All authors have read and agreed to the published version of the manuscript.

Data Availability Statement: Data supporting reported results can be acquired from the corresponding author M.-F.D.

Acknowledgments: M.F. is partially supported by the Slovak Research and Development Agency under the contract No. APVV-18-0308 and by the Slovak Grant Agency VEGA No. 1/0358/20 and No. 2/0127/20. N.K. and M.-F.D. acknowledge support from the Russian Science Foundation project 19-41-02002 (Section 3).

Conflicts of Interest: The authors declare no conflict of interest.

References

1. Oldham, K.; Spanier, J. *The Fractional Calculus: Theory and Applications of Differentiation and Integration to Arbitrary Order*; Academic Press: New York, NY, USA, 1974.
2. Podlubny, I. Geometric and physical interpretation of fractional integration and fractional differentiation. *Fract. Calc. Appl. Anal.* **2002**, *5*, 367–386.
3. Li, H.-L.; Jiang, H.; Cao, J. Global synchronization of fractional-order quaternion-valued neural networks with leakage and discrete delays. *Neurocomputing* **2020**, *385*, 211–219. [CrossRef]
4. Ray, S.A.; Atangana, A.; Noutchie, S.C.O.; Kurulay, M.; Bildik, N.; Kilicman, A. Fractional calculus and its applications in applied mathematics and other sciences. *Math. Probl. Eng.* **2014**, *2014*, 849395. [CrossRef]
5. Kang, Y.M.; Xie, Y.; Lu, J.; Jiang, J. On the nonexistence of non-constant exact periodic solutions in a class of the Caputo fractional-order dynamical systems. *Nonlinear Dyn.* **2015**, *82*, 1259–1267. [CrossRef]
6. Tavazoei, M.; Haeri, M. A proof for non existence of periodic solutions in time invariant fractional order systems. *Automatica* **2009**, *45*, 1886–1890. [CrossRef]
7. Tavazoei, M. A note on fractional-order derivatives of periodic functions. *Automatica* **2010**, *46*, 945–948. [CrossRef]
8. Yazdani, M.; Salarieh, H. On the existence of periodic solutions in time-invariant fractional order systems. *Automatica* **2011**, *47*, 1834–1837. [CrossRef]
9. Shen, J.; Lam, J. Non-existence of finite-time stable equilibria in fractional-order nonlinear systems. *Automatica* **2014**, *50*, 547–551. [CrossRef]
10. Fečkan, M. Note on periodic and asymptotically periodic solutions of fractional differential equations. *Stud. Syst. Decis. Control* **2020**, *177*, 153–185.
11. Kaslik, E.; Sivasundaram, S. Non-existence of periodic solutions in fractional-order dynamical systems and a remarkable difference between integer and fractional-order derivatives of periodic functions. *Nonlinear Anal. Real World Appl.* **2012**, *13*, 1489–1497. [CrossRef]
12. Area, I.; Losada, J.; Nieto, J. On Fractional Derivatives and Primitives of Periodic Functions. *Abstr. Appl. Anal.* **2014**, *2014*, 392598. [CrossRef]
13. Diblík, J.; Fečkan, M.; Pospisil, M. Nonexistence of periodic solutions and S-asymptotically periodic solutions in fractional difference equations. *Appl. Math. Comput.* **2015**, *257*, 230–240. [CrossRef]
14. Bin, H.; Huang, L.; Zhang, G. Convergence and periodicity of solutions for a class of difference systems. *Adv. Differ. Equ.* **2006**, *2006*, 70461. [CrossRef]

15. Jonnalagadda, J. Periodic solutions of fractional nabla difference equations. *Commun. Appl. Anal.* **2016**, *20*, 585–610.
16. Edelman, M. Cycles in asymptotically stable and chaotic fractional maps. *Nonlinear Dyn.* **2021**, *104*, 2829–2841. [CrossRef]
17. Pospíšil, M. Note on fractional difference equations with periodic and S-asymptotically periodic right-hand side. *Nonlinear Oscil.* **2021**, *24*, 99–109.
18. Danca, M.F.; Fečkan, M.; Kuznetsov, N.V.; Chen, G. Fractional-order PWC systems without zero Lyapunov exponents. *Nonlinear Dyn.* **2018**, *92*, 1061–1078. [CrossRef]
19. Leonov, G.; Kuznetsov, N. Hidden attractors in dynamical systems. From hidden oscillations in Hilbert-Kolmogorov, Aizerman, and Kalman problems to hidden chaotic attractors in Chua circuits. *Int. J. Bifurc. Chaos Appl. Sci. Eng.* **2013**, *23*, 1330002. [CrossRef]
20. Leonov, G.; Kuznetsov, N.; Mokaev, T. Homoclinic orbits, and self-excited and hidden attractors in a Lorenz-like system describing convective fluid motion. *Eur. Phys. J. Spec. Top.* **2015**, *224*, 1421–1458. [CrossRef]
21. Kuznetsov, N. Theory of hidden oscillations and stability of control systems. *J. Comput. Syst. Sci. Int.* **2020**, *59*, 647–668. [CrossRef]
22. Danca, M.F.; Kuznetsov, N.; Chen, G. Approximating hidden chaotic attractors via parameter switching. *Chaos* **2018**, *28*, 5007925. [CrossRef]
23. Danca, M.F. Hidden chaotic attractors in fractional-order systems. *Nonlinear Dyn.* **2017**, *89*, 577–586. [CrossRef]
24. Danca, M.F.; Bourke, P.; Kuznetsov, N. Graphical structure of attraction basins of hidden attractors: The Rabinovich-Fabrikant system. *Int. J. Bifurc. Chaos* **2019**, *29*, 1930001. [CrossRef]
25. Danca, M.F.; Kuznetsov, N.; Chen, G. Unusual dynamics and hidden attractors of the Rabinovich–Fabrikant system. *Nonlinear Dyn.* **2017**, *88*, 791–805. [CrossRef]
26. Danca, M.F. Hidden transient chaotic attractors of Rabinovich–Fabrikant system. *Nonlinear Dyn.* **2016**, *86*, 1263–1270. [CrossRef]
27. Danca, M.F.; Kuznetsov, N. Hidden chaotic sets in a Hopfield neural system. *Chaos Solitons Fractals* **2017**, *103*, 144–150. [CrossRef]
28. Danca, M.F. Coexisting Hidden and self-excited attractors in an economic system of integer or fractional order. *Int. J. Bifurc. Chaos* **2021**, *31*, 2150062. [CrossRef]
29. Danca, M.F.; Fečkan, M.; Kuznetsov, N.; Chen, G. Complex dynamics, hidden attractors and continuous approximation of a fractional-order hyperchaotic PWC system. *Nonlinear Dyn.* **2018**, *91*, 2523–2540. [CrossRef]
30. Jafari, S.; Sprott, J.; Nazarimehr, F. Recent new examples of hidden attractors. *Eur. Phys. J. Spec. Top.* **2015**, *224*, 1469–1476. [CrossRef]
31. Diethelm, K.; Ford, N.; Freed, A. A predictor-corrector approach for the numerical solution of fractional differential equations. *Nonlinear Dyn.* **2002**, *29*, 3–22. [CrossRef]
32. Garrappa, R. Numerical solution of fractional differential equations: A survey and a software tutorial. *Mathematics* **2018**, *6*, 16. [CrossRef]
33. Kuttner, B. On differences of fractional order. *Proc. Lond. Math. Soc.* **1957**, *3*, 453–466. [CrossRef]
34. Wang, Q.; Lu, D.; Fang, Y. Stability analysis of impulsive fractional differential systems with delay. *Appl. Math. Lett.* **2015**, *40*, 1–6. [CrossRef]
35. Wu, G.C.; Baleanu, D. Stability analysis of impulsive fractional difference equations. *Fract. Calc. Appl. Anal.* **2018**, *21*, 354–375. [CrossRef]
36. Edelman, M. On stability of fixed points and chaos in fractional systems. *Chaos* **2018**, *28*, 023112. [CrossRef] [PubMed]
37. Lopez-Ruiz, R.; Fournier-Prunaret, D. Indirect Allee effect, bistability and chaotic oscillations in a predator-prey discrete model of logistic type. *Chaos Solitons Fractals* **2005**, *24*, 85–101. [CrossRef]
38. Abdeljawad, T. On Riemann and Caputo fractional differences. *Comput. Math. Appl.* **2011**, *62*, 1602–1611. [CrossRef]
39. Atici, F.M.; Eloe, P.W. Discrete fractional calculus with the nabla operator. *Electron. J. Qual. Theory Differ. Equ.* **2009**, *3*, 1–12. [CrossRef]
40. Anastassiou, G.A. Discrete fractional calculus and inequalities. *arXiv* **2009**, arXiv:0911.3370.
41. Chen, F.; Luo, X.; Zhou, Y. Existence Results for Nonlinear Fractional Difference Equation. *Adv. Differ. Equ.* **2011**, *2011*, 713201. [CrossRef]
42. Danca, M.F.; Fečkan, M.; Kuznetsov, N. Chaos control in the fractional order logistic map via impulses. *Nonlinear Dyn.* **2019**, *98*, 1219–1230. [CrossRef]
43. Anh, P.; Babiarz, A.; Czornik, A.; Niezabitowski, M.; Siegmund, S. Asymptotic properties of discrete linear fractional equations. *Bull. Pol. Acad. Sci. Tech. Sci.* **2019**, *67*, 749–759.
44. Čermak, J.; Györi, I.; Nechvátal, L. On explicit stability conditions for a linear fractional difference system. *Fract. Calc. Appl. Anal.* **2015**, *18*, 651–672. [CrossRef]
45. Danca, M.F. Puu system of fractional order and its chaos suppression. *Symmetry* **2020**, *12*, 340. [CrossRef]
46. Wu, G.C.; Baleanu, D. Discrete chaos in fractional delayed logistic maps. *Nonlinear Dyn.* **2015**, *80*, 1697–1703. [CrossRef]
47. Danca, M.F. Hopfield neuronal network of fractional order: A note on its numerical integration. *Chaos Solitons Fractals* **2021**, *151*, 111219. [CrossRef]
48. Eckmann, J.P.; Ruelle, D. Ergodic theory of chaos and strange attractors. *Rev. Mod. Phys.* **1985**, *57*, 617–656. [CrossRef]
49. Fečkan, M.; Marynets, K. Approximation approach to periodic BVP for fractional differential systems. *Eur. Phys. J. Spec. Top.* **2017**, *226*, 3681–3692. [CrossRef]

50. Fečkan, M.; Marynets, K. Approximation approach to periodic BVP for mixed fractional differential systems. *J. Comput. Appl. Math.* **2018**, *339*, 208–217. [CrossRef]
51. Feckan, M.; Marynets, K.; Wang, J. Periodic boundary value problems for higher-order fractional differential systems. *Math. Methods Appl. Sci.* **2019**, *42*, 3616–3632. [CrossRef]

Article

Existence and Ulam–Hyers Stability of a Fractional-Order Coupled System in the Frame of Generalized Hilfer Derivatives

Abdulkafi M. Saeed [1,†], Mohammed S. Abdo [2,*,†] and Mdi Begum Jeelani [3,†]

1 Department of Mathematics, College of Science, Qassim University, Buraydah 51452, Saudi Arabia; abdulkafi.ahmed@qu.edu.sa
2 Department of Mathematics, Hodeidah University, Al-Hudaydah, Yemen
3 Department of Mathematics, Imam Mohammad Ibn Saud Islamic University, Riyadh 11564, Saudi Arabia; mbshaikh@imamu.edu.sa
* Correspondence: msabdo@hoduniv.net.ye
† These authors contributed equally to this work.

Abstract: In this research paper, we consider a class of a coupled system of fractional integrodifferential equations in the frame of Hilfer fractional derivatives with respect to another function. The existence and uniqueness results are obtained in weighted spaces by applying Schauder's and Banach's fixed point theorems. The results reported here are more general than those found in the literature, and some special cases are presented. Furthermore, we discuss the Ulam–Hyers stability of the solution to the proposed system. Some examples are also constructed to illustrate and validate the main results.

Keywords: ϑ-Hilfer fractional derivative; fractional coupled system; existence and stability of solutions; fixed point theorem

MSC: 26A33; 34A08; 34A12; 34D20; 47H10

1. Introduction

Recently, the theory of fractional differential equations (FDEs) has become an active space of exploration. This is because of its accurate outcomes compared with the classical differential equations (DEs). Indeed, fractional calculus has been improving the mathematical modeling of sundry phenomena in science and engineering, for more details, refer to the monographs [1–5]. The fundamental benefit of using fractional-order derivatives (FODs) rather than integer-order derivatives (IODs) is that IODs are local in nature, whereas FODs are global in nature. Numerous physical phenomena cannot be modeled for a single DE. To overcome this challenges, these kinds of phenomena can be given the assistance of coupled systems of DEs. As of late, coupled systems of FDEs have been investigated with various methodologies, see [6–10].

The existence and uniqueness results play a significant part in the theory of FDEs. The previously mentioned region has been investigated well for classical DEs. However, for FDEs, there are many theoretical aspects that need further investigation and exploration. The existence and uniqueness results of FDEs have been very much concentrated up by using Riemann–Liouville (R-L), Caputo, and Hilfer FDs, see [11–14].

Recently, notable consideration has been given to the qualitative analysis of initial and boundary value problems for FDEs with ψ-Caputo and ψ-Hilfer FDs introduced by Almedia [15] and Sousa et al. [16], respectively, see [17–24]. By considering physical phenomena which are modeled by utilizing classical FDs, the importance of ψ-Hilfer FD can be discussed by redesigning and remodeling such models under ψ-Hilfer FD.

In this regard, the most relaxing technique for stability for functional equations was presented by Ulam [25] and Hyers [26] which is famous for Hyers–Ulam (in short H-U)

stability. The first investigation into H-U's stability for DEs was presented by Obloza [27]. Moreover, Li and Zada in [28] provided connections between the stability of U-H and uniform exponential over Banach space. These types of stability have been very well-investigated for FDEs, see [29–34]. The existence and stability of solutions of the following ϑ-Hilfer type FDE:

$$\begin{cases} \mathbb{D}_{a^+,\vartheta(\varkappa)}^{\rho_1,\rho_2} v(\varkappa) = f(\varkappa, v(\varkappa), \mathbb{D}_{a^+,\vartheta(\varkappa)}^{\rho_1,\rho_2} v(\varkappa)), \quad \varkappa \in (a, T], \\ 0 < \rho_1 < 1, \quad 0 \le \rho_2 \le 1, \\ \mathbb{I}_{a^+,\vartheta(\varkappa)}^{1-\gamma} v(\varkappa) \Big|_{\varkappa=a} = v_a, \quad \gamma = \rho_1 + \rho_2(1-\rho_1) \end{cases}$$

have been investigated by Vanterler et al. [35]. Abdo and Panchal in [36] proved the existence, uniqueness and Ulam–Hyers stability of the following ϑ-Hilfer type fractional integrodifferential equation:

$$\begin{cases} \mathbb{D}_{a^+,\vartheta(\varkappa)}^{\rho_1,\rho_2} v(\varkappa) = f(\varkappa, v(\varkappa), \chi v(\varkappa)), \quad \varkappa \in (a, T], \\ 0 < \rho_1 < 1, \quad 0 \le \rho_2 \le 1, \\ \mathbb{I}_{a^+,\vartheta(\varkappa)}^{1-\gamma} v(\varkappa) \Big|_{\varkappa=a} = v_a, \quad \gamma = \rho_1 + \rho_2(1-\rho_1) \end{cases}$$

where $\chi v(\varkappa) = \int_0^{\varkappa} h(\varkappa, s, v(s)) ds$, $\mathbb{D}_{a^+,\vartheta(\varkappa)}^{\rho_1,\rho_2}$ and $\mathbb{I}_{a^+,\vartheta(\varkappa)}^{1-\gamma}$ represent ϑ-Hilfer FD and ϑ-Reimann-Liouville FI, respectively.

Motivated by the above discussion, we investigate the existence, uniqueness, and H-U stability of the solutions of a coupled system involving $a\vartheta$-Hilfer FD of the type:

$$\begin{cases} \mathbb{D}_{a^+,\vartheta(\varkappa)}^{\rho_1,\rho_2} v(\varkappa) = f(\varkappa, v(\varkappa), \mathbb{I}_{a^+,\vartheta(\varkappa)}^{\rho_3} w(\varkappa)), \quad \varkappa \in \mathbb{J} := (a, b], \\ \mathbb{D}_{a^+,\vartheta(\varkappa)}^{\rho_1,\rho_2} w(\varkappa) = g(\varkappa, w(\varkappa), \mathbb{I}_{a^+,\vartheta(\varkappa)}^{\rho_3} v(\varkappa)), \quad \varkappa \in \mathbb{J} := (a, b], \\ \mathbb{I}_{a^+,\vartheta(\varkappa)}^{1-\gamma} v(\varkappa) \Big|_{\varkappa=a} = v_a, \quad \mathbb{I}_{a^+,\vartheta(\varkappa)}^{1-\gamma} w(\varkappa) \Big|_{\varkappa=a} = w_a, \end{cases} \quad (1)$$

where

(i) $0 < \rho_1 < 1, 0 \le \rho_2 \le 1, \rho_3 > 0, \gamma = \rho_1 + \rho_2(1-\rho_1)$, and $v_a, w_a \in \mathbb{R}$;

(ii) $\mathbb{D}_{a^+,\vartheta(\varkappa)}^{\rho_1,\rho_2}$ represents the ϑ-Hilfer FD of order ρ_1 and type ρ_2.

(iii) $\mathbb{I}_{a^+,\vartheta(\varkappa)}^{\rho_3}$ and $\mathbb{I}_{a^+,\vartheta(\varkappa)}^{1-\gamma}$ represent the ϑ-R-L fractional integrals of order ρ_3 and $1-\gamma$, respectively;

(iv) $f, g : \mathbb{J} \times \mathcal{C} \times \mathcal{C} \to \mathbb{R}$ are continuous and nonlinear functions on a Banach space $\mathcal{C}$;

(v) $\vartheta \in \mathcal{C}^1(\mathbb{J}, \mathbb{R})$ are an increasing function with $\vartheta'(\varkappa) \ne 0$, for all $\varkappa \in \mathbb{J}$.

We pay attention to the topic of a novel operator with respect to another function, as it covers many fractional systems that are special cases for various values of ϑ. More precisely, the existence, uniqueness, and U-H stability of solutions to the system (1) are obtained in weighted spaces by using standard fixed point theorems (Banach-type and Schauder type) along with Arzelà–Ascoli's theorem.

The content of this paper is organized as follows: Section 2 presents some required results and preliminaries about ϑ-Hilfer FD. Our main results for the system (1) are addressed in Section 3. Some examples to explain the acquired results are given in Section 4. In the end, we epitomize our study in the Conclusion section.

2. Preliminaries

In this section, we recall the concept of advanced fractional calculus. Throughout the paper, we assume that $\mathbb{J} := (a, b] \subset \mathbb{R}$, $(a < b)$, $\gamma = \rho_1 + \rho_2(1-\rho_1)$, $0 < \rho_1 < 1$, $0 \le \rho_2 \le 1$, and $\vartheta : \mathbb{J} \to \mathbb{R}$ is an increasing linear function which satisfies $\vartheta'(\varkappa) \ne 0$, for all $\varkappa \in \mathbb{J}$. Let

$$\mathcal{C} = \mathcal{C}(\mathbb{J}, \mathbb{R}) = \left\{ \phi : \mathbb{J} \to \mathbb{R}; \ \|\phi\|_\infty = \max_{\varkappa \in \mathbb{J}} |\phi(\varkappa)| \right\}$$

and

$$\mathcal{C}_{1-\gamma,\vartheta} = \mathcal{C}_{1-\gamma,\vartheta}(\mathbb{J},\mathbb{R}) = \left\{\phi : \mathbb{J} \to \mathbb{R}; \ \mathbb{D}_{a^+,\vartheta}^{\rho_1,\rho_2}\phi \in \mathcal{C}; \ \|\phi\|_{1-\gamma,\vartheta} = \left\|(\vartheta(\varkappa) - \vartheta(a))^{1-\gamma}\phi(\varkappa)\right\|_\infty\right\}.$$

where $0 \leq \gamma < 1$. Obviously, $\mathcal{C}$ and $\mathcal{C}_{1-\gamma,\vartheta}$ are Banach spaces under $\|\phi\|_\infty$ and $\|\phi\|_{1-\gamma,\vartheta}$, respectively. Hence the products $\mathcal{C} \times \mathcal{C}$ and $\mathcal{C}_{1-\gamma,\vartheta} \times \mathcal{C}_{1-\gamma,\vartheta}$ are also Banach spaces with norms

$$\|(\phi_1,\phi_2)\|_\infty = \|\phi_1\|_\infty + \|\phi_2\|_\infty$$

and

$$\|(\phi_1,\phi_2)\|_{1-\gamma,\vartheta} = \|\phi_1\|_{1-\gamma,\vartheta} + \|\phi_2\|_{1-\gamma,\vartheta}$$

respectively. Let $z \in \mathbb{C}$ with $Re(z) > 0$. Then, the gamma function $\Gamma(z)$ is defined by [37]

$$\Gamma(z) = \int_0^\infty u^{z-1} e^{-u} du, \tag{2}$$

and let $z_1, z_2 \in \mathbb{C}$ with $Re(z_1), Re(z_2) > 0$. Then, the beta function $\mathcal{B}(z_1, z_2)$ is defined by [37]

$$\mathcal{B}(z_1, z_2) = \int_0^1 u^{z_1-1}(1-u)^{z_2-1} du.$$

Note that, beta function and gamma function have the following relation

$$\mathcal{B}(z_1, z_2) = \frac{\Gamma(z_1)\Gamma(z_2)}{\Gamma(z_1 + z_2)}. \tag{3}$$

Definition 1 ([2]). *The ϑ-R-L fractional integral of order $\rho_1 > 0$ for a function $\phi(\varkappa)$ is given by*

$$\mathbb{I}_{a^+,\vartheta(\varkappa)}^{\rho_1} \phi(\varkappa) = \frac{1}{\Gamma(\rho_1)} \int_a^\varkappa \vartheta'(t)(\vartheta(\varkappa) - \vartheta(t))^{\rho_1-1} \phi(t) dt,$$

where $\Gamma(\cdot)$ is the gamma function defined by (2).

Definition 2 ([16]). *The ϑ-Hilfer FD of a function $\phi(\varkappa)$ of order ρ_1 and type ρ_2 is defined by*

$$\mathbb{D}_{a^+,\vartheta(\varkappa)}^{\rho_1,\rho_2} \phi(\varkappa) = \mathbb{I}_{a^+,\vartheta(\varkappa)}^{\rho_2(1-\rho_1)} \left(\frac{1}{\vartheta'(\varkappa)} \frac{d}{d\varkappa}\right) \mathbb{I}_{a^+,\vartheta(\varkappa)}^{(1-\rho_2)(1-\rho_1)} \phi(\varkappa),$$

where $0 < \rho_1 < 1, 0 \leq \rho_2 \leq 1$, and $\varkappa > a$.

Lemma 1 ([2,16]). *Let $\rho_1, \eta, \delta > 0$. Then*

1. $\mathbb{I}_{a^+,\vartheta(\varkappa)}^{\rho_1} \mathbb{I}_{a^+,\vartheta(\varkappa)}^{\eta} \phi(\varkappa) = \mathbb{I}_{a^+,\vartheta(\varkappa)}^{\rho_1+\eta} \phi(\varkappa).$
2. $\mathbb{I}_{a^+,\vartheta(\varkappa)}^{\rho_1} (\vartheta(\varkappa) - \vartheta(a))^{\delta-1} = \frac{\Gamma(\delta)}{\Gamma(\rho_1+\delta)} (\vartheta(\varkappa) - \vartheta(a))^{\rho_1+\delta-1}.$

We note also that $\mathbb{D}_{a^+,\vartheta(\varkappa)}^{\rho_1,\rho_2} (\vartheta(\varkappa) - \vartheta(a))^{\gamma-1} = 0$, where $\gamma = \rho_1 + \rho_2(1-\rho_1)$.

Lemma 2 ([16]). *Let $\phi \in \mathcal{C}, \rho_1 \in (0,1)$ and $\rho_2 \in [0,1]$, then*

$$\left(\mathbb{I}_{a^+,\vartheta(\varkappa)}^{\rho_1} \mathbb{D}_{a^+,\vartheta(\varkappa)}^{\rho_1,\rho_2} \phi\right)(\varkappa) = \phi(\varkappa) - \frac{(\vartheta(\varkappa) - \vartheta(a))^{\zeta-1}}{\Gamma(\gamma)} \lim_{\varkappa \to a} \left(\mathbb{I}_{a^+,\vartheta(\varkappa)}^{(1-\rho_2)(1-\rho_1)} \phi\right)(\varkappa),$$

where $\phi_\vartheta^{[n-k]}(\varkappa) = \left(\frac{1}{\vartheta'(\varkappa)} \frac{d}{d\varkappa}\right)^{[n-k]} \phi(\varkappa)$ and $\gamma = \rho_1 + \rho_2(1-\rho_1)$.

Theorem 1 ([38] (Banach's Theorem)). *Let $\Omega \neq \emptyset$ be a closed subset of a Banach space $\mathcal{X}$. Then any contraction mapping $\mathcal{T} : \Omega \to \Omega$ has a unique fixed point.*

Theorem 2 ([39] (Schauder's Theorem)). *Let Ω be a non-empty closed and convex subset of a Banach space $\mathcal{X}$. If $\mathcal{T}: \Omega \to \Omega$ is a continuous such that $\mathcal{T}(\Omega)$ is a relatively compact subset of $\mathcal{X}$, then $\mathcal{T}$ has at least one fixed point in Ω.*

3. Main Results

In this section, we establish the existence, uniqueness, and U-H stability results for the system (1). To obtain our principle results, we consider the following assumptions:

(Hy$_1$) $f, g : \mathbb{J} \times \mathcal{C} \times \mathcal{C} \to \mathbb{R}$ are continuous such that for each $(\varkappa, v, \omega), (\varkappa, v^*, \omega^*) \in \mathbb{J} \times \mathcal{C} \times \mathcal{C}$ there exist $\kappa_f, \kappa_g, \overline{\kappa}_f, \overline{\kappa}_g > 0$ with

$$|f(\varkappa, v, \omega) - f(\varkappa, v^*, \omega^*)| \le \kappa_f |v - v^*| + \overline{\kappa}_f |\omega - \omega^*|,$$

$$|g(\varkappa, v, \omega) - g(\varkappa, v^*, \omega^*)| \le \kappa_g |v - v^*| + \overline{\kappa}_g |\omega - \omega^*|.$$

(Hy$_2$) $f, g : \mathbb{J} \times \mathcal{C} \times \mathcal{C} \to \mathbb{R}$ are completely continuous such that for each $(\varkappa, v, \omega) \in \mathbb{J} \times \mathcal{C} \times \mathcal{C}$ there exist $\varphi_f, \varphi_g, \overline{\varphi}_f, \overline{\varphi}_g > 0$ with

$$|f(\varkappa, v, \omega)| \le \varphi_f |v| + \overline{\varphi}_f |\omega|,$$

$$|g(\varkappa, v, \omega)| \le \varphi_g |v| + \overline{\varphi}_g |\omega|.$$

Theorem 3. *Let $0 < \rho_1 < 1$, $0 \le \rho_2 \le 1$ and $\gamma = \rho_1 + \rho_2(1 - \rho_1)$. If $(v, \omega) \in \mathcal{C}_{1-\gamma, \vartheta} \times \mathcal{C}_{1-\gamma, \vartheta}$ satisfies*

$$\begin{cases} \mathbb{D}_{a^+, \vartheta(\varkappa)}^{\rho_1, \rho_2} v(\varkappa) = h_1(\varkappa), & \varkappa \in \mathbb{J}, \\ \mathbb{D}_{a^+, \vartheta(\varkappa)}^{\rho_1, \rho_2} \omega(\varkappa) = h_2(\varkappa), & \varkappa \in \mathbb{J}, \\ \mathbb{I}_{a^+, \vartheta(\varkappa)}^{1-\gamma} v(\varkappa) \Big|_{\varkappa = a} = v_a, \\ \mathbb{I}_{a^+, \vartheta(\varkappa)}^{1-\gamma} \omega(\varkappa) \Big|_{\varkappa = a} = \omega_a, \end{cases}$$

then

$$\begin{cases} v(\varkappa) = \frac{(\vartheta(\varkappa) - \vartheta(a))^{\gamma - 1}}{\Gamma(\gamma)} v_a + \mathbb{I}_{a^+, \vartheta(\varkappa)}^{\rho_1} h_1(\varkappa), & \varkappa \in \mathbb{J}, \\ \omega(\varkappa) = \frac{(\vartheta(\varkappa) - \vartheta(a))^{\gamma - 1}}{\Gamma(\gamma)} \omega_a + \mathbb{I}_{a^+, \vartheta(\varkappa)}^{\rho_1} h_2(\varkappa), & \varkappa \in \mathbb{J}. \end{cases}$$

Proof. Let

$$\begin{cases} \mathbb{D}_{a^+, \vartheta(\varkappa)}^{\rho_1, \rho_2} v(\varkappa) = h_1(\varkappa), & \varkappa \in \mathbb{J}, \\ \mathbb{I}_{a^+, \vartheta(\varkappa)}^{1-\gamma} v(\varkappa) \Big|_{\varkappa = a} = v_a. \end{cases}$$

Applying the integral $\mathbb{I}_{a^+, \vartheta(\varkappa)}^{\rho_1}$ on the equation $\mathbb{D}_{a^+, \vartheta(\varkappa)}^{\rho_1, \rho_2} v(\varkappa) = h_1(\varkappa)$ and using Lemma 2, we have

$$v(\varkappa) - \frac{(\vartheta(\varkappa) - \vartheta(a))^{\gamma - 1}}{\Gamma(\gamma)} \mathbb{I}_{a^+, \vartheta(\varkappa)}^{(1-\rho_2)(1-\rho_1)} v(a) = \mathbb{I}_{a^+, \vartheta(\varkappa)}^{\rho_1} h_1(\varkappa),$$

which implies

$$\begin{aligned} v(\varkappa) &= \frac{(\vartheta(\varkappa) - \vartheta(a))^{\gamma - 1}}{\Gamma(\gamma)} \mathbb{I}_{a^+, \vartheta(\varkappa)}^{1-\gamma} v(a) + \mathbb{I}_{a^+, \vartheta(\varkappa)}^{\rho_1} h_1(\varkappa) \\ &= \frac{(\vartheta(\varkappa) - \vartheta(a))^{\gamma - 1}}{\Gamma(\gamma)} v_a + \mathbb{I}_{a^+, \vartheta(\varkappa)}^{\rho_1} h_1(\varkappa). \end{aligned}$$

Similarly,

$$\omega(\varkappa) = \frac{(\vartheta(\varkappa) - \vartheta(a))^{\gamma - 1}}{\Gamma(\gamma)} \omega_a + \mathbb{I}_{a^+, \vartheta(\varkappa)}^{\rho_1} h_2(\varkappa).$$

□

3.1. Existence Result

Theorem 4. *Assume that* (Hy_1) *and* (Hy_2) *hold. If* $\aleph_1 := \frac{\Lambda}{2}(\vartheta(b) - \vartheta(a))^{\rho_1 + \rho_3} < 1$, *then system* (1) *has at least one solution, where* $\Lambda := \left(\left(\varphi_f + \varphi_g\right)\frac{\mathcal{B}(\gamma,\rho_1)}{\Gamma(\rho_1)} + \left(\overline{\varphi}_f + \overline{\varphi}_g\right)\frac{\mathcal{B}(\gamma,\rho_1+\rho_3)}{\Gamma(\rho_1+\rho_3)}\right)$, *and* $\mathcal{B}(\cdot,\cdot)$ *is a beta function defined by* (3).

Proof. Consider a closed ball

$$\mathcal{S}_\beta = \left\{(v,\omega) \in \mathcal{C}_{1-\gamma,\vartheta} \times \mathcal{C}_{1-\gamma,\vartheta} : \|(v,\omega)\|_{\mathcal{C}_{1-\gamma,\vartheta}} \leq \beta, \|v\|_{\mathcal{C}_{1-\gamma,\vartheta}} \leq \frac{\beta}{2}, \|\omega\|_{\mathcal{C}_{1-\gamma,\vartheta}} \leq \frac{\beta}{2}\right\},$$

where $\beta \geq \frac{\aleph_1^\star}{1-\aleph_1}$ with $\aleph_1^\star := \frac{|v_a|+|\omega_a|}{\Gamma(\gamma)}$. In view of Theorem 3, we transform system (1) into a fixed point system. Define the operator $\Pi = (\Pi_1, \Pi_2)$ on $\mathcal{S}_\beta$, where

$$\begin{cases} \Pi_1(v(\varkappa),\omega(\varkappa)) = \frac{(\vartheta(\varkappa)-\vartheta(a))^{\gamma-1}}{\Gamma(\gamma)}v_a + \mathbb{I}^{\rho_1}_{a^+,\vartheta(\varkappa)}f(\varkappa,v(\varkappa),\mathbb{I}^{\rho_3}_{a^+,\vartheta(\varkappa)}\omega(\varkappa)), & \varkappa \in \mathbb{J}, \\ \Pi_2(\omega(\varkappa),v(\varkappa)) = \frac{(\vartheta(\varkappa)-\vartheta(a))^{\gamma-1}}{\Gamma(\gamma)}\omega_a + \mathbb{I}^{\rho_1}_{a^+,\vartheta(\varkappa)}g(\varkappa,\omega(\varkappa),\mathbb{I}^{\rho_3}_{a^+,\vartheta(\varkappa)}v(\varkappa)), & \varkappa \in \mathbb{J}. \end{cases} \quad (4)$$

For any $(v,\omega) \in \mathcal{S}_\beta$, we have

$$\|\Pi(v,\omega)\|_{\mathcal{C}_{1-\gamma,\vartheta}} \leq \|\Pi_1(v,\omega)\|_{\mathcal{C}_{1-\gamma,\vartheta}} + \|\Pi_2(\omega,v)\|_{\mathcal{C}_{1-\gamma,\vartheta}}. \quad (5)$$

From (4), we obtain

$$\begin{aligned}
|\Pi_1(v(\varkappa),\omega(\varkappa))| &\leq \frac{(\vartheta(\varkappa)-\vartheta(a))^{\gamma-1}}{\Gamma(\gamma)}|v_a| + \mathbb{I}^{\rho_1}_{a^+,\vartheta(\varkappa)}\left|f(\varkappa,v(\varkappa),\mathbb{I}^{\rho_3}_{a^+,\vartheta(\varkappa)}\omega(\varkappa))\right| \\
&\leq \frac{(\vartheta(\varkappa)-\vartheta(a))^{\gamma-1}}{\Gamma(\gamma)}|v_a| + \mathbb{I}^{\rho_1}_{a^+,\vartheta(\varkappa)}\left(\varphi_f|v(\varkappa)| + \overline{\varphi}_f \mathbb{I}^{\rho_3}_{a^+,\vartheta(\varkappa)}|\omega(\varkappa)|\right) \\
&\leq \frac{(\vartheta(\varkappa)-\vartheta(a))^{\gamma-1}}{\Gamma(\gamma)}|v_a| + \varphi_f\left(\mathbb{I}^{\rho_1}_{a^+,\vartheta(\varkappa)}|v(\varkappa)|\right) + \overline{\varphi}_f\left(\mathbb{I}^{\rho_1+\rho_3}_{a^+,\vartheta(\varkappa)}|\omega(\varkappa)|\right) \\
&\leq \frac{(\vartheta(\varkappa)-\vartheta(a))^{\gamma-1}}{\Gamma(\gamma)}|v_a| + \varphi_f\|v\|_{\mathcal{C}_{1-\gamma,\vartheta}}\mathbb{I}^{\rho_1}_{a^+,\vartheta(\varkappa)}(\vartheta(\varkappa)-\vartheta(a))^{\gamma-1} \\
&\quad + \overline{\varphi}_f\|\omega\|_{\mathcal{C}_{1-\gamma,\vartheta}}\mathbb{I}^{\rho_1+\rho_3}_{a^+,\vartheta(\varkappa)}(\vartheta(\varkappa)-\vartheta(a))^{\gamma-1} \\
&= \frac{(\vartheta(\varkappa)-\vartheta(a))^{\gamma-1}}{\Gamma(\gamma)}|v_a| + \varphi_f\|v\|_{\mathcal{C}_{1-\gamma,\vartheta}}\frac{\Gamma(\gamma)}{\Gamma(\rho_1+\gamma)}(\vartheta(\varkappa)-\vartheta(a))^{\rho_1+\gamma-1} \\
&\quad + \overline{\varphi}_f\|\omega\|_{\mathcal{C}_{1-\gamma,\vartheta}}\frac{\Gamma(\gamma)}{\Gamma(\rho_1+\rho_3+\gamma)}(\vartheta(\varkappa)-\vartheta(a))^{\rho_1+\rho_3+\gamma-1},
\end{aligned}$$

which implies

$$\begin{aligned}
\|\Pi_1(v,\omega)\|_{\mathcal{C}_{1-\gamma,\vartheta}} &\leq \frac{|v_a|}{\Gamma(\gamma)} + \frac{\varphi_f\beta}{2}\frac{\Gamma(\gamma)}{\Gamma(\rho_1+\gamma)}(\vartheta(b)-\vartheta(a))^{\rho_1} \\
&\quad + \frac{\overline{\varphi}_f\beta}{2}\frac{\Gamma(\gamma)}{\Gamma(\rho_1+\rho_3+\gamma)}(\vartheta(b)-\vartheta(a))^{\rho_1+\rho_3} \\
&\leq \frac{|v_a|}{\Gamma(\gamma)} + \frac{\beta}{2}\left(\varphi_f\frac{\mathcal{B}(\gamma,\rho_1)}{\Gamma(\rho_1)} + \overline{\varphi}_f\frac{\mathcal{B}(\gamma,\rho_1+\rho_3)}{\Gamma(\rho_1+\rho_3)}\right)(\vartheta(b)-\vartheta(a))^{\rho_1+\rho_3}. \quad (6)
\end{aligned}$$

Similarly, we obtain

$$\|\Pi_2(\omega,v)\|_{\mathcal{C}_{1-\gamma,\vartheta}} \leq \frac{|\omega_a|}{\Gamma(\gamma)} + \frac{\beta}{2}\left(\varphi_g\frac{\mathcal{B}(\gamma,\rho_1)}{\Gamma(\rho_1)} + \overline{\varphi}_g\frac{\mathcal{B}(\gamma,\rho_1+\rho_3)}{\Gamma(\rho_1+\rho_3)}\right)(\vartheta(b)-\vartheta(a))^{\rho_1+\rho_3}. \quad (7)$$

In Equations (6) and (7) along with (5), give

$$\|\Pi(v,\omega)\|_{\mathcal{C}_{1-\gamma,\vartheta}} \leq \frac{|v_a| + |\omega_a|}{\Gamma(\gamma)} + \frac{\beta}{2}\Lambda(\vartheta(b) - \vartheta(a))^{\rho_1+\rho_3}$$
$$\leq \aleph_1^* + \beta\aleph_1 \leq \beta(1-\aleph_1) + \beta\aleph_1 = \beta. \tag{8}$$

Hence $\Pi(\mathcal{S}_\beta) \subset \mathcal{S}_\beta$.

Now, we prove that Π is continuous and compact. Let a sequence (v_n, ω_n) in $\mathcal{S}_\beta$ such that $(v_n, \omega_n) \to (v, \omega)$ in $\mathcal{S}_\beta$ as $n \to \infty$, so, we have

$$\|\Pi(v_n, \omega_n)(\varkappa) - \Pi(v, \omega)(\varkappa)\|_{\mathcal{C}_{1-\gamma,\vartheta}}$$
$$= \|\Pi_1(v_n, \omega_n)(\varkappa) + \Pi_2(\omega_n, v_n)(\varkappa) - \Pi_1(v, \omega)(\varkappa) - \Pi_2(\omega, v)(\varkappa)\|_{\mathcal{C}_{1-\gamma,\vartheta}}$$
$$\leq \|(\Pi_1(v_n, \omega_n) - \Pi_1(v, \omega))(\varkappa)\|_{\mathcal{C}_{1-\gamma,\vartheta}} + \|(\Pi_2(\omega_n, v_n) - \Pi_2(\omega, v))(\varkappa)\|_{\mathcal{C}_{1-\gamma,\vartheta}}$$
$$\leq (\vartheta(\varkappa) - \vartheta(a))^{1-\gamma} \mathbb{I}^{\rho_1}_{a^+,\vartheta(\varkappa)} \left| f(\varkappa, v_n(\varkappa), \mathbb{I}^{\rho_3}_{a^+,\vartheta(\varkappa)}\omega_n(\varkappa)) - f(\varkappa, v(\varkappa), \mathbb{I}^{\rho_3}_{a^+,\vartheta(\varkappa)}\omega(\varkappa)) \right|$$
$$+ (\vartheta(\varkappa) - \vartheta(a))^{1-\gamma} \mathbb{I}^{\rho_1}_{a^+,\vartheta(\varkappa)} \left| g(\varkappa, \omega_n(\varkappa), \mathbb{I}^{\rho_3}_{a^+,\vartheta(\varkappa)}v_n(\varkappa)) - g(\varkappa, \omega(\varkappa), \mathbb{I}^{\rho_3}_{a^+,\vartheta(\varkappa)}v(\varkappa)) \right|$$
$$\leq (\vartheta(\varkappa) - \vartheta(a))^{1-\gamma} \mathbb{I}^{\rho_1}_{a^+,\vartheta(\varkappa)} \left(\kappa_f |v_n(\varkappa) - v(\varkappa)| + \overline{\kappa}_f \mathbb{I}^{\rho_3}_{a^+,\vartheta(\varkappa)} |\omega_n(\varkappa) - \omega(\varkappa)| \right)$$
$$+ (\vartheta(\varkappa) - \vartheta(a))^{1-\gamma} \mathbb{I}^{\rho_1}_{a^+,\vartheta(\varkappa)} \left(\kappa_g |\omega_n(\varkappa) - \omega(\varkappa)| + \overline{\kappa}_g \mathbb{I}^{\rho_3}_{a^+,\vartheta(\varkappa)} |v_n(\varkappa) - v(\varkappa)| \right)$$
$$\leq (\vartheta(\varkappa) - \vartheta(a))^{1-\gamma} \left(\kappa_f \|v_n - v\|_{\mathcal{C}_{1-\gamma,\vartheta}} \mathbb{I}^{\rho_1}_{a^+,\vartheta(\varkappa)} (\vartheta(\varkappa) - \vartheta(a))^{\gamma-1} \right.$$
$$\left. + \overline{\kappa}_f \|\omega_n - \omega\|_{\mathcal{C}_{1-\gamma,\vartheta}} \mathbb{I}^{\rho_1+\rho_3}_{a^+,\vartheta(\varkappa)} (\vartheta(\varkappa) - \vartheta(a))^{\gamma-1} \right)$$
$$+ (\vartheta(\varkappa) - \vartheta(a))^{1-\gamma} \left(\kappa_g \|\omega_n - \omega\|_{\mathcal{C}_{1-\gamma,\vartheta}} \mathbb{I}^{\rho_1}_{a^+,\vartheta(\varkappa)} (\vartheta(\varkappa) - \vartheta(a))^{\gamma-1} \right.$$
$$\left. + \overline{\kappa}_g \|v_n - v\|_{\mathcal{C}_{1-\gamma,\vartheta}} \mathbb{I}^{\rho_1+\rho_3}_{a^+,\vartheta(\varkappa)} (\vartheta(\varkappa) - \vartheta(a))^{\gamma-1} \right)$$
$$\leq \left(\kappa_f \frac{\Gamma(\gamma)(\vartheta(b) - \vartheta(a))^{\rho_1}}{\Gamma(\rho_1+\gamma)} + \overline{\kappa}_g \frac{\Gamma(\gamma)(\vartheta(b) - \vartheta(a))^{\rho_1+\rho_3}}{\Gamma(\rho_1+\rho_3+\gamma)} \right) \|v_n - v\|_{\mathcal{C}_{1-\gamma,\vartheta}}$$
$$+ \left(\kappa_g \frac{\Gamma(\gamma)(\vartheta(b) - \vartheta(a))^{\rho_1}}{\Gamma(\rho_1+\gamma)} + \overline{\kappa}_f \frac{\Gamma(\gamma)(\vartheta(b) - \vartheta(a))^{\rho_1+\rho_3}}{\Gamma(\rho_1+\rho_3+\gamma)} \right) \|\omega_n - \omega\|_{\mathcal{C}_{1-\gamma,\vartheta}}.$$

This implies that $\|\Pi(v_n, \omega_n) - \Pi(v, \omega)\|_{\mathcal{C}_{1-\gamma,\vartheta}} \to 0$ as $n \to \infty$. So, Π is continuous. Moreover, Π is bounded on $\mathcal{S}_\beta$. Therefore, Π is uniformly bounded on $\mathcal{S}_\beta$.

To prove that Π is equicontinuous, we take $\varkappa_1, \varkappa_2 \in \mathbb{J}$ with $\varkappa_1 < \varkappa_2$ and for any $(v, \omega) \in \mathcal{S}_\beta$, we obtain

$$|\Pi(v, \omega)(\varkappa_2) - \Pi(v, \omega)(\varkappa_1)|$$
$$\leq |\Pi_1(v, \omega)(\varkappa_2) - \Pi_1(v, \omega)(\varkappa_1)| + |\Pi_2(\omega, v)(\varkappa_2) - \Pi_2(\omega, v)(\varkappa_1)|$$
$$\leq \left| \frac{(\vartheta(\varkappa_2) - \vartheta(a))^{\gamma-1} - \vartheta(\varkappa_1) - \vartheta(a))^{\gamma-1}}{\Gamma(\gamma)} v_a + \mathbb{I}^{\rho_1}_{a^+,\vartheta(\varkappa_2)} f(\varkappa_2, v(\varkappa_2), \mathbb{I}^{\rho_3}_{a^+,\vartheta(\varkappa_2)}\omega(\varkappa_2)) \right.$$
$$\left. - \mathbb{I}^{\rho_1}_{a^+,\vartheta(\varkappa_1)} f(\varkappa_1, v(\varkappa_1), \mathbb{I}^{\rho_3}_{a^+,\vartheta(\varkappa_1)}\omega(\varkappa_1)) \right|$$
$$+ \left| \frac{(\vartheta(\varkappa_2) - \vartheta(a))^{\gamma-1} - \vartheta(\varkappa_1) - \vartheta(a))^{\gamma-1}}{\Gamma(\gamma)} \omega_a + \mathbb{I}^{\rho_1}_{a^+,\vartheta(\varkappa_2)} g(\varkappa_2, \omega(\varkappa_2), \mathbb{I}^{\rho_3}_{a^+,\vartheta(\varkappa_2)}v(\varkappa_2)) \right.$$
$$\left. - \mathbb{I}^{\rho_1}_{a^+,\vartheta(\varkappa_1)} g(\varkappa_1, \omega(\varkappa_1), \mathbb{I}^{\rho_3}_{a^+,\vartheta(\varkappa_1)}v(\varkappa_1)) \right|. \tag{9}$$

Since $f(\cdot, v(\cdot), \mathbb{I}^{\rho_3}_{a^+,\vartheta(\cdot)}\omega(\cdot))$ and $g(\cdot, \omega(\cdot), \mathbb{I}^{\rho_3}_{a^+,\vartheta(\cdot)}v(\cdot))$ are continuous on $\mathbb{J}$. Therefore, there exist $\xi_f, \xi_g \in \mathbb{R}$ such that

$$\left| f(\cdot, v(\cdot), \mathbb{I}^{\rho_3}_{a^+,\vartheta(\cdot)}\omega(\cdot)) \right| \leq \xi_f, \text{ and } \left| g(\cdot, \omega(\cdot), \mathbb{I}^{\rho_3}_{a^+,\vartheta(\cdot)}v(\cdot)) \right| \leq \xi_g.$$

Hence

$$\left|\mathbb{I}^{\rho_1}_{a^+,\vartheta(\varkappa_2)} f(\varkappa_2, v(\varkappa_2), \mathbb{I}^{\rho_3}_{a^+,\vartheta(\varkappa_2)}\omega(\varkappa_2)) - \mathbb{I}^{\rho_1}_{a^+,\vartheta(\varkappa_1)} f(\varkappa_1, v(\varkappa_1), \mathbb{I}^{\rho_3}_{a^+,\vartheta(\varkappa_1)}\omega(\varkappa_1))\right|$$
$$\leq \frac{1}{\Gamma(\rho_1)} \int_a^{\varkappa_1} \vartheta'(t)\left[(\vartheta(\varkappa_1)-\vartheta(t))^{\rho_1-1} - (\vartheta(\varkappa_2)-\vartheta(t))^{\rho_1-1}\right]\left|f(t,v(t),\mathbb{I}^{\rho_3}_{a^+,\vartheta(t)}\omega(t))\right|dt$$
$$+ \frac{1}{\Gamma(\rho_1)} \int_{\varkappa_1}^{\varkappa_2} \vartheta'(t)(\vartheta(\varkappa_2)-\vartheta(t))^{\rho_1-1}\left|f(t,v(t),\mathbb{I}^{\rho_3}_{a^+,\vartheta(t)}\omega(t))\right|dt$$
$$\leq \frac{\xi_f}{\Gamma(\rho_1)} \int_a^{\varkappa_1} \vartheta'(t)\left[(\vartheta(\varkappa_1)-\vartheta(t))^{\rho_1-1} - (\vartheta(\varkappa_2)-\vartheta(t))^{\rho_1-1}\right]dt$$
$$+ \frac{\xi_f}{\Gamma(\rho_1)} \int_{\varkappa_1}^{\varkappa_2} \vartheta'(t)(\vartheta(\varkappa_2)-\vartheta(t))^{\rho_1-1}dt$$
$$= \frac{\xi_f}{\Gamma(\rho_1+1)}\left[(\vartheta(\varkappa_1)-\vartheta(a))^{\rho_1} + 2(\vartheta(\varkappa_2)-\vartheta(\varkappa_1))^{\rho_1} - (\vartheta(\varkappa_2)-\vartheta(a))^{\rho_1}\right]$$
$$\leq \frac{2\xi_f}{\Gamma(\rho_1+1)}(\vartheta(\varkappa_2)-\vartheta(\varkappa_1))^{\rho_1}. \tag{10}$$

Similarly,

$$\left|\mathbb{I}^{\rho_1}_{a^+,\vartheta(\varkappa_2)} g(\varkappa_2, \omega(\varkappa_2), \mathbb{I}^{\rho_3}_{a^+,\vartheta(\varkappa_2)}v(\varkappa_2)) - \mathbb{I}^{\rho_1}_{a^+,\vartheta(\varkappa_1)} g(\varkappa_1, \omega(\varkappa_1), \mathbb{I}^{\rho_3}_{a^+,\vartheta(\varkappa_1)}v(\varkappa_1))\right|$$
$$\leq \frac{2\xi_g}{\Gamma(\rho_1+1)}(\vartheta(\varkappa_2)-\vartheta(\varkappa_1))^{\rho_1}. \tag{11}$$

Substituting (10) and (11) into (9), we obtain

$$|\Pi(v,\omega)(\varkappa_2) - \Pi(v,\omega)(\varkappa_1)| \leq \frac{(\vartheta(\varkappa_2)-\vartheta(a))^{\gamma-1} - (\vartheta(\varkappa_1)-\vartheta(a))^{\gamma-1}}{\Gamma(\gamma)}(v_a+\omega_a)$$
$$+ \frac{2(\xi_f+\xi_g)}{\Gamma(\rho_1+1)}(\vartheta(\varkappa_2)-\vartheta(\varkappa_1))^{\rho_1}.$$

Thus, $|\Pi(v,\omega)(\varkappa_2) - \Pi(v,\omega)(\varkappa_1)| \to 0$, as $\varkappa_1 \to \varkappa_2$. Thus, Π is relatively compact on $\mathcal{S}_\beta$. It follows that Π is completely continuous due to the Arzela–Ascolli theorem. An application Theorem 2 shows that system (1) has at least one solution. □

3.2. Uniqueness Result

Theorem 5. Assume that (Hy_1) holds. If $\max_{\varkappa\in\mathbb{J}}\{\zeta_1,\zeta_2\} = \zeta < 1$, then the system (1) has a unique solution on $\mathbb{J}$, where

$$\zeta_1 := \frac{(\vartheta(b)-\vartheta(a))^{\rho_1}}{\Gamma(\rho_1+1)}\kappa_f + \frac{(\vartheta(b)-\vartheta(a))^{\rho_1+\rho_3}}{\Gamma(\rho_1+\rho_3+1)}\overline{\kappa}_g,$$
$$\zeta_2 := \frac{(\vartheta(b)-\vartheta(a))^{\rho_1}}{\Gamma(\rho_1+1)}\kappa_g + \frac{(\vartheta(b)-\vartheta(a))^{\rho_1+\rho_3}}{\Gamma(\rho_1+\rho_3+1)}\overline{\kappa}_f.$$

Proof. To demonstrate the desired result, we show that Π is a contraction. For each $\varkappa \in \mathbb{J}$ and $(v,\omega), (v^\star,\omega^\star) \in \mathcal{S}_\beta$, we have

$$\|\Pi(v,\omega) - \Pi(v^*,\omega^*)\|_{\mathcal{C}_{1-\gamma,\vartheta}}$$
$$\leq \|\Pi_1(v,\omega) - \Pi_1(v^*,\omega^*)\|_{\mathcal{C}_{1-\gamma,\vartheta}} + \|\Pi_2(\omega,v) - \Pi_2(\omega^*,v^*)\|_{\mathcal{C}_{1-\gamma,\vartheta}}$$
$$\leq \left\|\mathbb{I}_{a^+,\vartheta(\varkappa)}^{\rho_1} f(\varkappa, v(\varkappa), \mathbb{I}_{a^+,\vartheta(\varkappa)}^{\rho_3}\omega(\varkappa)) - \mathbb{I}_{a^+,\vartheta(\varkappa)}^{\rho_1} f(\varkappa, v^*(\varkappa), \mathbb{I}_{a^+,\vartheta(\varkappa)}^{\rho_3}\omega^*(\varkappa))\right\|_{\mathcal{C}_{1-\gamma,\vartheta}}$$
$$+ \left\|\mathbb{I}_{a^+,\vartheta(\varkappa)}^{\rho_1} g(\varkappa, \omega(\varkappa), \mathbb{I}_{a^+,\vartheta(\varkappa)}^{\rho_3}v(\varkappa)) - \mathbb{I}_{a^+,\vartheta(\varkappa)}^{\rho_1} g(\varkappa, \omega^*(\varkappa), \mathbb{I}_{a^+,\vartheta(\varkappa)}^{\rho_3}v^*(\varkappa))\right\|_{\mathcal{C}_{1-\gamma,\vartheta}}$$
$$\leq \max_{\varkappa\in\mathbb{J}}(\vartheta(\varkappa)-\vartheta(a))^{1-\gamma}\mathbb{I}_{a^+,\vartheta(\varkappa)}^{\rho_1}\left|f(\varkappa, v(\varkappa), \mathbb{I}_{a^+,\vartheta(\varkappa)}^{\rho_3}\omega(\varkappa)) - f(\varkappa, v^*(\varkappa), \mathbb{I}_{a^+,\vartheta(\varkappa)}^{\rho_3}\omega^*(\varkappa))\right|$$
$$+ \max_{\varkappa\in\mathbb{J}}(\vartheta(\varkappa)-\vartheta(a))^{1-\gamma}\mathbb{I}_{a^+,\vartheta(\varkappa)}^{\rho_1}\left|g(\varkappa, \omega(\varkappa), \mathbb{I}_{a^+,\vartheta(\varkappa)}^{\rho_3}v(\varkappa)) - g(\varkappa, \omega^*(\varkappa), \mathbb{I}_{a^+,\vartheta(\varkappa)}^{\rho_3}v^*(\varkappa))\right|$$
$$\leq \max_{\varkappa\in\mathbb{J}}(\vartheta(\varkappa)-\vartheta(a))^{1-\gamma}\mathbb{I}_{a^+,\vartheta(\varkappa)}^{\rho_1}\left[\kappa_f|v(\varkappa)-v^*(\varkappa)| + \overline{\kappa}_f \mathbb{I}_{a^+,\vartheta(\varkappa)}^{\rho_3}|\omega(\varkappa)-\omega^*(\varkappa)|\right]$$
$$+ \max_{\varkappa\in\mathbb{J}}(\vartheta(\varkappa)-\vartheta(a))^{1-\gamma}\mathbb{I}_{a^+,\vartheta(\varkappa)}^{\rho_1}\left[\kappa_g|\omega(\varkappa)-\omega^*(\varkappa)| + \overline{\kappa}_g \mathbb{I}_{a^+,\vartheta(\varkappa)}^{\rho_3}|v(\varkappa)-v^*(\varkappa)|\right]$$
$$\leq \frac{(\vartheta(b)-\vartheta(a))^{\rho_1}}{\Gamma(\rho_1+1)}\kappa_f\|v-v^*\|_{\mathcal{C}_{1-\gamma,\vartheta}} + \frac{(\vartheta(b)-\vartheta(a))^{\rho_1+\rho_3}}{\Gamma(\rho_1+\rho_3+1)}\overline{\kappa}_f\|\omega-\omega^*\|_{\mathcal{C}_{1-\gamma,\vartheta}}$$
$$+ \frac{(\vartheta(b)-\vartheta(a))^{\rho_1}}{\Gamma(\rho_1+1)}\kappa_g\|\omega-\omega^*\|_{\mathcal{C}_{1-\gamma,\vartheta}} + \frac{(\vartheta(b)-\vartheta(a))^{\rho_1+\rho_3}}{\Gamma(\rho_1+\rho_3+1)}\overline{\kappa}_g\|v-v^*\|_{\mathcal{C}_{1-\gamma,\vartheta}}$$
$$= \zeta_1\|v-v^*\|_{\mathcal{C}_{1-\gamma,\vartheta}} + \zeta_2\|\omega-\omega^*\|_{\mathcal{C}_{1-\gamma,\vartheta}},$$

which implies

$$\|\Pi(v,\omega) - \Pi(v^*,\omega^*)\|_{\mathcal{C}_{1-\gamma,\vartheta}} \leq \zeta\|(v,\omega) - (v^*,\omega^*)\|_{\mathcal{C}_{1-\gamma,\vartheta}}.$$

Since $\zeta < 1$, Π is a contraction map. Thus, a unique solution exists on $\mathbb{J}$ for system (1) in view of Theorem 1, and this completes the proof. □

3.3. Special Cases

In this subsection, we present some special cases according to our previous findings:

Case 1: If $\vartheta(\varkappa) = \varkappa$, then the system (1) is reduced to a Hilfer type coupled system of FIDE of the form

$$\begin{cases} \mathbb{D}_{a^+,\varkappa}^{\rho_1,\rho_2} v(\varkappa) = f(\varkappa, v(\varkappa), \mathbb{I}_{a^+,\varkappa}^{\rho_3}\omega(\varkappa)), & \varkappa \in \mathbb{J}, \\ \mathbb{D}_{a^+,\varkappa}^{\rho_1,\rho_2} \omega(\varkappa) = g(\varkappa, \omega(\varkappa), \mathbb{I}_{a^+,\varkappa}^{\rho_3}v(\varkappa)), & \varkappa \in \mathbb{J}, \\ \mathbb{I}_{a^+,\varkappa}^{1-\gamma} v(\varkappa)\big|_{\varkappa=a} = v_a, \quad \mathbb{I}_{a^+,\varkappa}^{1-\gamma}\omega(\varkappa)\big|_{\varkappa=a} = \omega_a, \end{cases} \quad (12)$$

where $\mathbb{D}_{a^+,\varkappa}^{\rho_1,\rho_2}$ and $\mathbb{I}_{a^+,\varkappa}^{1-\gamma}$ represent the Hilfer FD of order (ρ_1,ρ_2) and the R-L fractional integral of order $1-\gamma$, respectively (see [5]). Therefore, the results in Theorems 4 and 5 can be presented by

$$\begin{cases} v(\varkappa) = \frac{(\varkappa-a)^{\gamma-1}}{\Gamma(\gamma)}v_a + \mathbb{I}_{a^+,\varkappa}^{\rho_1}f(\varkappa, v(\varkappa), \mathbb{I}_{a^+,\varkappa}^{\rho_3}\omega(\varkappa)), & \varkappa \in \mathbb{J}, \\ \omega(\varkappa) = \frac{(\varkappa-a)^{\gamma-1}}{\Gamma(\gamma)}\omega_a + \mathbb{I}_{a^+,\varkappa}^{\rho_1}g(\varkappa, \omega(\varkappa), \mathbb{I}_{a^+,\varkappa}^{\rho_3}v(\varkappa)), & \varkappa \in \mathbb{J}. \end{cases}$$

Let

$$\mathcal{C}_{1-\gamma} = \left\{\phi : \mathbb{J} \to \mathbb{R}; \mathbb{D}_{a^+,\varkappa}^{\rho_1,\rho_2}\phi \in \mathcal{C}; \|\phi\|_{1-\gamma} = \left\|(\varkappa-a)^{1-\gamma}\phi(\varkappa)\right\|_{\infty}\right\}, \ 0 \leq \gamma < 1.$$

Then the next two corollaries are a special case of the Theorems 4 and 5.

Corollary 1. Assume that (Hy_1) and (Hy_2) are satisfied. If $\frac{\Lambda}{2}(b-a)^{\rho_1+\rho_3} < 1$, then system (12) has at least one solution $(v,\omega) \in \mathcal{C}_{1-\gamma} \times \mathcal{C}_{1-\gamma}$, where Λ as in Theorem 4.

Corollary 2. Assume that (Hy_1) and (Hy_2) are satisfied. If $\max_{\varkappa \in \mathbb{J}}\{\zeta_1^\star, \zeta_2^\star\} = \zeta^\star < 1$, then the system (12) has a unique solution $(v,\omega) \in \mathcal{C}_{1-\gamma} \times \mathcal{C}_{1-\gamma}$, where

$$\zeta_1^\star := \frac{(b-a)^{\rho_1}}{\Gamma(\rho_1+1)}\kappa_f + \frac{(b-a)^{\rho_1+\rho_3}}{\Gamma(\rho_1+\rho_3+1)}\overline{\kappa}_g,$$

$$\zeta_2^\star := \frac{(b-a)^{\rho_1}}{\Gamma(\rho_1+1)}\kappa_g + \frac{(b-a)^{\rho_1+\rho_3}}{\Gamma(\rho_1+\rho_3+1)}\overline{\kappa}_f.$$

Case 2: Let $a > 0$, and $\vartheta(\varkappa) = \log \varkappa$, then the system (1) is reduced to a Hilfer–Hadamard type coupled system of FIDE of the form

$$\begin{cases} \mathbb{D}^{\rho_1,\rho_2}_{a^+,\log \varkappa} v(\varkappa) = f(\varkappa, v(\varkappa), \mathbb{I}^{\rho_3}_{a^+,\log \varkappa} \omega(\varkappa)), & \varkappa \in \mathbb{J}, \\ \mathbb{D}^{\rho_1,\rho_2}_{a^+,\log \varkappa} \omega(\varkappa) = g(\varkappa, \omega(\varkappa), \mathbb{I}^{\rho_3}_{a^+,\log \varkappa} v(\varkappa)), & \varkappa \in \mathbb{J}, \\ \mathbb{I}^{1-\gamma}_{a^+,\log \varkappa} v(\varkappa)\big|_{\varkappa=a} = v_a, \; \mathbb{I}^{1-\gamma}_{a^+,\log \varkappa} \omega(\varkappa)\big|_{\varkappa=a} = \omega_a. \end{cases} \quad (13)$$

where $\mathbb{D}^{\rho_1,\rho_2}_{a^+,\log \varkappa}$ and $\mathbb{I}^{1-\gamma}_{a^+,\log \varkappa}$ represent the Hilfer–Hadamard FD of order (ρ_1,ρ_2) and the Hadamard fractional integral of order $1-\gamma$, respectively, (see [40,41]). Consequently, the results in Theorems 4 and 5 can be offered by

$$\begin{cases} v(\varkappa) = \frac{(\log \frac{\varkappa}{a})^{\gamma-1}}{\Gamma(\gamma)} v_a + \mathbb{I}^{\rho_1}_{a^+,\log \varkappa} f(\varkappa, v(\varkappa), \mathbb{I}^{\rho_3}_{a^+,\log \varkappa} \omega(\varkappa)), & \varkappa \in \mathbb{J}, \\ \omega(\varkappa) = \frac{(\log \frac{\varkappa}{a})^{\gamma-1}}{\Gamma(\gamma)} \omega_a + \mathbb{I}^{\rho_1}_{a^+,\log \varkappa} g(\varkappa, \omega(\varkappa), \mathbb{I}^{\rho_3}_{a^+,\log \varkappa} v(\varkappa)), & \varkappa \in \mathbb{J}. \end{cases}$$

Let

$$\mathcal{C}_{1-\gamma,\log \varkappa} = \left\{\phi : \mathbb{J} \to \mathbb{R}; \; \mathbb{D}^{\rho_1,\rho_2}_{a^+,\log \varkappa} \phi \in \mathcal{C}; \; \|\phi\|_{1-\gamma,\log \varkappa} = \left\|(\log \frac{\varkappa}{a})^{1-\gamma} \phi(\varkappa)\right\|_\infty\right\}, \; 0 \le \gamma < 1.$$

Then the following two results are a special case of the Theorems 4 and 5.

Corollary 3. Assume that (Hy_1) and (Hy_2) hold. If $\frac{\Lambda}{2}(\log \frac{b}{a})^{\rho_1+\rho_3} < 1$, then system (13) has at least one solution $(v,\omega) \in \mathcal{C}_{1-\gamma,\log \varkappa} \times \mathcal{C}_{1-\gamma,\log \varkappa}$, where Λ is as in Theorem 4.

Corollary 4. Assume that (Hy_1) and (Hy_2) are satisfied. If $\max_{\varkappa \in \mathbb{J}}\{\zeta_3^\star, \zeta_4^\star\} = \overline{\zeta} < 1$, then the system (13) has a unique solution in $\mathcal{C}_{1-\gamma,\log \varkappa} \times \mathcal{C}_{1-\gamma,\log \varkappa}$, where

$$\zeta_3^\star := \frac{(\log \frac{b}{a})^{\rho_1}}{\Gamma(\rho_1+1)}\kappa_f + \frac{(\log \frac{b}{a})^{\rho_1+\rho_3}}{\Gamma(\rho_1+\rho_3+1)}\overline{\kappa}_g,$$

$$\zeta_4^\star := \frac{(\log \frac{b}{a})^{\rho_1+\rho_3}}{\Gamma(\rho_1+\rho_3+1)}\overline{\kappa}_f + \frac{(\log \frac{b}{a})^{\rho_1}}{\Gamma(\rho_1+1)}\kappa_g.$$

Case 3: If $\vartheta(\varkappa) = \varkappa^\rho$, for $\rho > 0$, then the system (1) is reduced to a Hilfer–Katugumpola type coupled system of FIDE of the form

$$\begin{cases} \mathbb{D}^{\rho_1,\rho_2}_{a^+,\varkappa^\rho} v(\varkappa) = f(\varkappa, v(\varkappa), \mathbb{I}^{\rho_3}_{a^+,\varkappa^\rho} \omega(\varkappa)), & \varkappa \in \mathbb{J}, \\ \mathbb{D}^{\rho_1,\rho_2}_{a^+,\varkappa^\rho} \omega(\varkappa) = g(\varkappa, \omega(\varkappa), \mathbb{I}^{\rho_3}_{a^+,\varkappa^\rho} v(\varkappa)), & \varkappa \in \mathbb{J}, \\ \mathbb{I}^{1-\gamma}_{a^+,\varkappa^\rho} v(\varkappa)\big|_{\varkappa=a} = v_a, \; \mathbb{I}^{1-\gamma}_{a^+,\varkappa^\rho} \omega(\varkappa)\big|_{\varkappa=a} = \omega_a, \end{cases} \quad (14)$$

where $\mathbb{D}_{a^+,\varkappa^\rho}^{\rho_1,\rho_2}$ and $\mathbb{I}_{a^+,\varkappa^\rho}^{1-\gamma}$ represent the Hilfer–Katugumpola FD of order (ρ_1,ρ_2) and the Katugumpola fractional integral of order $1-\gamma$, respectively, (see [42,43]). So, the results in Theorems 4 and 5 can be given by

$$\begin{cases} v(\varkappa) = \frac{(\varkappa^\rho - a^\rho)^{\gamma-1}}{\Gamma(\gamma)} v_a + \mathbb{I}_{a^+,\varkappa^\rho}^{\rho_1} f(\varkappa, v(\varkappa), \mathbb{I}_{a^+,\varkappa^\rho}^{\rho_3} w(\varkappa)), & \varkappa \in \mathbb{J}, \\ w(\varkappa) = \frac{(\varkappa^\rho - a^\rho)^{\gamma-1}}{\Gamma(\gamma)} w_a + \mathbb{I}_{a^+,\varkappa^\rho}^{\rho_1} g(\varkappa, w(\varkappa), \mathbb{I}_{a^+,\varkappa^\rho}^{\rho_3} v(\varkappa)), & \varkappa \in \mathbb{J}. \end{cases}$$

Let

$$\mathcal{C}_{1-\gamma,\varkappa^\rho} = \left\{ \phi : \mathbb{J} \to \mathbb{R}; \; \mathbb{D}_{a^+,\varkappa^\rho}^{\rho_1,\rho_2} \phi \in \mathcal{C}; \; \|\phi\|_{1-\gamma,\varkappa^\rho} = \left\| (\varkappa^\rho - a^\rho)^{1-\gamma} \phi(\varkappa) \right\|_\infty \right\}, \; 0 \leq \gamma < 1.$$

Then the following results are a special case of the Theorems 4 and 5.

Corollary 5. *Assume that* (Hy_1) *and* (Hy_2) *hold. If* $\frac{\Lambda}{2}(b^\rho - a^\rho))^{\rho_1+\rho_3} < 1$, *then system* (14) *has at least one solution* $(v,w) \in \mathcal{C}_{1-\gamma,\varkappa^\rho} \times \mathcal{C}_{1-\gamma,\varkappa^\rho}$, *where* Λ *as in Theorem 4.*

Corollary 6. *Assume that* (Hy_1) *and* (Hy_2) *are satisfied. If* $\max_{\varkappa \in \mathbb{J}}\{\zeta_5^\star, \zeta_6^\star\} = \widetilde{\zeta} < 1$, *then the system* (14) *has a unique solution in* $\mathcal{C}_{1-\gamma,\varkappa^\rho} \times \mathcal{C}_{1-\gamma,\varkappa^\rho}$, *where*

$$\zeta_5^\star \; : \; = \frac{(b^\rho - a^\rho)^{\rho_1}}{\Gamma(\rho_1 + 1)} \overline{\kappa}_f + \frac{(b^\rho - a^\rho)^{\rho_1+\rho_3}}{\Gamma(\rho_1 + \rho_3 + 1)} \overline{\kappa}_g,$$

$$\zeta_6^\star \; : \; = \frac{(b^\rho - a^\rho)^{\rho_1+\rho_3}}{\Gamma(\rho_1 + \rho_3 + 1)} \overline{\kappa}_f + \frac{(b^\rho - a^\rho)^{\rho_1}}{\Gamma(\rho_1 + 1)} \overline{\kappa}_g.$$

Remark 1. *Many other special cases of function* ϑ *and parameter* ρ_2 *generate similar problems and systems some of them addressed in the literature, to name a few, the* ϑ-*Hilfer type system* (1) *reduces to*

(1) *The R-L type system, for* $\vartheta(\varkappa) = \varkappa$, *and* $\rho_2 = 0$ *(see* [2]*);*
(2) *The Caputo type system, for* $\vartheta(\varkappa) = \varkappa$, *and* $\rho_2 = 1$ *(see* [2]*);*
(3) *The Hilfer type system, for* $\vartheta(\varkappa) = \varkappa$ *(see* [5]*);*
(4) *The Katugampola type system, for* $\vartheta(\varkappa) = \varkappa^\rho$, *and* $\rho_2 = 0$ *(see* [42]*);*
(5) *The Caputo–Katugampola type system, for* $\vartheta(\varkappa) = \varkappa^\rho$, *and* $\rho_2 = 1$ *(see* [44]*);*
(6) *The Hilfer–Katugampola type system, for* $\vartheta(\varkappa) = \varkappa^\rho$ *(see* [43]*);*
(7) *The Hadamard type system, for* $\vartheta(\varkappa) = \log \varkappa$, *and* $\rho_2 = 0$ *(see* [40]*);*
(8) *The Caputo–Hadamard type system, for* $\vartheta(\varkappa) = \log \varkappa$, *and* $\rho_2 = 1$ *(see* [45]*);*
(9) *The Hilfer–Hadamard type system, for* $\vartheta(\varkappa) = \log \varkappa$ *(see* [41]*).*

3.4. U-H Stability Analysis

In this subsection, we discuss the U-H Stability of the considered system.

Definition 3. *System* (1) *is said to be U-H stable if there exists a constant* $Y_{1,2} = \max\{Y_1, Y_2\} > 0$ $(Y_1, Y_2 > 0)$ *such that for each* $\varepsilon = \max\{\varepsilon_1, \varepsilon_2\}$, *where* $\varepsilon_1, \varepsilon_2 > 0$, *and every solution* $(\widetilde{v}, \widetilde{w}) \in \mathcal{C}_{1-\gamma,\vartheta} \times \mathcal{C}_{1-\gamma,\vartheta}$ *of the inequalities*

$$\begin{cases} \left| \mathbb{D}_{a^+,\vartheta(\varkappa)}^{\rho_1,\rho_2} \widetilde{v}(\varkappa) - f(\varkappa, \widetilde{v}(\varkappa), \mathbb{I}_{a^+,\vartheta(\varkappa)}^{\rho_3} \widetilde{w}(\varkappa)) \right| \leq \varepsilon_1, & \varkappa \in \mathbb{J}, \\ \left| \mathbb{D}_{a^+,\vartheta(\varkappa)}^{\rho_1,\rho_2} \widetilde{w}(\varkappa) - g(\varkappa, \widetilde{w}(\varkappa), \mathbb{I}_{a^+,\vartheta(\varkappa)}^{\rho_3} \widetilde{v}(\varkappa)) \right| \leq \varepsilon_2, & \varkappa \in \mathbb{J}, \end{cases} \tag{15}$$

there exists a solution $(v, w) \in \mathcal{C}_{1-\gamma,\vartheta} \times \mathcal{C}_{1-\gamma,\vartheta}$ *of system* (1) *which satisfies*

$$\|(\widetilde{v}, \widetilde{w}) - (v, w)\|_{\mathcal{C}_{1-\gamma,\vartheta}} \leq Y_{1,2}\varepsilon. \tag{16}$$

Remark 2. $(\widetilde{v}, \widetilde{\omega}) \in \mathcal{C}_{1-\gamma,\vartheta} \times \mathcal{C}_{1-\gamma,\vartheta}$ satisfies (15) if and only if there exist functions $\sigma_1, \sigma_2 \in \mathcal{C}_{1-\gamma,\vartheta}$ such that:

(i) $|\sigma_1(\varkappa)| \leq \varepsilon_1$, and $|\sigma_2(\varkappa)| \leq \varepsilon_2$, $\varkappa \in \mathbb{J}$;

(ii) For all $\varkappa \in \mathbb{J}$,

$$\begin{cases} \mathbb{D}_{a^+,\vartheta(\varkappa)}^{\rho_1,\rho_2} \widetilde{v}(\varkappa) = f(\varkappa, \widetilde{v}(\varkappa), \mathbb{I}_{a^+,\vartheta(\varkappa)}^{\rho_3} \widetilde{\omega}(\varkappa)) + \sigma_1(\varkappa), & \varkappa \in \mathbb{J}, \\ \mathbb{D}_{a^+,\vartheta(\varkappa)}^{\rho_1,\rho_2} \widetilde{\omega}(\varkappa) = g(\varkappa, \widetilde{\omega}(\varkappa), \mathbb{I}_{a^+,\vartheta(\varkappa)}^{\rho_3} \widetilde{v}(\varkappa)) + \sigma_2(\varkappa), & \varkappa \in \mathbb{J}, \end{cases} \quad (17)$$

Lemma 3. If $(\widetilde{v}, \widetilde{\omega}) \in \mathcal{C}_{1-\gamma,\vartheta} \times \mathcal{C}_{1-\gamma,\vartheta}$ satisfies (15), then $(\widetilde{v}, \widetilde{\omega})$ is the solution of the inequalities

$$\begin{cases} \left| \widetilde{v}(\varkappa) - \frac{(\vartheta(\varkappa) - \vartheta(a))^{\gamma-1}}{\Gamma(\gamma)} v_a + \mathbb{I}_{a^+,\vartheta(\varkappa)}^{\rho_1} f(\varkappa, \widetilde{v}(\varkappa), \mathbb{I}_{a^+,\vartheta(\varkappa)}^{\rho_3} \widetilde{\omega}(\varkappa)) \right| \leq \varepsilon_1 \frac{(\vartheta(\varkappa) - \vartheta(a))^{\rho_1}}{\Gamma(\rho_1+1)}, \\ \left| \widetilde{\omega}(\varkappa) - \frac{(\vartheta(\varkappa) - \vartheta(a))^{\gamma-1}}{\Gamma(\gamma)} \omega_a + \mathbb{I}_{a^+,\vartheta(\varkappa)}^{\rho_1} g(\varkappa, \widetilde{\omega}(\varkappa), \mathbb{I}_{a^+,\vartheta(\varkappa)}^{\rho_3} \widetilde{v}(\varkappa)) \right| \leq \varepsilon_2 \frac{(\vartheta(\varkappa) - \vartheta(a))^{\rho_1}}{\Gamma(\rho_1+1)}. \end{cases} \quad (18)$$

Proof. By virtue of Theorem 3 and Remark 2 (ii) the solution of (17) with

$$\mathbb{I}_{a^+,\vartheta(\varkappa)}^{1-\gamma} \widetilde{v}(\varkappa) \Big|_{\varkappa=a} = v_a, \quad \mathbb{I}_{a^+,\vartheta(\varkappa)}^{1-\gamma} \widetilde{\omega}(\varkappa) \Big|_{\varkappa=a} = \omega_a$$

is equivalent to:

$$\begin{cases} \widetilde{v}(\varkappa) = \frac{(\vartheta(\varkappa) - \vartheta(a))^{\gamma-1}}{\Gamma(\gamma)} v_a + \mathbb{I}_{a^+,\vartheta(\varkappa)}^{\rho_1} f(\varkappa, \widetilde{v}(\varkappa), \mathbb{I}_{a^+,\vartheta(\varkappa)}^{\rho_3} \widetilde{\omega}(\varkappa)) + \mathbb{I}_{a^+,\vartheta(\varkappa)}^{\rho_1} \sigma_1(\varkappa), \\ \widetilde{\omega}(\varkappa) = \frac{(\vartheta(\varkappa) - \vartheta(a))^{\gamma-1}}{\Gamma(\gamma)} \omega_a + \mathbb{I}_{a^+,\vartheta(\varkappa)}^{\rho_1} g(\varkappa, \widetilde{\omega}(\varkappa), \mathbb{I}_{a^+,\vartheta(\varkappa)}^{\rho_3} \widetilde{v}(\varkappa)) + \mathbb{I}_{a^+,\vartheta(\varkappa)}^{\rho_1} \sigma_2(\varkappa). \end{cases} \quad (19)$$

Hence,

$$\left| \widetilde{v}(\varkappa) - \frac{(\vartheta(\varkappa) - \vartheta(a))^{\gamma-1}}{\Gamma(\gamma)} v_a + \mathbb{I}_{a^+,\vartheta(\varkappa)}^{\rho_1} f(\varkappa, \widetilde{v}(\varkappa), \mathbb{I}_{a^+,\vartheta(\varkappa)}^{\rho_3} \widetilde{\omega}(\varkappa)) \right|$$
$$= \left| \mathbb{I}_{a^+,\vartheta(\varkappa)}^{\rho_1} \sigma_1(\varkappa) \right|$$
$$\leq \mathbb{I}_{a^+,\vartheta(\varkappa)}^{\rho_1} |\sigma_1(\varkappa)|$$
$$\leq \varepsilon_1 \frac{(\vartheta(\varkappa) - \vartheta(a))^{\rho_1}}{\Gamma(\rho_1+1)}.$$

Similarly, we obtain

$$\left| \widetilde{\omega}(\varkappa) - \frac{(\vartheta(\varkappa) - \vartheta(a))^{\gamma-1}}{\Gamma(\gamma)} \omega_a + \mathbb{I}_{a^+,\vartheta(\varkappa)}^{\rho_1} g(\varkappa, \widetilde{\omega}(\varkappa), \mathbb{I}_{a^+,\vartheta(\varkappa)}^{\rho_3} \widetilde{v}(\varkappa)) \right|$$
$$\leq \varepsilon_2 \frac{(\vartheta(\varkappa) - \vartheta(a))^{\rho_1}}{\Gamma(\rho_1+1)}.$$

□

Theorem 6. Under the hypothesis (Hy_1), if $\left(1 - \mathcal{L}_f\right)\left(1 - \mathcal{L}_g\right) - \mathcal{K}_f \mathcal{K}_g \neq 0$, then the solution of the coupled system (1) is H-U stable, where

$$\mathcal{L}_f := \kappa_f \frac{\mathcal{B}(\rho_1, \gamma)}{\Gamma(\rho_1)} (\vartheta(b) - \vartheta(a))^{\rho_1}, \quad \mathcal{K}_f := \overline{\kappa}_f \frac{\mathcal{B}(\rho_1 + \rho_3, \gamma)}{\Gamma(\rho_1 + \rho_3)} (\vartheta(b) - \vartheta(a))^{\rho_1 + \rho_3},$$

$$\mathcal{L}_g := \kappa_g \frac{\mathcal{B}(\rho_1, \gamma)}{\Gamma(\rho_1)} (\vartheta(b) - \vartheta(a))^{\rho_1}, \quad \mathcal{K}_g := \overline{\kappa}_g \frac{\mathcal{B}(\rho_1 + \rho_3, \gamma)}{\Gamma(\rho_1 + \rho_3)} (\vartheta(b) - \vartheta(a))^{\rho_1 + \rho_3}.$$

Proof. Let $(\widetilde{v}, \widetilde{\omega}) \in \mathcal{C}_{1-\gamma,\vartheta} \times \mathcal{C}_{1-\gamma,\vartheta}$ satisfies (15), and let $(v, \omega) \in \mathcal{C}_{1-\gamma,\vartheta} \times \mathcal{C}_{1-\gamma,\vartheta}$ the unique solution of the system

$$\begin{cases} \mathbb{D}^{\rho_1,\rho_2}_{a^+,\vartheta(\varkappa)} v(\varkappa) = f(\varkappa, v(\varkappa), \mathbb{I}^{\rho_3}_{a^+,\vartheta(\varkappa)} \omega(\varkappa)), & \varkappa \in \mathbb{J}, \\ \mathbb{D}^{\rho_1,\rho_2}_{a^+,\vartheta(\varkappa)} \omega(\varkappa) = g(\varkappa, \omega(\varkappa), \mathbb{I}^{\rho_3}_{a^+,\vartheta(\varkappa)} v(\varkappa)), & \varkappa \in \mathbb{J}, \\ \mathbb{I}^{1-\gamma}_{a^+,\vartheta(\varkappa)} v(\varkappa) \Big|_{\varkappa=a} = \mathbb{I}^{1-\gamma}_{a^+,\vartheta(\varkappa)} \widetilde{v}(\varkappa) \Big|_{\varkappa=a} = v_a, \\ \mathbb{I}^{1-\gamma}_{a^+,\vartheta(\varkappa)} \omega(\varkappa) \Big|_{\varkappa=a} = \mathbb{I}^{1-\gamma}_{a^+,\vartheta(\varkappa)} \widetilde{\omega}(\varkappa) \Big|_{\varkappa=a} = \omega_a, \end{cases} \quad (20)$$

By virtue of Theorem 3, we obtain

$$\begin{cases} v(\varkappa) = \mathcal{X}_v + \mathbb{I}^{\rho_1}_{a^+,\vartheta(\varkappa)} f(\varkappa, v(\varkappa), \mathbb{I}^{\rho_3}_{a^+,\vartheta(\varkappa)} \omega(\varkappa)), \\ \omega(\varkappa) = \mathcal{X}_\omega + \mathbb{I}^{\rho_1}_{a^+,\vartheta(\varkappa)} g(\varkappa, \omega(\varkappa), \mathbb{I}^{\rho_3}_{a^+,\vartheta(\varkappa)} v(\varkappa)), \end{cases} \quad (21)$$

where

$$\mathcal{X}_v = \frac{(\vartheta(\varkappa) - \vartheta(a))^{\gamma-1}}{\Gamma(\gamma)} v_a, \text{ and } \mathcal{X}_\omega = \frac{(\vartheta(\varkappa) - \vartheta(a))^{\gamma-1}}{\Gamma(\gamma)} \omega_a.$$

If $\mathbb{I}^{1-\gamma}_{a^+,\vartheta(\varkappa)} v(\varkappa) \Big|_{\varkappa=a} = \mathbb{I}^{1-\gamma}_{a^+,\vartheta(\varkappa)} \widetilde{v}(\varkappa) \Big|_{\varkappa=a}$ and $\mathbb{I}^{1-\gamma}_{a^+,\vartheta(\varkappa)} \omega(\varkappa) \Big|_{\varkappa=a} = \mathbb{I}^{1-\gamma}_{a^+,\vartheta(\varkappa)} \widetilde{\omega}(\varkappa) \Big|_{\varkappa=a}$, then $\mathcal{X}_v = \mathcal{X}_{\widetilde{v}}$ and $\mathcal{X}_\omega = \mathcal{X}_{\widetilde{\omega}}$. Consequently, we have

$$\begin{cases} v(\varkappa) = \mathcal{X}_{\widetilde{v}} + \mathbb{I}^{\rho_1}_{a^+,\vartheta(\varkappa)} f(\varkappa, v(\varkappa), \mathbb{I}^{\rho_3}_{a^+,\vartheta(\varkappa)} \omega(\varkappa)), \\ \omega(\varkappa) = \mathcal{X}_{\widetilde{\omega}} + \mathbb{I}^{\rho_1}_{a^+,\vartheta(\varkappa)} g(\varkappa, \omega(\varkappa), \mathbb{I}^{\rho_3}_{a^+,\vartheta(\varkappa)} v(\varkappa)), \end{cases} \quad (22)$$

Therefore, by (22), Lemma 3 and (Hy$_1$), we obtain

$$\begin{aligned} |\widetilde{v}(\varkappa) - v(\varkappa)| &\leq \left| \widetilde{v}(\varkappa) - \mathcal{X}_{\widetilde{v}} + \mathbb{I}^{\rho_1}_{a^+,\vartheta(\varkappa)} f(\varkappa, \widetilde{v}(\varkappa), \mathbb{I}^{\rho_3}_{a^+,\vartheta(\varkappa)} \widetilde{\omega}(\varkappa)) \right| \\ &\quad + \mathbb{I}^{\rho_1}_{a^+,\vartheta(\varkappa)} \left| f(\varkappa, \widetilde{v}(\varkappa), \mathbb{I}^{\rho_3}_{a^+,\vartheta(\varkappa)} \widetilde{\omega}(\varkappa)) - f(\varkappa, v(\varkappa), \mathbb{I}^{\rho_3}_{a^+,\vartheta(\varkappa)} \omega(\varkappa)) \right| \\ &\leq \varepsilon_1 \frac{(\vartheta(\varkappa) - \vartheta(a))^{\rho_1}}{\Gamma(\rho_1 + 1)} + \mathbb{I}^{\rho_1}_{a^+,\vartheta(\varkappa)} \left[\kappa_f |\widetilde{v}(\varkappa) - v(\varkappa)| + \overline{\kappa}_f \mathbb{I}^{\rho_3}_{a^+,\vartheta(\varkappa)} |\widetilde{\omega}(\varkappa) - \omega(\varkappa)| \right] \\ &\leq \varepsilon_1 \frac{(\vartheta(\varkappa) - \vartheta(a))^{\rho_1}}{\Gamma(\rho_1 + 1)} + \kappa_f \|\widetilde{v} - v\|_{\mathcal{C}_{1-\gamma,\vartheta}} \mathbb{I}^{\rho_1}_{a^+,\vartheta(\varkappa)} (\vartheta(\varkappa) - \vartheta(a))^{\gamma-1} \\ &\quad + \overline{\kappa}_f \|\widetilde{\omega} - \omega\|_{\mathcal{C}_{1-\gamma,\vartheta}} \mathbb{I}^{\rho_1+\rho_3}_{a^+,\vartheta(\varkappa)} (\vartheta(\varkappa) - \vartheta(a))^{\gamma-1} \\ &= \varepsilon_1 \frac{(\vartheta(\varkappa) - \vartheta(a))^{\rho_1}}{\Gamma(\rho_1 + 1)} + \kappa_f \|\widetilde{v} - v\|_{\mathcal{C}_{1-\gamma,\vartheta}} \frac{\mathcal{B}(\rho_1, \gamma)}{\Gamma(\rho_1)} (\vartheta(\varkappa) - \vartheta(a))^{\rho_1+\gamma-1} \\ &\quad + \overline{\kappa}_f \|\widetilde{\omega} - \omega\|_{\mathcal{C}_{1-\gamma,\vartheta}} \frac{\mathcal{B}(\rho_1+\rho_3, \gamma)}{\Gamma(\rho_1+\rho_3)} (\vartheta(\varkappa) - \vartheta(a))^{\rho_1+\rho_3+\gamma-1}. \end{aligned}$$

Thus

$$\begin{aligned} \|\widetilde{v} - v\|_{\mathcal{C}_{1-\gamma,\vartheta}} &\leq \varepsilon_1 \frac{(\vartheta(b) - \vartheta(a))^{\rho_1-\gamma+1}}{\Gamma(\rho_1+1)} + \kappa_f \|\widetilde{v} - v\|_{\mathcal{C}_{1-\gamma,\vartheta}} \frac{\mathcal{B}(\rho_1,\gamma)}{\Gamma(\rho_1)} (\vartheta(b) - \vartheta(a))^{\rho_1} \\ &\quad + \overline{\kappa}_f \|\widetilde{\omega} - \omega\|_{\mathcal{C}_{1-\gamma,\vartheta}} \frac{\mathcal{B}(\rho_1+\rho_3,\gamma)}{\Gamma(\rho_1+\rho_3)} (\vartheta(b) - \vartheta(a))^{\rho_1+\rho_3}, \end{aligned}$$

which implies

$$(1 - \mathcal{L}_f) \|\widetilde{v} - v\|_{\mathcal{C}_{1-\gamma,\vartheta}} \leq Y_1 \varepsilon_1 + \mathcal{K}_f \|\widetilde{\omega} - \omega\|_{\mathcal{C}_{1-\gamma,\vartheta}}. \quad (23)$$

Similarly

$$(1 - \mathcal{L}_g) \|\widetilde{\omega} - \omega\|_{\mathcal{C}_{1-\gamma,\vartheta}} \leq Y_2 \varepsilon_2 + \mathcal{K}_g \|\widetilde{v} - v\|_{\mathcal{C}_{1-\gamma,\vartheta}}. \quad (24)$$

where
$$Y_1 = Y_2 := \frac{(\vartheta(b) - \vartheta(a))^{\rho_1 - \gamma + 1}}{\Gamma(\rho_1 + 1)}.$$

Now, we can express (23) and (24) by

$$(1 - \mathcal{L}_f)\|\widetilde{v} - v\|_{\mathcal{C}_{1-\gamma,\vartheta}} - \mathcal{K}_f\|\widetilde{\omega} - \omega\|_{\mathcal{C}_{1-\gamma,\vartheta}} \leq Y_1\varepsilon_1, \qquad (25)$$

$$-\mathcal{K}_g\|\widetilde{v} - v\|_{\mathcal{C}_{1-\gamma,\vartheta}} + (1 - \mathcal{L}_g)\|\widetilde{\omega} - \omega\|_{\mathcal{C}_{1-\gamma,\vartheta}} \leq Y_2\varepsilon_2. \qquad (26)$$

The matrix formula of (25) and (26) is

$$\begin{pmatrix} 1 - \mathcal{L}_f & -\mathcal{K}_f \\ -\mathcal{K}_g & 1 - \mathcal{L}_g \end{pmatrix} \begin{pmatrix} \|\widetilde{v} - v\|_{\mathcal{C}_{1-\gamma,\vartheta}} \\ \|\widetilde{\omega} - \omega\|_{\mathcal{C}_{1-\gamma,\vartheta}} \end{pmatrix} \leq \begin{pmatrix} Y_1\varepsilon_1 \\ Y_2\varepsilon_2 \end{pmatrix}.$$

It follows that

$$\begin{pmatrix} \|\widetilde{v} - v\|_{\mathcal{C}_{1-\gamma,\vartheta}} \\ \|\widetilde{\omega} - \omega\|_{\mathcal{C}_{1-\gamma,\vartheta}} \end{pmatrix} \leq \frac{1}{\Delta} \begin{pmatrix} 1 - \mathcal{L}_g & \mathcal{K}_f \\ \mathcal{K}_g & 1 - \mathcal{L}_f \end{pmatrix} \begin{pmatrix} Y_1\varepsilon_1 \\ Y_2\varepsilon_2 \end{pmatrix},$$

where $\Delta = (1 - \mathcal{L}_f)(1 - \mathcal{L}_g) - \mathcal{K}_f\mathcal{K}_g \neq 0$. Hence

$$\|\widetilde{v} - v\|_{\mathcal{C}_{1-\gamma,\vartheta}} \leq \frac{(1 - \mathcal{L}_g)Y_1\varepsilon_1}{\Delta} + \frac{\mathcal{K}_f Y_2\varepsilon_2}{\Delta}, \qquad (27)$$

and

$$\|\widetilde{\omega} - \omega\|_{\mathcal{C}_{1-\gamma,\vartheta}} \leq \frac{\mathcal{K}_g Y_1\varepsilon_1}{\Delta} + \frac{(1 - \mathcal{L}_f)Y_2\varepsilon_2}{\Delta}, \qquad (28)$$

By (27) and (28), we find that

$$\begin{aligned}
\|(\widetilde{v},\widetilde{\omega}) - (v,\omega)\|_{\mathcal{C}_{1-\gamma,\vartheta}} &\leq \|\widetilde{v} - v\|_{\mathcal{C}_{1-\gamma,\vartheta}} + \|\widetilde{\omega} - \omega\|_{\mathcal{C}_{1-\gamma,\vartheta}} \\
&\leq \frac{(1 - \mathcal{L}_g)Y_1\varepsilon_1}{\Delta} + \frac{\mathcal{K}_f Y_2\varepsilon_2}{\Delta} \\
&\quad + \frac{\mathcal{K}_g Y_1\varepsilon_1}{\Delta} + \frac{(1 - \mathcal{L}_f)Y_2\varepsilon_2}{\Delta} \\
&\leq Y\varepsilon,
\end{aligned}$$

where $Y = \frac{2 - \mathcal{L}_g + \mathcal{K}_f + \mathcal{K}_g - \mathcal{L}_f}{\Delta} Y_{1,2}$ and $\varepsilon = \max\{\varepsilon_1, \varepsilon_2\}$. □

4. Examples

Consider the ϑ-Hilfer type system

$$\begin{cases} \mathbb{D}_{0^+,\frac{\varkappa}{3}}^{\frac{1}{3},\frac{1}{4}} v(\varkappa) = f(\varkappa, v(\varkappa), \mathbb{I}_{a^+,\vartheta(\varkappa)}^{\rho_3} \omega(\varkappa)), & \varkappa \in (0,1], \\ \mathbb{D}_{0^+,\frac{\varkappa}{3}}^{\frac{1}{3},\frac{1}{4}} \omega(\varkappa) = g(\varkappa, \omega(\varkappa), \mathbb{I}_{a^+,\vartheta(\varkappa)}^{\rho_3} v(\varkappa)), & \varkappa \in (0,1], \\ \mathbb{I}_{0^+,\frac{\varkappa}{3}}^{\frac{1}{2}} v(\varkappa)\Big|_{\varkappa=0} = 1, \; \mathbb{I}_{0^+,\frac{\varkappa}{3}}^{\frac{1}{2}} \omega(\varkappa)\Big|_{\varkappa=0} = 2, \end{cases} \qquad (29)$$

where $\rho_1 = \frac{1}{3}$, $\rho_2 = \frac{1}{4}$, $\rho_3 = \frac{1}{4}$, $\gamma = \frac{1}{2}$, $v_0 = 1$, and $\omega_0 = 2$.

1. In order to illustrate Theorem 5, we take $\vartheta(\varkappa) = \frac{\varkappa}{3}$ and

$$\begin{cases} f(\varkappa, v(\varkappa), \mathbb{I}^{\rho_3}_{a^+, \vartheta(\varkappa)} \omega(\varkappa)) = \frac{8}{20}\left(\sin v(\varkappa) + \sin\left(\mathbb{I}^{\frac{1}{4}}_{0^+, \frac{\varkappa}{3}} \omega(\varkappa)\right) + 1\right), \\ g(\varkappa, \omega(\varkappa), \mathbb{I}^{\rho_3}_{a^+, \vartheta(\varkappa)} v(\varkappa)) = \frac{1}{30}\left(\cos \varkappa + \omega(\varkappa) + \sin\left(\mathbb{I}^{\frac{1}{4}}_{0^+, \frac{\varkappa}{3}} v(\varkappa)\right)\right). \end{cases} \quad (30)$$

Then we have

$$\left| f(\varkappa, v(\varkappa), \mathbb{I}^{\rho_3}_{a^+, \vartheta(\varkappa)} \omega(\varkappa)) - f(\varkappa, \overline{v}(\varkappa), \mathbb{I}^{\rho_3}_{a^+, \vartheta(\varkappa)} \overline{\omega}(\varkappa)) \right|$$
$$\leq \frac{8}{20} |\sin v(\varkappa) - \sin \overline{v}(\varkappa)| + \left| \sin\left(\mathbb{I}^{\frac{1}{4}}_{0^+, \frac{\varkappa}{3}} \omega(\varkappa)\right) - \sin\left(\mathbb{I}^{\frac{1}{4}}_{0^+, \frac{\varkappa}{3}} \overline{\omega}(\varkappa)\right) \right|$$
$$\leq \frac{8}{20}\left(|v(\varkappa) - \overline{v}(\varkappa)| + \left|\mathbb{I}^{\frac{1}{4}}_{0^+, \frac{\varkappa}{3}} \omega(\varkappa) - \mathbb{I}^{\frac{1}{4}}_{0^+, \frac{\varkappa}{3}} \overline{\omega}(\varkappa)\right|\right)$$

and

$$\left| g(\varkappa, \omega(\varkappa), \mathbb{I}^{\rho_3}_{a^+, \vartheta(\varkappa)} v(\varkappa)) - g(\varkappa, \overline{\omega}(\varkappa), \mathbb{I}^{\rho_3}_{a^+, \vartheta(\varkappa)} \overline{v}(\varkappa)) \right|$$
$$\leq \frac{1}{30}\left(|\omega(\varkappa) - \overline{\omega}(\varkappa)| + \left|\sin\left(\mathbb{I}^{\frac{1}{4}}_{0^+, \frac{\varkappa}{3}} v(\varkappa)\right) - \sin\left(\mathbb{I}^{\frac{1}{4}}_{0^+, \frac{\varkappa}{3}} \overline{v}(\varkappa)\right)\right|\right)$$
$$\leq \frac{1}{30}\left(|\omega(\varkappa) - \overline{\omega}(\varkappa)| + \left|\mathbb{I}^{\frac{1}{4}}_{0^+, \frac{\varkappa}{3}} v(\varkappa) - \mathbb{I}^{\frac{1}{4}}_{0^+, \frac{\varkappa}{3}} \overline{v}(\varkappa)\right|\right).$$

Thus, (Hy$_1$) holds with $\kappa_f = \overline{\kappa}_f = \frac{8}{20}$ and $\kappa_g = \overline{\kappa}_g = \frac{1}{30}$. From the above data, we obtain $\zeta_1 \approx 0.33$ and $\zeta_2 \approx 0.26$. Hence $\max_{\varkappa \in \mathbb{J}}\{\zeta_1, \zeta_2\} = \zeta \approx 0.33 < 1$. Thus, with the assistance of Theorem 5, the system (29) with f and g given by (30) has a unique solution $(v(\varkappa), \omega(\varkappa))$ on $(0, 1]$.

2. In order to illustrate Theorem 4, we take

$$\begin{cases} f(\varkappa, v(\varkappa), \mathbb{I}^{\rho_3}_{a^+, \vartheta(\varkappa)} \omega(\varkappa)) = \frac{1}{40} v(\varkappa) \sin \omega(\varkappa) + \frac{3}{20} \cos v(\varkappa) \left(\mathbb{I}^{\frac{1}{4}}_{0^+, \frac{\varkappa}{3}} \omega(\varkappa)\right), \\ g(\varkappa, \omega(\varkappa), \mathbb{I}^{\rho_3}_{a^+, \vartheta(\varkappa)} v(\varkappa)) = \frac{1}{10+\varkappa} \sin\left(\mathbb{I}^{\frac{1}{4}}_{0^+, \frac{\varkappa}{3}} v(\varkappa)\right) + \frac{3}{100}\left(e^{-\frac{\varkappa}{2}} \omega(\varkappa)\right). \end{cases} \quad (31)$$

It is easy to see that

$$\left| f(\varkappa, v(\varkappa), \mathbb{I}^{\rho_3}_{a^+, \vartheta(\varkappa)} \omega(\varkappa)) \right| \leq \frac{1}{40} |v(\varkappa)| + \frac{3}{20}\left|\mathbb{I}^{\frac{1}{4}}_{0^+, \frac{\varkappa}{3}} \omega(\varkappa)\right|,$$

$$\left| g(\varkappa, \omega(\varkappa), \mathbb{I}^{\rho_3}_{a^+, \vartheta(\varkappa)} v(\varkappa)) \right| \leq \frac{1}{10}\left|\left(\mathbb{I}^{\frac{1}{4}}_{0^+, \frac{\varkappa}{3}} v(\varkappa)\right)\right| + \frac{3}{100}|\omega(\varkappa)|.$$

So, condition (Hy$_2$) is satisfied with $\varphi_f = \frac{1}{40}, \overline{\varphi}_f = \frac{3}{20}, \varphi_g = \frac{1}{10}, \overline{\varphi}_g = \frac{3}{100}$. Moreover, $\Lambda = \frac{\sqrt{\pi}}{8\Gamma(\frac{5}{6})} + \frac{9\sqrt{\pi}}{50\Gamma(\frac{13}{12})}$ and $\aleph_1 \approx 0.14 < 1$. Thus, Theorem 4 is applied to system (29) with f and g given by (31).

3. In order to illustrate Theorem 6, we have from case 1 that (Hy$_1$) is satisfied. As has been shown in Theorem 6, for $\varepsilon_1 = \frac{1}{2}$ and $\varepsilon_2 = \frac{1}{4}$, if $(\widetilde{v}, \widetilde{\omega}) \in \mathcal{C}_{\frac{1}{2}, \frac{\varkappa}{3}}([0,1], \mathbb{R}) \times \mathcal{C}_{\frac{1}{2}, \frac{\varkappa}{3}}([0,1], \mathbb{R})$ satisfies

$$\begin{cases} \left| \mathbb{D}^{\frac{3}{4}, \frac{1}{4}}_{0^+, \frac{\varkappa}{3}} \widetilde{v}(\varkappa) - \frac{8}{20}\left(\sin \widetilde{v}(\varkappa) + \sin\left(\mathbb{I}^{\frac{1}{4}}_{0^+, \frac{\varkappa}{3}} \widetilde{\omega}(\varkappa)\right) + 1\right) \right| \leq \frac{1}{2}, \quad \varkappa \in (0,1], \\ \left| \mathbb{D}^{\frac{3}{4}, \frac{1}{4}}_{0^+, \frac{\varkappa}{3}} \widetilde{\omega}(\varkappa) - \frac{1}{30}\left(\cos \varkappa + \widetilde{\omega}(\varkappa) + \sin\left(\mathbb{I}^{\frac{1}{4}}_{0^+, \frac{\varkappa}{3}} \widetilde{v}(\varkappa)\right)\right) \right| \leq \frac{1}{4}, \quad \varkappa \in (0,1], \end{cases}$$

there exists a unique solution $(v, \omega) \in \mathcal{C}_{\frac{1}{2}, \frac{x}{3}}([0,1], \mathbb{R}) \times \mathcal{C}_{\frac{1}{2}, \frac{x}{3}}([0,1], \mathbb{R})$ of the problem (29) with f and g given by (30) such that

$$\|(\widetilde{v}, \widetilde{\omega}) - (v, \omega)\|_{\mathcal{C}_{\frac{1}{2}, \frac{x}{3}}} \leq \frac{1}{2} Y.$$

where $Y = \frac{2 - \mathcal{L}_g + \mathcal{K}_f + \mathcal{K}_g - \mathcal{L}_f}{\Delta} Y_{1,2} = 0.952857 > 0$, $\varepsilon = \max\{\varepsilon_1, \varepsilon_2\} = \frac{1}{2}$, $Y_{1,2} = \max\{Y_1, Y_2\} = \frac{1}{(3)^{\frac{5}{6}} \Gamma(\frac{4}{3})}$,

$$Y_1 = Y_2 = \frac{1}{(3)^{\frac{5}{6}} \Gamma(\frac{4}{3})} > 0,$$

and

$$\mathcal{L}_f = \frac{2\sqrt{\pi}}{5 \sqrt[3]{3} \Gamma(\frac{5}{6})}, \quad \mathcal{K}_f = \frac{2\sqrt{\pi}}{5 \sqrt[12]{3^7} \Gamma(\frac{13}{12})},$$

$$\mathcal{L}_g = \frac{\sqrt{\pi}}{30 \sqrt[3]{3} \Gamma(\frac{5}{6})}, \quad \mathcal{K}_g = \frac{\sqrt{\pi}}{30 \sqrt[12]{3^7} \Gamma(\frac{13}{12})}.$$

Hence $\Delta = \left(1 - \mathcal{L}_f\right)\left(1 - \mathcal{L}_g\right) - \mathcal{K}_f \mathcal{K}_g = 0.88 \neq 0$, which implies that system (29) is H-U stable.

5. Conclusions

Recently, FDEs have attracted the interest of several researchers with prosperous applications, especially those involving generalized fractional operators. It is important that we investigate the fractional systems with generalized Hilfer derivatives since these derivatives cover many systems in the literature and they contain a kernel with different values that generates many special cases. As an additional contribution in this topic, existence, uniqueness, and U-H stability results of a coupled system for a new class of fractional integrodifferential equations in the generalized Hilfer sense are examined. The analysis of obtained results is based on applying Schauder's and Banach's fixed point theorems, and Arzelà-Ascoli's theorem.

It should be noted that in light of our obtained results, our use of the generalized Hilfer operator covers many systems associated with different values of the function ϑ and the parameter ρ_2, as is the case in the Special Cases section.

Author Contributions: Conceptualization, M.S.A., A.M.S. and M.B.J.; formal analysis, M.S.A., A.M.S. and M.B.J.; methodology, M.S.A. All authors have read and agreed to the published version of the manuscript.

Funding: The Deanship of Scientific Research at Qassim University supported this work.

Institutional Review Board Statement: Not applicable.

Informed Consent Statement: Not applicable.

Data Availability Statement: Not applicable.

Acknowledgments: The authors thank the anonymous referees for their careful reading of the manuscript and their insightful comments, which have helped improve the quality of the manuscript. Moreover, the first author would like to thank the Department of Mathematics, College of Science, and the Deanship of Scientific Research at Qassim University for encouraging scientific research and supporting this work.

Conflicts of Interest: The authors declare no conflict of interest.

References

1. Diethelm, K. *The Analysis of Fractional Differential Equations, Lecture Notes in Mathematics*; Springer: New York, NY, USA, 2010.
2. Kilbas, A.A.; Srivastava, H.M.; Trujillo, J.J. *Theory and Applications of the Fractional Differential Equations*; Elsevier: Amsterdam, The Netherlands, 2006; Volume 204.
3. Miller, K.S.; Ross, B. *An Introduction to the Fractional Calculus and Differential Equations*; John Wiley: New York, NY, USA, 1993.
4. Samko, S.G.; Kilbas, A.A.; Marichev, O.I. *Fractional Integrals and Derivatives*; Gordon and Breach Science: Yverdon, Switzerland, 1993.
5. Hilfer, R. *Applications of Fractional Calculus in Physics*; World Scientific: Singapore, 2000.
6. Abdo, M.S.; Abdeljawad, T.; Shah, K.; Ali, S.M. On nonlinear coupled evolution system with nonlocal subsidiary conditions under fractal-fractional order derivative. *Math. Meth. Appl. Sci.* **2021**, *44*, 6581–6600. [CrossRef]
7. Wang, J.; Shah, K.; Ali, A. Existence and Hyers–Ulam stability of fractional nonlinear impulsive switched coupled evolution equations. *Math. Meth. Appl. Sci.* **2018**, *41*, 1–11. [CrossRef]
8. Ahmad, M.; Zada, A.; Alzabut, J. Hyers-Ulam stability of a coupled system of fractional differential equations of Hilfer–Hadamard type. *Demon. Math.* **2019**, *52*, 283–295. [CrossRef]
9. Almalahi, M.A.; Abdo, M.S.; Panchal, S.K. Existence and Ulam–Hyers stability results of a coupled system of ψ-Hilfer sequential fractional differential equations. *Results Appl. Math.* **2021**, *10*, 100142. [CrossRef]
10. Abbas, S.; Benchohra, M.; Graef, J.R. Coupled systems of Hilfer fractional differential inclusions in Banach spaces. *Commun. Pure Appl. Anal.* **2018**, *17*, 2479. [CrossRef]
11. Khan, H.; Khan, A.; Abdeljawad, T.; Alkhazzan, A. Existence results in Banach space for a nonlinear impulsive system. *Adv. Differ. Equ.* **2019**, *2019*, 18. [CrossRef]
12. Khan, R.A.; Shah, K. Existence and uniqueness of solutions to fractional order multi-point boundary value problems. *Commun. Appl. Anal.* **2015**, *19*, 515–526.
13. Furati, K.F.; Kassim, M.D.; Tatar, N.E. Existence and uniqueness for a problem involving Hilfer fractional derivative. *Comput. Math. Appl.* **2012**, *64*, 1616–1626. [CrossRef]
14. Salim, A.; Benchohra, M.; Karapınar, E.; Lazreg, J.E. Existence and Ulam stability for impulsive generalized Hilfer-type fractional differential equations. *Adv. Differ. Equ.* **2020**, *2020*, 1–21. [CrossRef]
15. Almeida, R. A Caputo fractional derivative of a function with respect to another function. *Commun. Nonlinear Sci. Numer. Simul.* **2017**, *44*, 460–481. [CrossRef]
16. Vanterler, C.S.J.; Capelas, O.E. On the ψ–Hilfer fractional derivative. *Commun. Nonlinear Sci. Numer. Simul.* **2018**, *60*, 72–91. [CrossRef]
17. Vanterler, C.S.J.; Kucche, K.D.; Capelas, O.E. On the Ulam-Hyers stabilities of the solutions of ψ–Hilfer fractional differential equation with abstract Volterra operator. *Math. Methods Appl. Sci.* **2019**, *42*, 3021–3032.
18. Luo, D.; Shah, K.; Luo, Z. On the Novel Ulam–Hyers Stability for a Class of Nonlinear ψ–Hilfer Fractional Differential Equation with Time-Varying Delays. *Mediterranean J. Math.* **2019**, *16*, 1–15. [CrossRef]
19. Wahash, H.A.; Abdo, M.S.; Panchal, K.S. Fractional integrodifferential equations with nonlocal conditions and generalized Hilfer fractional derivative. *Ufa Math. J.* **2019**, *11*, 151–171. [CrossRef]
20. Abdo, M.S.; Hanan, A.W.; Panchal, S.K. Ulam–Hyers–Mittag-Leffler stability for a ψ-Hilfer problem with fractional order and infinite delay. *Results Appl. Math.* **2020**, *7*, 100115. [CrossRef]
21. Abdo, M.S.; Thabet, S.T.; Ahmad, B. The existence and Ulam–Hyers stability results for ψ–Hilfer fractional integrodifferential equations. *J. Pseudo-Differ. Oper. Appl.* **2020**, *11*, 1757–1780. [CrossRef]
22. Asawasamrit, S.; Kijjathanakorn, A.; Ntouyas, S.K.; Tariboon, J. Nonlocal boundary value problems for Hilfer fractional differential equations. *Bull. Korean Math. Soc.* **2018**, *55*, 1639–1657.
23. Ntouyas, S.K.; Vivek, D. Existence and uniqueness results for sequential ψ-Hilfer fractional differential equations with multi-point boundary conditions. *Acta Math. Univ. Comenianae* **2021**, *90*, 171–185.
24. Sudsutad, W.; Thaiprayoon, C.; Ntouyas, S.K. Existence and stability results for ψ-Hilfer fractional integro-differential equation with mixed nonlocal boundary conditions. *AIMS Math.* **2021**, *6*, 4119–4141. [CrossRef]
25. Ulam, S.M. *Problems in Modern Mathematics*; John Wiley and Sons: New York, NY, USA, 1940.
26. Hyers, D.H. On the stability of the linear functional equation. *Proc. Natl. Acad. Sci. USA* **1941**, *27*, 222–224. [CrossRef]
27. Obloza, M. Hyers stability of the linear differential equation, Rocznik Nauk-Dydakt. *Prac. Mat.* **1993**, *13*, 259–270.
28. Li, T.; Zada, A. Connections between Hyers–Ulam stability and uniform exponential stability of discrete evolution families of bounded linear operators over Banach spaces. *Adv. Differ. Equ.* **2016**, *2016*, 153. [CrossRef]
29. Rus, I.A. Ulam stabilities of ordinary differential equations in a Banach space. *Carpathian J. Math.* **2010**, *26*, 103–107.
30. Kumam, P.; Ali, A.; Shah, K.; Khan, R. Existence results and Hyers-Ulam stability to a class of nonlinear arbitrary order differential equations. *J. Nonlinear Sci. Applic. JNSA* **2017**, *10*, 2986–2997. [CrossRef]
31. Wang, J.; Li, X. Ulam-Hyers stability of fractional Langevin equations. *Appl. Math. Comput.* **2015**, *258*, 72–83. [CrossRef]
32. Ali, Z.; Zada, A.; Shah, K. On Ulam's Stability for a Coupled Systems of Nonlinear Implicit Fractional Differential Equations. *Bull. Malays. Math. Sci. Soc.* **2019**, *42*, 2681–2699. [CrossRef]
33. Kassim, M.D.; Abdeljawad, T.; Shatanawi, W.; Saeed, M.A.; Abdo, M.S. A qualitative study on generalized Caputo fractional integro-differential equations. *Adv. Differ. Equ.* **2021**, *2021*, 375. [CrossRef]

34. Abdo, M.S.; Shah, K.; Panchal, S.K.; Wahash, H.A. Existence and Ulam stability results of a coupled system for terminal value problems involving ψ-Hilfer fractional operator. Advances in Difference Equations. *Adv. Differ. Equ.* **2020**, *2020*, 316. [CrossRef]
35. Da Vanterler, C.S.J.; Capelas, O.E. On the Ulam–Hyers–Rassias stability for nonlinear fractional differential equations using the ψ-Hilfer operator. *J. Fixed Point Theory Appl.* **2018**, *20*, 96.
36. Abdo, M.S.; Panchal, S.K. Fractional integro-differential equations involving ψ–Hilfer fractional derivative. *Adv. Appl. Math. Mech.* **2019**, *11*, 338–359.
37. Andrews, G.E.; Askey, R.; Roy, R. *Special Functions*; Encyclopedia of Mathematics and its Applications 71; Cambridge University Press: Cambridge, UK, 1999; Volume 71.
38. Granas, A.; Dugundji, J. *Fixed Point Theory*; Springer: New York, NY, USA, 2003.
39. Smart, D.R. *Fixed Point Theorems*; Cambridge University Press: Cambridge, UK, 1980.
40. Hadamard, J. Essai sur létude des fonctions donnees par leur developpment de Taylor. *J. Mat. Pure Appl. Ser.* **1892**, *8*, 101–186.
41. Qassim, M.D.; Furati, K.M.; Tatar, N.E. On a differential equation involving Hilfer-Hadamard fractional derivative. *Abstr. Appl. Anal.* **2012**, *2012*, 391062. [CrossRef]
42. Katugampola, U.N. A new approach to generalized fractional derivatives. *Bull. Math. Anal. Appl.* **2014**, *6*, 1–15.
43. Oliveira, D.S.; de Oliveira, E.C. Hilfer–Katugampola fractional derivatives. *Comput. Appl. Math.* **2018**, *37*, 3672–3690. [CrossRef]
44. Almeida, R.; Malinowska, A.B.; Odzijewicz, T. Fractional differential equations with dependence on the Caputo–Katugampola derivative. *J. Comput. Nonlinear Dyn.* **2016**, *11*, 061017. [CrossRef]
45. Jarad, F.; Abdeljawad, T.; Baleanu, D. Caputo-type modification of the Hadamard fractional derivatives. *Adv. Differ. Equ.* **2012**, *2012*, 142. [CrossRef]

Article

On a System of ψ- Caputo Hybrid Fractional Differential Equations with Dirichlet Boundary Conditions

Muath Awadalla [1,*], Kinda Abuasbeh [1], Muthaiah Subramanian [2] and Murugesan Manigandan [3]

[1] Department of Mathematics and Statistics, College of Science, King Faisal University, Al Ahsa 31982, Saudi Arabia; kabuasbeh@kfu.edu.sa

[2] Department of Mathematics, KPR Institute of Engineering and Technology, Coimbatore 641020, India; subramanian.m@kpriet.ac.in

[3] Department of Mathematics, Sri Ramakrishna Mission Vidyalaya College of Arts and Science, Coimbatore 641020, India; yogimani22@rmv.ac.in

* Correspondence: mawadalla@kfu.edu.sa

Abstract: In this article, we investigate sufficient conditions for the existence and stability of solutions to a coupled system of ψ-Caputo hybrid fractional derivatives of order $1 < v \leq 2$ subjected to Dirichlet boundary conditions. We discuss the existence and uniqueness of solutions with the assistance of the Leray–Schauder alternative theorem and Banach's contraction principle. In addition, by using some mathematical techniques, we examine the stability results of Ulam–Hyers. Finally, we provide one example in order to show the validity of our results.

Keywords: ψ-Caputo fractional derivative; existence; fixed point theorems; Ulam–Hyers stability

MSC: 26A33; 34K37; 34A08

Citation: Awadalla, M.; Abuasbeh, K.; Subramanian, M.; Manigandan, M. On a System of ψ-Caputo Hybrid Fractional Differential Equations with Dirichlet Boundary Conditions. *Mathematics* **2022**, *10*, 1681. https://doi.org/10.3390/math10101681

Academic Editor: Vilém Novák

Received: 31 March 2022
Accepted: 5 May 2022
Published: 13 May 2022

Publisher's Note: MDPI stays neutral with regard to jurisdictional claims in published maps and institutional affiliations.

Copyright: © 2022 by the authors. Licensee MDPI, Basel, Switzerland. This article is an open access article distributed under the terms and conditions of the Creative Commons Attribution (CC BY) license (https://creativecommons.org/licenses/by/4.0/).

1. Introduction

Fractional calculus has a long history, going all the way back to Leibniz's 17th-century explanation of the derivative order in 1965. Mathematicians use fractional calculus to study how derivatives and integrals of noninteger order work and how they change over time. Since then, the new theory has proven to be very appealing to mathematicians, biologists, chemists, economists, engineers, and physicists. Subsequently, the subject attracted the interest of numerous famous mathematicians, including Fourier, Laplace, Abel, Liouville, Riemann, and Letnikov. For current and wide-ranging analyses of fractional derivatives and their applications, we recommend the monographs [1–4]. In [5], the authors investigated new results of the existence and uniqueness of systems of nonlinear coupled DEs and inclusions involving Caputo-type sequential derivatives of fractional order and new kinds of boundary conditions. In [6], the authors investigated a new type of SFDE and inclusions involving ψ-Hilfer fractional derivatives, associated with integral multi-point BCs.

Fractional derivatives have played a very important role in mathematical modeling in many diverse applied sciences, see [7]. In [8], the authors applied a new technique called "local fractional Laplace homotopy perturbation method" (LFLHPM) on Helmholtz and coupled Helmholtz equations to obtain analytical approximate solutions. In [9], the authors present a new analytical method called the "local fractional Laplace variational iteration method" (LFLVIM) for solving the two-dimensional Helmholtz and coupled Helmholtz equations. In [10], the authors find the solution of the LFFPE on the Cantor set. They make a comparison between the RDTM and LFSEM used in LFFPE. For example, the authors in [11] employed the LFLVIM and LFLDM to obtain approximate solutions for solving the damped wave equation and dissipative wave equation within LFDOs. The authors in [12] employed the fractional derivative of the ψ-Caputo type in modeling the logistic population equation, through which they were able to show that the model with the fractional derivative led to a better approximation of the variables than the classical model. In addition, the authors in [13] employ the fractional derivative of the ψ-Caputo type, and use the kernel Rayleigh, to improve the model again in modeling the logistic population equation. Various research has studied the existence and uniqueness of solutions to initial and boundary value problems utilizing ψ-fractional derivatives, see [14–18].

Fractional differential equations have been used to describe a wide variety of occurrences in a number of different engineering and scientific areas. Differential equations of fractional order are suitable for critical aspects in finance, electromagnetics, acoustics, viscoelasticity, biochemistry, and material science, see [19–21].

Additionally, it is essential to examine coupled systems through the use of fractional differential equations, as these systems are found in a wide range of applications. A number of scholars have also investigated coupled fractional differential equation systems. Some theoretical work on coupled fractional differential equations is included in this article, see [22–24].

The fractional derivatives of an unknown function are included in hybrid differential equations, as is the nonlinearity that relies on them. This class of equations arises in a wide variety of applications and physical science areas, for example, in the redirection of a bent pillar with a constant or variable cross-area, a three-layer shaft, electromagnetic waves, or gravity-driven streams. In the literature, hybrid FDEs have been examined by employing a variety of different forms of fractional derivatives; see [23,25,26]. Some recent results on the existence and uniqueness of initial and boundary value problems and Ulam–Hyers stability can be found in [27–29] and the references therein. For recent results from the ψ-Caputo hybrid fractional derivatives (CHFDs), we refer to [22,23,30,31] and the references cited therein. Choukri Derbazi et al. recently investigated the existence of extremal solutions to the nonlinear coupled system in [32]. Using the so-called "monotone iterative technique" together with the method of upper and lower solutions, the authors investigate the existence of extremal solutions of the following BVP that involves the ψ-Caputo derivative with ICs.

$$\begin{cases} {}^C\mathcal{D}_{a^+}^{v,\psi}\varphi(\omega) = \mathfrak{f}(\omega,\varphi(\omega),\zeta(\omega)), & \omega \in \mathcal{J} \quad [a,b]; \\ {}^C\mathcal{D}_{a^+}^{v,\psi}\zeta(\omega) = \mathfrak{g}(\omega,\varphi(\omega),\zeta(\omega)), & \omega \in \mathcal{J} \quad [a,b]; \\ \varphi(a) = \varphi_a \quad \zeta(b) = \zeta_b, \end{cases}$$

where ${}^C\mathcal{D}_{a^+}^{v,\psi}$ denote the ψ-Caputo fractional derivatives (CFDs) of order v and $\mathfrak{f},\mathfrak{g}:[a,b] \times \mathcal{R}_e^2 \to \mathcal{R}_e$ are continuous functions and $\varphi_a, \zeta_b \in \mathcal{R}_e$ with $\varphi_a \leq \zeta_b$.

Mohamed I Abbas [30] investigated the uniqueness of solutions for the following coupled system of fractional differential equations (CSFDEs). Based on the Leray–Schauder alternative and Banach's fixed point theorem, the authors investigated the existence and uniqueness of the following BVP associated with four-point BCs.

$$\begin{cases} {}^C\mathcal{D}_{0^+}^{v,\psi}\varphi(\omega) = \mathfrak{f}(\omega,\varphi(\omega),\zeta(\omega)), & \omega \in [0,1] \quad 1 < v < 2; \\ {}^C\mathcal{D}_{0^+}^{\beta,\psi}\zeta(\omega) = \mathfrak{g}(\omega,\varphi(\omega),\zeta(\omega)), & \omega \in [0,1] \quad 1 < \beta < 2; \\ \varphi(0) = \zeta(0) = 0, \\ \varphi(1) = \lambda\varphi(\eta), \quad \zeta(1) = \mu\zeta(\zeta), \quad 0 < \eta < \zeta < 1, \quad \lambda,\mu > 0, \end{cases}$$

where ${}^C\mathcal{D}_{0^+}^{v,\psi}, {}^C\mathcal{D}_{0^+}^{\beta,\psi}$ denote the ψ-CFDs of order v, β and $\mathfrak{f},\mathfrak{g}:[0,1] \times \mathcal{R}_e^2 \to \mathcal{R}_e$ are continuous functions.

In 2020, the authors of [33] studied the existence and uniqueness of the following BVP associated with multi-point BCs, with results obtained via topological degree theory and Banach's contraction principle:

$$\begin{cases} {}^C\mathcal{D}_{a^+}^{\alpha;\psi}z(\tau) + h(\tau, z(\tau)) = 0, & 2 < \alpha \leq 3, \ a \leq \tau \leq b, \\ z(a) = z'(a) = 0, \ z(b) = \sum_{k=1}^{n} \delta_k z(\mu_k), & a < \mu_k < b, \end{cases}$$

where ${}^C\mathcal{D}_{a^+}^{\alpha;\psi}$ denotes ψ-Caputo fractional derivatives, $h : [a,b] \times \mathcal{R}_e \to \mathcal{R}_e$ is assumed to be continous and $\delta_k \in \mathcal{R}_e, k = 1, 2, \ldots, n$.

In previous works, researchers investigated the existence and uniqueness of linear fractional differential equations involving ψ-Caputo.

This work is devoted to investigating the existence and uniqueness of the solutions for the following system of equations with Dirichlet BCs. Adding to this, we show that BVP is stable via the Ulam–Hyers technique.

$$\begin{cases} {}^C\mathcal{D}^{v_1;\psi}\left(\dfrac{\varphi(\omega)}{\mathfrak{f}(\omega, \varphi(\omega), \zeta(\omega))}\right) = \mathfrak{h}_1(\omega, \varphi(\omega), \zeta(\omega)), & \omega \in [\xi, \mathcal{T}] \quad 1 < v_1 \leq 2; \\ {}^C\mathcal{D}^{v_2;\psi}\left(\dfrac{\zeta(\omega)}{\mathfrak{g}(\omega, \varphi(\omega), \zeta(\omega))}\right) = \mathfrak{h}_2(\omega, \varphi(\omega), \zeta(\omega)), & \omega \in [\xi, \mathcal{T}] \quad 1 < v_2 \leq 2; \\ \varphi(\xi) = \varphi(\mathcal{T}) = 0, \\ \zeta(\xi) = \zeta(\mathcal{T}) = 0, \end{cases} \quad (1)$$

where ${}^C\mathcal{D}_{0^+}^{v_i;\psi}, i = 1, 2.$ is the ψ-CFDs of order v_i, and $\mathfrak{f}, \mathfrak{g} : [\xi, \mathcal{T}] \times \mathcal{R}_e^2 \to \mathcal{R}_e$ are continuous functions. To be valuable, the findings of this paper must be novel and generalize several earlier findings that are important to the research. To the best of our knowledge, there are no articles that discuss boundary value problems for systems of fractional differential equations with ψ-Caputo and no articles that investigate Ulam–Hyers stability for differential equations that contain ψ-Caputo derivatives. This paper is organized as follows. In Section 2, we will briefly recall some basic definitions and some preliminary concepts about fractional calculus and auxiliary results used in the following sections. In Section 3, we establish the existence of solutions to the ψ-Caputo fractional hybrid differential equation by using the Leray–Schauder alternative and Banach's fixed point theorem. In Section 4, the stability of Ulam–Hyers solutions is shown. In Section 5, we finally give an example to illustrate the application of the results obtained and we give our conclusion in Section 6.

2. Preliminaries

There are some basic definitions, lemmas and results of the ψ-CFDs with regard to another function ([1–4]).

Definition 1. *Let $v > 0, \mathfrak{f} \in L'([\xi, \mathcal{T}], \mathcal{R}_e)$ and $\psi : [\xi, \mathcal{T}] \to \mathcal{R}_e$ such that $\psi'(\omega) > 0$ $\forall \omega \in [\xi, \mathcal{T}]$. The ψ-Riemann–Liouville fractional integral of order v for the function $\mathfrak{f}$ is given by*

$$\mathcal{I}_\xi^{v;\psi}\mathfrak{f}(\omega) = \frac{1}{\Gamma(v)} \int_\xi^\omega (\psi(\omega) - \psi(\mathfrak{s}))^{v-1} \mathfrak{f}(\mathfrak{s})\psi'(\mathfrak{s})\partial\mathfrak{s}, \quad (2)$$

where Γ denotes the standard Euler gamma function.

Definition 2. *Let $v > 0, \mathfrak{f} \in \mathcal{C}^{m-1}([\xi, \mathcal{T}], \mathcal{R}_e)$ and $\psi \in \mathcal{C}^m([\xi, \mathcal{T}], \mathcal{R}_e)$ such that $\psi'(\omega) > 0$ $\forall \omega \in ([\xi, \mathcal{T}], \mathcal{R}_e)$. The ψ-Caputo fractional derivative (CFD) of order v for the function $\mathfrak{f}$ is given by*

$${}^C\mathcal{D}_\xi^{v;\psi}\mathfrak{f}(\omega) = \frac{1}{\Gamma(n-v)} \int_\xi^\omega \psi'(\mathfrak{s})(\psi(\omega) - \psi(\mathfrak{s}))^{n-v-1}\mathfrak{f}_\psi^{[n]}(\mathfrak{s})\partial\mathfrak{s}, \quad (3)$$

where

$$\mathfrak{f}_\psi^{[n]}(\mathfrak{s}) = \left(\frac{1}{\psi'(\mathfrak{s})}\frac{d}{d\mathfrak{s}}\right)^n \mathfrak{f}(\mathfrak{s}) \ \ and \ \ n = [v] + 1,$$

and $[v]$ denotes the integer part of the real number v.

Remark 1. If $v \in (0,1)$, then Equation (3) can be written as follows:

$$^C\mathcal{D}_\xi^{v;\psi}\mathfrak{f}(\omega) = \frac{1}{\Gamma(v)} \int_\xi^\omega (\psi(\omega) - \psi(\mathfrak{s}))^{v-1} \mathfrak{f}'(\mathfrak{s}) \partial \mathfrak{s}.$$

In another way, we have

$$^C\mathcal{D}_\xi^{v;\psi}\mathfrak{f}(\omega) = \mathcal{I}^{1-v,\psi}\left(\frac{\mathfrak{f}'(\omega)}{\psi'(\omega)}\right).$$

Remark 2. Note that if $\psi(\omega) = \omega$ and $\psi(\omega) = \log(\omega)$, then Equation (2) is reduced to the Riemann–Liouville and Hadamard fractional integrals, respectively.

Remark 3. In particular, note that if $\psi(\omega) = \omega$ and $\psi(\omega) = \log(\omega)$, then Equation (3) is reduced to the CFDs and Caputo–Hadamard fractional integrals, respectively.

Definition 3. Let $v > 0$ and an increasing function $\psi : [\xi, \mathcal{T}] \to \mathcal{R}_e$ satisfy $\psi'(\omega)\ 0$ for all $\omega \in [\xi, \mathcal{T}]$. We define the left-side ψ-Riemann–Liouville integral of an integrable function $\mathfrak{f}$ on $[\xi, \mathcal{T}]$ in the fractional framework with regard to another differentiable function ψ as

$$(_\xi\mathcal{I}^{v;\psi}\mathfrak{f})(\omega) = \frac{1}{\Gamma(v)} \int_\xi^\omega (\psi(\omega) - \psi(\mathfrak{s}))^{v-1} \mathfrak{f}(\mathfrak{s}) \psi'(\mathfrak{s}) \partial \mathfrak{s},$$

where Γ denotes the standard Euler gamma function.

Definition 4. Let $m \in \mathbb{N}$ with $m = [v] + 1$. The left-sided ψ-Riemann–Liouville fractional derivative of an existing function $\mathfrak{f} \in \mathcal{C}^m([\xi, \mathcal{T}], \mathcal{R}_e)$ with regard to a nondecreasing function ψ such that $\psi'(\omega) = 0$, for all $\omega \in [\xi, \mathcal{T}]$ in the functional framework, is represented as follows:

$$\mathcal{D}_{\xi^+}^{v;\psi}\mathfrak{f}(\omega) = \left(\frac{1}{\psi'(\omega)} \frac{\partial}{\partial t}\right)^m (\mathcal{I}_\xi^{m-v;\psi}\mathfrak{f})(\omega),$$

$$= \frac{1}{\Gamma(m-v)} \left(\frac{1}{\psi'(\omega)} \frac{\partial}{\partial t}\right)^m \int_\xi^\omega (\psi(\omega) - \psi(\mathfrak{s}))^{m-v-1} \mathfrak{f}(\mathfrak{s}) \psi'(\mathfrak{s}) \partial \mathfrak{s}.$$

Definition 5. Let $m \in \mathbb{N}$ with $m = [v] + 1$. The left-sided ψ-Caputo fractional derivative of an existing function $\mathfrak{f} \in \mathcal{C}^m([\xi, \mathcal{T}], \mathcal{R}_e)$ with regard to a nondecreasing function ψ such that $\psi'(\omega) = 0$, for all $\omega \in [\xi, \mathcal{T}]$ in the functional framework, is represented as follows:

$$^c\mathcal{D}_{\xi^+}^{v;\psi}\mathfrak{f}(\omega) = \mathcal{I}_{\xi^+}^{m-v;\psi}\left(\frac{1}{\psi'(\omega)} \frac{\partial}{\partial t}\right)^m \mathfrak{f}(\omega),$$

$$= \frac{1}{\Gamma(m-v)} \left(\frac{1}{\psi'(\omega)} \frac{\partial}{\partial t}\right)^m \int_\xi^\omega (\psi(\omega) - \psi(\mathfrak{s}))^{m-v-1} \mathfrak{f}(\mathfrak{s}) \psi'(\mathfrak{s}) \partial \mathfrak{s}.$$

Definition 6. Let $\psi \in \mathcal{C}^n([\xi, \mathcal{T}])$ be such that $\psi'(\omega) > 0$ on $[\xi, \mathcal{T}]$. Then,

$$\mathcal{AC}^{m;\psi}([\xi, \mathcal{T}]) = \left\{\mathfrak{f}: [\xi, \mathcal{T}] \to \mathbb{C} \text{ and } \mathfrak{f}^{[m-1]} = \left(\frac{1}{\psi'(\omega)} \frac{\partial}{\partial t}\right)^{m-1} \mathfrak{f}\right\}.$$

Proposition 1. Let $v > 0$ and $\beta > 0$, then

(1) $\mathcal{I}_{\xi^+}^{v;\psi}(\psi(\omega) - \psi(\xi))^{\beta-1} = \frac{\Gamma(\beta)}{\Gamma(v+\beta)}(\psi(\omega) - \psi(\xi))^{v+\beta-1}$,

(2) $^c\mathcal{D}_{\xi^+}^{v;\psi}(\psi(\omega) - \psi(\xi))^{\beta-1} = \frac{\Gamma(\beta)}{\Gamma(\beta-v)}(\psi(\omega) - \psi(\xi))^{\beta-v-1}$,

(3) $^c\mathcal{D}_{\xi^+}^{v;\psi}(\psi(\omega) - \psi(\xi))^k = 0$, for any $k = 0, \ldots, m-1; m \in \mathbb{N}$.

Proposition 2. Let $v > 0$, if $\mathfrak{f} \in \mathcal{C}^{m-1}([\xi, \mathcal{T}], \mathcal{R}_e)$, then we have

(1) $^C\mathcal{D}_{\xi^+}^{v,\psi} \mathcal{I}_{\xi^+}^{v,\psi} \mathfrak{f}(\omega) = \mathfrak{f}(\omega)$,

(2) $\mathcal{I}_{\xi^+}^{v,\psi} {}^C\mathcal{D}_{\xi^+}^{v,\psi} \mathfrak{f}(\omega) = \mathfrak{f}(\omega) - \sum_{j=0}^{n-1} \frac{\mathfrak{f}^{[k]}_{\psi}(0)}{k!} (\psi(\omega) - \psi(0))^k$.

(3) $\mathcal{I}_{\xi^+}^{v,\psi}$ is linear and bounded from $\mathcal{C}([\xi, \mathcal{T}], \mathcal{R}_e)$ to $\mathcal{C}([\xi, \mathcal{T}], \mathcal{R}_e)$.

Lemma 1 (Hybrid Fixed Point Theorem). Let $\mathcal{X}$ be a convex, bounded and closed set contained in the Banach algebra $\mathcal{Y}$ and the operators $\mathcal{P}, \mathcal{S} : \mathcal{Y} \to \mathcal{Y}$ and $\mathcal{Q} : \mathcal{X} \to \mathcal{Y}$ be such that:

(1) $\mathcal{P}$ and $\mathcal{S}$ are Lipschitz maps with Lipschitz constant $\mathcal{L}_{\mathcal{P}}$ and $\mathcal{L}_{\mathcal{S}}$, respectively;
(2) $\mathcal{Q}$ is continuous and compact;
(3) $\varphi = \mathcal{P}\varphi \mathcal{Q}\zeta + \mathcal{S}\varphi \; \forall \; \zeta \in \mathcal{X} \implies \varphi \in \mathcal{X}$; and
(4) $\mathcal{L}_{\mathcal{P}} \mathcal{M}_{\mathcal{Q}} + \mathcal{L}_{\mathcal{S}} < 1$, where $\mathcal{M}_{\mathcal{Q}} = ||\mathcal{Q}(\mathcal{X})|| = \sup\{||\mathcal{Q}\varphi|| : \varphi \in \mathcal{X}\}$, then the operator equation $\varphi = \mathcal{P}\varphi + \mathcal{S}\varphi$ possesses a solution in $\mathcal{X}$.

Theorem 1. A contraction mapping $\mathcal{T} : \Omega \to \Omega$ possesses a unique fixed point where Ω is a nonempty closed set contained in a Banach space $\mathcal{Y}$.

Theorem 2 (Banach Contraction Mapping Principle). A contraction mapping on a complete metric space has exactly one fixed point.

Theorem 3 (Arzelà–Ascoli Theorem). A set of functions in $\mathcal{C}([a,b])$ with supremum norm is relatively compact if, and only if, it is uniformly bounded and equicontinuous on $[a,b]$.

Before presenting our main results, the following auxiliary lemma is presented.

Lemma 2. The solution of the following boundary value problem (BVP):

$$\begin{cases} {}^C\mathcal{D}^{v_1;\psi}\left(\dfrac{\varphi(\omega)}{\mathfrak{f}(\omega, \varphi(\omega), \zeta(\omega))}\right) = \mathfrak{H}_1(\omega), & \omega \in [\xi, \mathcal{T}] \quad 1 < v_1 \leq 2; \\ {}^C\mathcal{D}^{v_2;\psi}\left(\dfrac{\zeta(\omega)}{\mathfrak{g}(\omega, \varphi(\omega), \zeta(\omega))}\right) = \mathfrak{H}_2(\omega), & \omega \in [\xi, \mathcal{T}] \quad 1 < v_2 \leq 2; \\ \varphi(\xi) = \varphi(\mathcal{T}) = 0, \\ \zeta(\xi) = \zeta(\mathcal{T}) = 0, \end{cases} \quad (4)$$

is given by

$$\varphi(\omega) = \mathfrak{f}(\omega, \varphi(\omega), \zeta(\omega)) \left(\frac{1}{\Gamma(v_1)} \int_\xi^\omega \psi'(\varsigma)(\psi(\omega) - \psi(\varsigma))^{v_1 - 1} \mathfrak{H}_1(\varsigma) \partial \varsigma \right) \quad (5)$$
$$- \frac{(\psi(\omega) - \psi(\xi))}{\Gamma(v_1)(\psi(\mathcal{T}) - \psi(\xi))} \int_\xi^{\mathcal{T}} \psi'(\varsigma)(\psi(\mathcal{T}) - \psi(\varsigma))^{v_1 - 1} \mathfrak{H}_1(\varsigma) \partial \varsigma,$$

and

$$\zeta(\omega) = \mathfrak{g}(\omega, \varphi(\omega), \zeta(\omega)) \left(\frac{1}{\Gamma(v_2)} \int_\xi^\omega \psi'(\varsigma)(\psi(\omega) - \psi(\varsigma))^{v_2 - 1} \mathfrak{H}_2(\varsigma) \partial \varsigma \right) \quad (6)$$
$$- \frac{(\psi(\omega) - \psi(\xi))}{\Gamma(v_2)(\psi(\mathcal{T}) - \psi(\xi))} \int_\xi^{\mathcal{T}} \psi'(\varsigma)(\psi(\mathcal{T}) - \psi(\varsigma))^{v_2 - 1} \mathfrak{H}_2(\varsigma) \partial \varsigma.$$

Proof. First, we apply the fractional integral ${}^{\psi}\mathcal{I}_{\xi^+}^{v_1}$ to the equation

$$^C\mathcal{D}^{v_1;\psi}\left(\frac{\varphi(\omega)}{\mathfrak{f}(\omega, \varphi(\omega), \zeta(\omega))}\right) = \mathfrak{H}_1(\omega),$$

and we obtain

$$\left(\frac{\varphi(\omega)}{\mathfrak{f}(\omega, \varphi(\omega), \zeta(\omega))}\right) = {}^{\psi}\mathcal{I}_{\xi^+}^{v_1} \mathfrak{H}_1(\omega) + \mathfrak{b}_0 + \mathfrak{b}_1(\psi(\omega) - \psi(\xi)), \quad (7)$$

the first boundary condition $\varphi(\xi) = 0$, which yields

$$\mathfrak{b}_0 = 0,$$

and the second boundary condition $\varphi(\mathcal{T})$, which implies

$$\mathfrak{b}_1 = \frac{-{}^\psi\mathcal{I}_{\xi^+}^{v_1}\mathfrak{H}_1(\mathcal{T})}{(\psi(\omega) - \psi(\xi))}.$$

Substituting the obtained values of $\mathfrak{b}_0$ and $\mathfrak{b}_1$ in Equation (7), we have

$$\left(\frac{\varphi(\omega)}{\mathfrak{f}(\omega, \varphi(\omega), \zeta(\omega))}\right) = {}^\psi\mathcal{I}_{\xi^+}^{v_1}\mathfrak{H}_1(\omega) - \frac{1}{(\psi(\omega) - \psi(\xi))}{}^\psi\mathcal{I}_{\xi^+}^{v_1}\mathfrak{H}_1(\mathcal{T}),$$

$$\left(\frac{\varphi(\omega)}{\mathfrak{f}(\omega, \varphi(\omega), \zeta(\omega))}\right) = \left(\frac{1}{\Gamma(v_1)}\int_\xi^\omega \psi'(\varsigma)(\psi(\omega) - \psi(\varsigma))^{v_1-1}\mathfrak{H}_1(\varsigma)\partial\varsigma\right)$$
$$- \frac{(\psi(\omega) - \psi(\xi))}{\Gamma(v_1)(\psi(\mathcal{T}) - \psi(\xi))}\int_\xi^\mathcal{T} \psi'(\varsigma)(\psi(\mathcal{T}) - \psi(\varsigma))^{v_1-1}\mathfrak{H}_1(\varsigma)\partial\varsigma,$$

which completes the proof. □

3. Main Result

Defining the space $\mathcal{B} = \{(\varphi(\omega), \zeta(\omega)) : (\varphi, \zeta) \in \mathcal{C}([\xi, \mathcal{T}], \mathcal{R}_e) \times \mathcal{C}([\xi, \mathcal{T}], \mathcal{R}_e)\}$, it is obvious that $\mathcal{B}$ is a Banach space. Furthermore, this space is endowed with the norm

$$||(\varphi, \zeta)||_\mathcal{B} = ||\varphi|| + ||\zeta|| \; \forall (\varphi, \zeta) \in \mathcal{B}.$$

By Lemma 2, we define an operator $\Phi : \mathcal{B} \to \mathcal{B}$ as

$$\Phi(\varphi, \zeta)(\omega) = \begin{cases} \Phi_1(\varphi, \zeta)(\omega), \\ \Phi_2(\varphi, \zeta)(\omega), \end{cases} \tag{8}$$

where

$$\Phi_1((\varphi, \zeta)(\omega))$$
$$= \mathfrak{f}(\omega, \varphi(\omega), \zeta(\omega))\left(\frac{1}{\Gamma(v_1)}\int_\xi^\omega \psi'(\varsigma)(\psi(\omega) - \psi(\varsigma))^{v_1-1}\mathfrak{H}_1(\omega, \varphi(\omega), \zeta(\omega))\partial\varsigma\right) \tag{9}$$
$$- \frac{(\psi(\omega) - \psi(\xi))}{\Gamma(v_1)(\psi(\mathcal{T}) - \psi(\xi))}\int_\xi^\mathcal{T} \psi'(\varsigma)(\psi(\mathcal{T}) - \psi(\varsigma))^{v_1-1}\mathfrak{H}_1(\omega, \varphi(\omega), \zeta(\omega))\partial\varsigma,$$

and

$$\Phi_2((\varphi, \zeta)(\omega))$$
$$= \mathfrak{g}(\omega, \varphi(\omega), \zeta(\omega))\left(\frac{1}{\Gamma(v_2)}\int_\xi^\omega \psi'(\varsigma)(\psi(\omega) - \psi(\varsigma))^{v_2-1}\mathfrak{H}_2(\omega, \varphi(\omega), \zeta(\omega))\partial\varsigma\right) \tag{10}$$
$$- \frac{(\psi(\omega) - \psi(\xi))}{\Gamma(v_2)(\psi(\mathcal{T}) - \psi(\xi))}\int_\xi^\mathcal{T} \psi'(\varsigma)(\psi(\mathcal{T}) - \psi(\varsigma))^{v_2-1}\mathfrak{H}_2(\omega, \varphi(\omega), \zeta(\omega))\partial\varsigma.$$

Now, let us assume that the following assumptions hold true:

($\mathcal{A}_1$) φ, ζ are assumed to be continuous and bounded, and there exist $\partial_\mathfrak{f}, \partial_\mathfrak{g} > 0$ such that

$$|\mathfrak{f}(\omega, \varphi, \zeta)| \leq \partial_\mathfrak{f}, \text{ and } |\mathfrak{g}(\omega, \varphi, \zeta)| \leq \partial_\mathfrak{g}, \forall (\omega, \varphi, \zeta) \in [\xi, \mathcal{T}] \times \mathcal{R}_e^2.$$

($\mathcal{A}_2$) Both $\mathfrak{H}_1$ and $\mathfrak{H}_2$ are assumed to be continuous and there exist $\delta_i, \varepsilon_i > 0, i = 1, 2$ such that

$$|\mathfrak{H}_1(\omega, \varphi_1, \zeta_1) - \mathfrak{H}_1(\omega, \varphi_2, \zeta_2)| \leq \delta_1|\varphi_1 - \varphi_2| + \delta_2|\zeta_1 - \zeta_2|,$$
$$|\mathfrak{H}_2(\omega, \varphi_1, \zeta_1) - \mathfrak{H}_2(\omega, \varphi_2, \zeta_2)| \leq \varepsilon_1|\varphi_1 - \varphi_2| + \varepsilon_2|\zeta_1 - \zeta_2|,$$

$\forall \; \omega \in [\xi, \mathcal{T}], \varphi_i, \zeta_i \in \mathcal{R}_e, i = 1, 2.$

($\mathcal{A}_3$) There exist $\lambda_0, \mu_0 > 0$, and $\lambda_i, \mu_i \leq 0, i = 1, 2$ such that

$$|\mathfrak{H}_1(\omega, \varphi, \zeta)| \leq \lambda_0 + \lambda_1|\varphi| + \lambda_2|\zeta|,$$
$$|\mathfrak{H}_2(\omega, \varphi, \zeta)| \leq \mu_0 + \mu_1|\varphi| + \mu_2|\zeta|, \;\; \forall \omega \in [\xi, \mathcal{T}], \varphi, \zeta \in \mathcal{R}_e.$$

($\mathcal{A}_4$) Let $\mathcal{S} \subset \mathcal{B}$ be a bounded set, then there exist $\mathcal{K}_i > 0, i = 1, 2$ such that

$$|\mathfrak{H}_1(\omega, \varphi(\omega), \zeta(\omega))| \leq \mathcal{K}_1,$$
$$|\mathfrak{H}_2(\omega, \varphi(\omega), \zeta(\omega))| \leq \mathcal{K}_2, \;\; \forall \; \omega \in [\xi, \mathcal{T}], \;\; \forall \varphi, \zeta \in \mathcal{S}.$$

Using $\mathcal{A}_4$, observe that $\forall \; i = 1, 2$.

$$\left| \left(\frac{1}{\Gamma(v_i)} \int_\xi^\omega \psi'(\varsigma)(\psi(\omega) - \psi(\varsigma))^{v_i-1} \mathfrak{H}_i(\varsigma, \varphi(\varsigma), \zeta(\varsigma)) \partial\varsigma \right) \right.$$
$$\left. - \frac{(\psi(\omega) - \psi(\xi))}{\Gamma(v_i)(\psi(\mathcal{T}) - \psi(\xi))} \int_\xi^\mathcal{T} \psi'(\varsigma)(\psi(\mathcal{T}) - \psi(\varsigma))^{v_i-1} \mathfrak{H}_1(\varsigma, \varphi(\varsigma), \zeta(\varsigma)) \partial\varsigma \right|$$
$$\leq \frac{2\mathcal{K}_i(\psi(\mathcal{T}) - \psi(\xi))^{v_i}}{\Gamma(v_i + 1)}.$$

For computational convenience, we let

$$\mathcal{L}_i = \frac{(\psi(\mathcal{T}) - \psi(\xi))^{v_i}}{\Gamma(v_i + 1)}. \tag{11}$$

Next, we introduce our main result by setting two theorems with their proofs.

Theorem 4. *If the assumptions $\mathcal{A}_1$ and $\mathcal{A}_2$ hold, and*

$$\mathcal{P} = 2(\partial_\mathfrak{f}\mathcal{L}_1(\delta_1 + \delta_2) + \partial_\mathfrak{g}\mathcal{L}_2(\varepsilon_1 + \varepsilon_2)) < 1, \tag{12}$$

then the BVP in (1) has a unique solution on $[\xi, \mathcal{T}]$.

Proof. Considering the operator given by (1), let

$$\hat{\mathcal{B}}_\mathfrak{r} = \{(\varphi, \zeta) \in \mathcal{B} : ||(\varphi, \zeta)|| \leq \mathfrak{r}\}$$

be closed ball in $\mathcal{B}$ with

$$\mathfrak{r} \geq \frac{2(\partial_\mathfrak{f}\mathcal{L}_1(\mathcal{N}_{\mathfrak{H}_1}) + \partial_\mathfrak{g}\mathcal{L}_2(\mathcal{N}_{\mathfrak{H}_2}))}{1 - [2(\partial_\mathfrak{f}\mathcal{L}_1(\delta_1 + \delta_2) + \partial_\mathfrak{g}\mathcal{L}_2(\varepsilon_1 + \varepsilon_2))]'}$$

where

$$\mathcal{N}_{\mathfrak{H}_1} = \sup_{\xi \leq \omega \leq \mathcal{T}} |\mathfrak{H}_1(\omega, 0, 0)| \text{ and } \mathcal{N}_{\mathfrak{H}_2} = \sup_{\xi \leq \omega \leq \mathcal{T}} |\mathfrak{H}_2(\omega, 0, 0)|.$$

Observe that

$$|\mathfrak{H}_1(\omega, \varphi, \zeta)| = |\mathfrak{H}_1(\omega, \varphi, \zeta) - \mathfrak{H}_1(\omega, 0, 0) + \mathfrak{H}_1(\omega, 0, 0)|,$$
$$\leq \delta_1\|\varphi\| + \delta_2\|\zeta\| + \mathcal{N}_{\mathfrak{H}_1},$$

$$\leq (\delta_1 + \delta_2)\mathfrak{r} + \mathcal{N}_{\mathfrak{H}_1}.$$

Now, we demonstrate that $\Phi \hat{\mathcal{B}}_{\mathfrak{r}} \subset \hat{\mathcal{B}}_{\mathfrak{r}}, \forall \, (\varphi, \zeta) \in \hat{\mathcal{B}}_{\mathfrak{r}}, \omega \in [\xi, \mathcal{T}]$, then

$$|\Phi_1((\varphi,\zeta)(\omega))|$$
$$= \left| \mathfrak{f}(\omega, \varphi(\omega), \zeta(\omega)) \left(\frac{1}{\Gamma(v_1)} \int_\xi^\omega \psi'(\varsigma)(\psi(\omega) - \psi(\varsigma))^{v_1 - 1} \mathfrak{H}_1(\omega, \varphi(\omega), \zeta(\omega)) \partial \varsigma \right) \right.$$
$$\left. - \frac{(\psi(\omega) - \psi(\xi))}{\Gamma(v_1)(\psi(\mathcal{T}) - \psi(\xi))} \int_\xi^{\mathcal{T}} \psi'(\varsigma)(\psi(\mathcal{T}) - \psi(\varsigma))^{v_1 - 1} \mathfrak{H}_1(\omega, \varphi(\omega), \zeta(\omega)) \partial \varsigma \right|,$$
$$\leq \partial_\mathfrak{f} \sup_{\xi \leq \omega \leq \mathcal{T}} \left\{ \left(\frac{1}{\Gamma(v_1)} \int_\xi^\omega \psi'(\varsigma)(\psi(\omega) - \psi(\varsigma))^{v_1 - 1} |\mathfrak{H}_1(\omega, \varphi(\omega), \zeta(\omega))| \partial \varsigma \right) \right.$$
$$\left. + \frac{(\psi(\omega) - \psi(\xi))}{\Gamma(v_1)(\psi(\mathcal{T}) - \psi(\xi))} \int_\xi^{\mathcal{T}} \psi'(\varsigma)(\psi(\mathcal{T}) - \psi(\varsigma))^{v_1 - 1} |\mathfrak{H}_1(\omega, \varphi(\omega), \zeta(\omega))| \partial \varsigma \right\},$$
$$\leq \partial_\mathfrak{f} ((\delta_1 + \delta_2)\mathfrak{r} + \mathcal{N}_{\mathfrak{H}_1}) \sup_{\xi \leq \omega \leq \mathcal{T}} \left\{ \left(\frac{1}{\Gamma(v_1)} \int_\xi^\omega \psi'(\varsigma)(\psi(\omega) - \psi(\varsigma))^{v_1 - 1} \partial \varsigma \right) \right.$$
$$\left. + \frac{(\psi(\omega) - \psi(\xi))}{\Gamma(v_1)(\psi(\mathcal{T}) - \psi(\xi))} \int_\xi^{\mathcal{T}} \psi'(\varsigma)(\psi(\mathcal{T}) - \psi(\varsigma))^{v_1 - 1} \partial \varsigma \right\},$$

$$|\Phi_1((\varphi,\zeta)(\omega))| \leq \partial_\mathfrak{f} (2\mathcal{L}_1)[(\delta_1 + \delta_2)\mathfrak{r} + \mathcal{N}_{\mathfrak{H}_1}],$$

and

$$\|\Phi_1((\varphi,\zeta)(\omega))\| \leq \partial_\mathfrak{f} (2\mathcal{L}_1)[(\delta_1 + \delta_2)\mathfrak{r} + \mathcal{N}_{\mathfrak{H}_1}], \tag{13}$$

similarly,

$$\|\Phi_2((\varphi,\zeta)(\omega))\| \leq \partial_\mathfrak{g} (2\mathcal{L}_1)[(\varepsilon_1 + \varepsilon_2)\mathfrak{r} + \mathcal{N}_{\mathfrak{H}_2}]. \tag{14}$$

Equations (13) and (14) yield

$$\|\Phi(\varphi,\zeta)\| \leq \mathfrak{r}.$$

Next, we show that Φ is a contraction. Let $(\varphi_1, \zeta_1), (\varphi_2, \zeta_2) \in \mathcal{B}$, then

$$|\Phi_1(\varphi_1, \zeta_1)(\omega) - \Phi_1(\varphi_2, \zeta_2)(\omega)|$$
$$\leq \partial_\mathfrak{f} \sup_{\xi \leq \omega \leq \mathcal{T}} \left\{ \left(\frac{1}{\Gamma(v_1)} \int_\xi^\omega \psi'(\varsigma)(\psi(\omega) - \psi(\varsigma))^{v_1 - 1} \right. \right.$$
$$|\mathfrak{H}_1(\omega, \varphi_1(\omega), \zeta_1(\omega)) - \mathfrak{H}_1(\omega, \varphi_2(\omega), \zeta_2(\omega))| \partial \varsigma)$$
$$+ \frac{(\psi(\omega) - \psi(\xi))}{\Gamma(v_1)(\psi(\mathcal{T}) - \psi(\xi))} \int_\xi^{\mathcal{T}} \psi'(\varsigma)(\psi(\mathcal{T}) - \psi(\varsigma))^{v_1 - 1}$$
$$|\mathfrak{H}_1(\omega, \varphi_1(\omega), \zeta_1(\omega)) - \mathfrak{H}_1(\omega, \varphi_2(\omega), \zeta_2(\omega))| \partial \varsigma, \},$$
$$\leq \partial_\mathfrak{f} (\delta_1 \|\varphi_1 - \varphi_2\| + \delta_2 \|\zeta_1 - \zeta_2\|)(2\mathcal{L}_1),$$

$$\|\Phi_1(\varphi_1, \zeta_1) - \Phi_1(\varphi_2, \zeta_2)\|$$
$$\leq \partial_\mathfrak{f} (\delta_1 + \delta_2)(\|\varphi_1 - \varphi_2\| + \|\zeta_1 - \zeta_2\|)(2\mathcal{L}_1). \tag{15}$$

Similarly,

$$\|\Phi_2(\varphi_1, \zeta_1) - \Phi_2(\varphi_2, \zeta_2)\|$$
$$\leq \partial_\mathfrak{g} (\varepsilon_1 + \varepsilon_2)(\|\varphi_1 - \varphi_2\| + \|\zeta_1 - \zeta_2\|)(2\mathcal{L}_2). \tag{16}$$

Equations (15) and (16) give

$$\|\Phi(\varphi_1,\zeta_1) - \Phi(\varphi_2,\zeta_2)\| \tag{17}$$
$$\leq [\partial_{\mathfrak{f}}(2\mathcal{L}_1)(\delta_1+\delta_2) + \partial_{\mathfrak{g}}(2\mathcal{L}_2)(\varepsilon_1+\varepsilon_2)](\|\varphi_1-\varphi_2\|+\|\zeta_1-\zeta_2\|)$$
$$\leq \|\varphi_1-\varphi_2\| + \|\zeta_1-\zeta_2\|.$$

Operator Φ is a contraction, and the Banach contraction mapping principle applies, that is, on $[\xi,\mathcal{T}]$, the BVP (1) has a unique solution. □

Theorem 5. *If* $(\mathcal{A}_1), (\mathcal{A}_3)$ *and* $(\mathcal{A}_4)$ *are satisfied, and if*

$$2(\partial_{\mathfrak{f}}\mathcal{L}_1\lambda_1 + \partial_{\mathfrak{g}}\mathcal{L}_2\mu_1) < 1$$

and

$$2(\partial_{\mathfrak{f}}\mathcal{L}_1\lambda_2 + \partial_{\mathfrak{g}}\mathcal{L}_2\mu_2) < 1,$$

then the proposed problem given by (1) *has at least one solution on* $[\xi,\mathcal{T}]$.

Proof. To begin, we show that Φ is (c.c), if $\mathfrak{H}_1, \mathfrak{H}_2, \mathfrak{f}$ and $\mathfrak{g}$ are both continuous, which implies that Φ is continuous.

By $\mathcal{A}_4$, for any $(\mathfrak{f}, \mathfrak{g}) \in \mathcal{S}$, we have

$$|\Phi_1((\varphi,\zeta)(\omega))|$$
$$\leq \partial_{\mathfrak{f}} \sup_{\xi \leq \omega \leq \mathcal{T}} \left\{ \left(\frac{1}{\Gamma(v_1)} \int_\xi^\omega \psi'(\varsigma)(\psi(\omega)-\psi(\varsigma))^{v_1-1}|\mathfrak{H}_1(\omega,\varphi(\omega),\zeta(\omega))|\partial\varsigma \right) \right.$$
$$\left. + \frac{(\psi(\omega)-\psi(\xi))}{\Gamma(v_1)(\psi(\mathcal{T})-\psi(\xi))} \int_\xi^{\mathcal{T}} \psi'(\varsigma)(\psi(\mathcal{T})-\psi(\varsigma))^{v_1-1}|\mathfrak{H}_1(\omega,\varphi(\omega),\zeta(\omega))|\partial\varsigma \right\},$$

that is

$$\|\Phi_1(\varphi,\zeta)\| \leq \partial_{\mathfrak{f}}(2\mathcal{L}_1)\mathcal{K}_1, \tag{18}$$

similarly,

$$\|\Phi_2(\varphi,\zeta)\| \leq \partial_{\mathfrak{g}}(2\mathcal{L}_2)\mathcal{K}_2, \tag{19}$$

and, from (18) and (19), we obtain

$$\|\Phi(\varphi,\zeta)\| \leq \partial_{\mathfrak{f}}(2\mathcal{L}_1)\mathcal{K}_1 + \partial_{\mathfrak{g}}(2\mathcal{L}_2)\mathcal{K}_2, \tag{20}$$

which implies that our operator Φ is uniformly bounded.

Next, we investigate the equicontinuity of our operator to see this, $\forall \omega_1, \omega_2 \in [\xi,\mathcal{T}]$ with $\omega_1 < \omega_2, i = 1,2$. We have

$$|\Phi_1((\varphi,\zeta)(\omega_2)) - \Phi_1((\varphi,\zeta)(\omega_1))|$$
$$\leq \partial_{\mathfrak{f}} \left\{ \left(\frac{1}{\Gamma(v_1)} \int_\xi^{\omega_1} \psi'(\varsigma)\left[(\psi(\omega_1)-\psi(\varsigma))^{v_1-1} - (\psi(\omega_2)-\psi(\varsigma))^{v_1-1}\right]|\mathfrak{H}_1(\omega,\varphi(\omega),\zeta(\omega))|\partial\varsigma \right) \right.$$
$$+ \left(\frac{1}{\Gamma(v_1)} \int_{\omega_1}^{\omega_2} \psi'(\varsigma)\left[(\psi(\omega_2)-\psi(\varsigma))^{v_1-1}\right]|\mathfrak{H}_1(\omega,\varphi(\omega),\zeta(\omega))|\partial\varsigma \right)$$
$$\left. + \frac{(\psi(\omega_2)-\psi(\omega_1))}{\Gamma(v_1)(\psi(\mathcal{T})-\psi(\xi))} \int_\xi^{\mathcal{T}} \psi'(\varsigma)(\psi(\mathcal{T})-\psi(\varsigma))^{v_1-1}|\mathfrak{H}_1(\omega,\varphi(\omega),\zeta(\omega))|\partial\varsigma \right\},$$

$$\leq \frac{\partial_{\mathfrak{f}}\mathcal{K}_1}{\Gamma(v_1)} \left\{ \left(\int_\xi^{\omega_1} \psi'(\varsigma)\left[(\psi(\omega_1)-\psi(\varsigma))^{v_1-1} - (\psi(\omega_2)-\psi(\varsigma))^{v_1-1}\right]\partial\varsigma \right) \right.$$
$$+ \left(\int_{\omega_1}^{\omega_2} \psi'(\varsigma)\left[(\psi(\omega_2)-\psi(\varsigma))^{v_1-1}\right]\partial\varsigma \right)$$
$$\left. + \frac{(\psi(\omega_2)-\psi(\omega_1))}{(\psi(\mathcal{T})-\psi(\xi))} \int_\xi^{\mathcal{T}} \psi'(\varsigma)(\psi(\mathcal{T})-\psi(\varsigma))^{v_1-1}\partial\varsigma \right\},$$

and

$$|\Phi_2((\varphi,\zeta)(\omega_2)) - \Phi_2((\varphi,\zeta)(\omega_1))|$$
$$\leq \partial_{\mathfrak{g}}\left\{\left(\frac{1}{\Gamma(v_2)}\int_{\xi}^{\omega_1}\psi'(\varsigma)\left[(\psi(\omega_1)-\psi(\varsigma))^{v_2-1}-(\psi(\omega_2)-\psi(\varsigma))^{v_2-1}\right]|\mathfrak{H}_2(\omega,\varphi(\omega),\zeta(\omega))|\partial\varsigma\right)\right.$$
$$+\left(\frac{1}{\Gamma(v_2)}\int_{\omega_1}^{\omega_2}\psi'(\varsigma)\left[(\psi(\omega_2)-\psi(\varsigma))^{v_2-1}\right]|\mathfrak{H}_2(\omega,\varphi(\omega),\zeta(\omega))|\partial\varsigma\right)$$
$$+\frac{(\psi(\omega_2)-\psi(\omega_1))}{\Gamma(v_2)(\psi(\mathcal{T})-\psi(\xi))}\int_{\xi}^{\mathcal{T}}\psi'(\varsigma)(\psi(\mathcal{T})-\psi(\varsigma))^{v_2-1}|\mathfrak{H}_2(\omega,\varphi(\omega),\zeta(\omega))|\partial\varsigma\bigg\},$$

$$\leq \frac{\partial_{\mathfrak{g}}\mathscr{K}_2}{\Gamma(v_2)}\left\{\left(\int_{\xi}^{\omega_1}\psi'(\varsigma)\left[(\psi(\omega_1)-\psi(\varsigma))^{v_2-1}-(\psi(\omega_2)-\psi(\varsigma))^{v_1-1}\right]\partial\varsigma\right)\right.$$
$$+\left(\int_{\omega_1}^{\omega_2}\psi'(\varsigma)\left[(\psi(\omega_2)-\psi(\varsigma))^{v_2-1}\right]\partial\varsigma\right)$$
$$+\frac{(\psi(\omega_2)-\psi(\omega_1))}{(\psi(\mathcal{T})-\psi(\xi))}\int_{\xi}^{\mathcal{T}}\psi'(\varsigma)(\psi(\mathcal{T})-\psi(\varsigma))^{v_2-1}\partial\varsigma\bigg\}.$$

Note that the above inequality approaches zero and is independent of $(\mathfrak{f},\mathfrak{g})$, that is, Φ is equicontinuous. Finally, we let $\Delta = \{(\varphi,\zeta) \in \mathcal{B} : (\varphi,\zeta) = \mathfrak{r}\Phi(\varphi,\zeta), \mathfrak{r} \in [0,1]\} \forall \omega \in [0,1]$ and we obtain $\varphi(\omega) = \mathfrak{r}\Phi_1(\varphi,\zeta)(\omega)$ and $\zeta(\omega) = \mathfrak{r}\Phi_2(\varphi,\zeta)(\omega)$. By $(\mathcal{A}_3)$, we obtain

$$||\varphi|| \leq \partial_{\mathfrak{f}}(2\mathcal{L}_1)(\lambda_0 + \lambda_1||\varphi|| + \lambda_2||\zeta||) \qquad (21)$$
$$||\zeta|| \leq \partial_{\mathfrak{g}}(2\mathcal{L}_2)(\mu_0 + \mu_1||\varphi|| + \mu_2||\zeta||), \qquad (22)$$

and adding (21) and (22), we obtain

$$||\varphi|| + ||\zeta|| \leq (\partial_{\mathfrak{f}}(2\mathcal{L}_1)\lambda_0 + \partial_{\mathfrak{g}}(2\mathcal{L}_2)\mu_0)$$
$$+ (\partial_{\mathfrak{f}}(2\mathcal{L}_1)\lambda_1 + \partial_{\mathfrak{g}}(2\mathcal{L}_2)\mu_1)||\varphi||$$
$$+ (\partial_{\mathfrak{f}}(2\mathcal{L}_1)\lambda_2 + \partial_{\mathfrak{g}}(2\mathcal{L}_2)\mu_2)||\zeta||. \qquad (23)$$

Equation (23) can be rewritten as

$$||(\varphi,\zeta)|| \leq \frac{(\partial_{\mathfrak{f}}(2\mathcal{L}_1)\lambda_0 + \partial_{\mathfrak{g}}(2\mathcal{L}_2)\mu_0)}{\min\{1-(\partial_{\mathfrak{f}}(2\mathcal{L}_1)\lambda_1 + \partial_{\mathfrak{g}}(2\mathcal{L}_2)\mu_1), 1-(\partial_{\mathfrak{f}}(2\mathcal{L}_1)\lambda_2 + \partial_{\mathfrak{g}}(2\mathcal{L}_2)\mu_2)\}}, \qquad (24)$$

which shows that the defined subset Δ is bounded. Now, applying the Leray–Schauder alternative, the problem (1) has at least one solution on $[\xi,\mathcal{T}]$. □

4. Ulam–Hyers Stability

This section is devoted to the investigation of Hyers–Ulam stability for our system. Consider the following equations:

$$\varphi(\omega) = \Phi_1(\varphi,\zeta)(\omega), \qquad (25)$$
$$\zeta(\omega) = \Phi_2(\varphi,\zeta)(\omega),$$

where Φ_1 and Φ_2 are given by (9) and (10), respectively. Consider the following definitions of nonlinear operators $\mathfrak{h}_1, \mathfrak{h}_2 \in \mathcal{C}([\xi,\mathcal{T}],\mathcal{R}_e) \times \mathcal{C}([\xi,\mathcal{T}],\mathcal{R}_e) \to \mathcal{C}([\xi,\mathcal{T}],\mathcal{R}_e)$:

$$^{C}\mathcal{D}^{v_1;\psi}\left(\frac{\varphi(\omega)}{\mathfrak{f}(\omega,\varphi(\omega),\zeta(\omega))}\right) - \mathfrak{h}_1(\omega,\varphi(\omega),\zeta(\omega)) = \mathfrak{H}_1(\omega,\varphi(\omega),\zeta(\omega)), \qquad \omega \in [a,\mathcal{T}],$$

$$^{C}\mathcal{D}^{v_2;\psi}\left(\frac{\zeta(\omega)}{\mathfrak{g}(\omega,\varphi(\omega),\zeta(\omega))}\right) - \mathfrak{h}_2(\omega,\varphi(\omega),\zeta(\omega)) = \mathfrak{H}_2(\omega,\varphi(\omega),\zeta(\omega)), \qquad \omega \in [a,\mathcal{T}].$$

Considering the following inequalities for some $\hat{\Lambda}_1$ and $\hat{\Lambda}_2$,

$$||\mathfrak{H}_1(\omega,\varphi(\omega),\zeta(\omega))|| \leq \hat{\Lambda}_1, \qquad (26)$$

$$\|\mathfrak{H}_2(\omega, \varphi(\omega), \zeta(\omega))\| \leq \hat{\Lambda}_2.$$

Definition 7. *The coupled system 1 is said to have Hyers–Ulam stability, if there exist $\mathcal{M}_1, \mathcal{M}_2 > 0$, showing that, for every solution $(\varphi', \zeta') \in \mathcal{C}([\xi, \mathcal{T}], \mathcal{R}_e) \times \mathcal{C}([\xi, \mathcal{T}], \mathcal{R}_e)$ of the inequalities (26),*

$$\|\varphi(\omega) - \varphi'(\omega)\| \leq \mathcal{M}_1 \hat{\Lambda}_1,$$
$$\|\zeta(\omega) - \zeta'(\omega)\| \leq \mathcal{M}_2 \hat{\Lambda}_2, \text{ and } \omega \in [\xi, \mathcal{T}].$$

Theorem 6. *If all conditions of Theorem 4 are satisfied, the CSFDEs given by (1) are U-H stable.*

Proof. Let $\mathcal{C}([\xi, \mathcal{T}], \mathcal{R}_e) \times \mathcal{C}([\xi, \mathcal{T}], \mathcal{R}_e)$ be the solution to (1).

Let (φ, ζ) be any solution that meets the condition (26):

$${}^C\mathcal{D}^{v_1;\psi}\left(\frac{\varphi(\omega)}{\mathfrak{f}(\omega, \varphi(\omega), \zeta(\omega))}\right) = \mathfrak{h}_1(\omega, \varphi(\omega), \zeta(\omega)) + \mathfrak{H}_1(\omega, \varphi(\omega), \zeta(\omega)), \quad \omega \in [\xi, \mathcal{T}],$$

$${}^C\mathcal{D}^{v_2;\psi}\left(\frac{\zeta(\omega)}{\mathfrak{g}(\omega, \varphi(\omega), \zeta(\omega))}\right) = \mathfrak{h}_2(\omega, \varphi(\omega), \zeta(\omega)) + \mathfrak{H}_2(\omega, \varphi(\omega), \zeta(\omega)), \quad \omega \in [\xi, \mathcal{T}],$$

so,

$$\varphi(\omega)$$
$$= \varphi'(\omega) + \mathfrak{f}(\omega, \varphi(\omega), \zeta(\omega))\left(\frac{1}{\Gamma(v_1)}\int_\xi^\omega \psi'(\varsigma)(\psi(\omega) - \psi(\varsigma))^{v_1-1}\mathfrak{H}_1(\omega, \varphi(\omega), \zeta(\omega))\partial\varsigma\right)$$
$$- \frac{(\psi(\omega) - \psi(\xi))}{\Gamma(v_1)(\psi(\mathcal{T}) - \psi(\xi))}\int_\xi^\mathcal{T} \psi'(\varsigma)(\psi(\mathcal{T}) - \psi(\varsigma))^{v_1-1}\mathfrak{H}_1(\omega, \varphi(\omega), \zeta(\omega))\partial\varsigma,$$

$$|\varphi(\omega) - \varphi'(\omega)|$$
$$= \mathfrak{f}(\omega, \varphi(\omega), \zeta(\omega))\left(\frac{1}{\Gamma(v_1)}\int_\xi^\omega \psi'(\varsigma)(\psi(\omega) - \psi(\varsigma))^{v_1-1}|\mathfrak{H}_1(\omega, \varphi(\omega), \zeta(\omega))|\partial\varsigma\right)$$
$$- \frac{(\psi(\omega) - \psi(\xi))}{\Gamma(v_1)(\psi(\mathcal{T}) - \psi(\xi))}\int_\xi^\mathcal{T} \psi'(\varsigma)(\psi(\mathcal{T}) - \psi(\varsigma))^{v_1-1}|\mathfrak{H}_1(\omega, \varphi(\omega), \zeta(\omega))|\partial\varsigma,$$
$$\leq \frac{(\psi(\mathcal{T}) - \psi(\xi))^{v_1}}{\Gamma(v_1 + 1)}\hat{\Lambda}_1$$
$$\leq \mathcal{L}_1 \hat{\Lambda}_1, \tag{27}$$

and

$$\zeta(\omega)$$
$$= \zeta'(\omega) + \mathfrak{g}(\omega, \varphi(\omega), \zeta(\omega))\left(\frac{1}{\Gamma(v_2)}\int_\xi^\omega \psi'(\varsigma)(\psi(\omega) - \psi(\varsigma))^{v_2-1}\mathfrak{H}_2(\omega, \varphi(\omega), \zeta(\omega))\partial\varsigma\right)$$
$$- \frac{(\psi(\omega) - \psi(\xi))}{\Gamma(v_2)(\psi(\mathcal{T}) - \psi(\xi))}\int_\xi^\mathcal{T} \psi'(\varsigma)(\psi(\mathcal{T}) - \psi(\varsigma))^{v_2-1}\mathfrak{H}_2(\omega, \varphi(\omega), \zeta(\omega))\partial\varsigma,$$

$$|\zeta(\omega) - \zeta'(\omega)|$$
$$= \mathfrak{g}(\omega, \varphi(\omega), \zeta(\omega))\left(\frac{1}{\Gamma(v_2)}\int_\xi^\omega \psi'(\varsigma)(\psi(\omega) - \psi(\varsigma))^{v_2-1}\mathfrak{H}_2(\omega, \varphi(\omega), \zeta(\omega))\partial\varsigma\right)$$
$$- \frac{(\psi(\omega) - \psi(\xi))}{\Gamma(v_2)(\psi(\mathcal{T}) - \psi(\xi))}\int_\xi^\mathcal{T} \psi'(\varsigma)(\psi(\mathcal{T}) - \psi(\varsigma))^{v_2-1}|\mathfrak{H}_2(\omega, \varphi(\omega), \zeta(\omega))|\partial\varsigma,$$
$$\leq \frac{(\psi(\mathcal{T}) - \psi(\xi))^{v_2}}{\Gamma(v_2 + 1)}\hat{\Lambda}_2$$
$$\leq \mathcal{L}_2 \hat{\Lambda}_2, \tag{28}$$

where $\mathcal{L}_1$ and $\mathcal{L}_2$ are defined in (11). Hence, Definition (7) is verified, with the help of (27) and (28). Hence, the problem (1) is Ulam–Hyers stable. □

5. Example

Example 1. *Let us consider the following CSFDEs:*

$$\begin{cases} {}^C\mathcal{D}^{v_1;\psi}\left(\frac{\varphi(\omega)}{\mathfrak{f}(\omega,\varphi(\omega),\zeta(\omega))}\right) = \mathfrak{h}_1(\omega,\varphi(\omega),\zeta(\omega)), & \omega \in [\xi,\mathcal{T}] \quad 1 < v_1 \leq 2; \\ {}^C\mathcal{D}^{v_2;\psi}\left(\frac{\zeta(\omega)}{\mathfrak{g}(\omega,\varphi(\omega),\zeta(\omega))}\right) = \mathfrak{h}_2(\omega,\varphi(\omega),\zeta(\omega)), & \omega \in [\xi,\mathcal{T}] \quad 1 < v_2 \leq 2; \\ \varphi(\xi) = \varphi(\mathcal{T}) = 0; \\ \zeta(\xi) = \zeta(\mathcal{T}) = 0. \end{cases} \quad (29)$$

The problem (29) has a coupled system of hybrid FDEs (1), where $v_1 = \frac{1}{2}, v_2 = \frac{1}{3}$, $\mathcal{T} = 1, \psi(\omega) = \omega, \xi = 0$. To prove Theorem 4, let $\omega \in [\xi,\mathcal{T}]$ and $\varphi, \zeta \in \mathcal{R}_e$, then we have

$$\mathfrak{h}_1(\omega,\varphi(\omega),\zeta(\omega)) = \frac{1}{99}\left(\frac{\omega\zeta(\omega)}{2+\zeta(\omega)} - \frac{\zeta(\omega)}{2+\zeta(\omega)}\right),$$

$$\mathfrak{h}_2(\omega,\varphi(\omega),\zeta(\omega)) = \frac{e^{-\omega}}{87}\left(\frac{\omega^2 - \varphi(\omega)\zeta(\omega)}{2+\zeta(\omega)\varphi(\omega)}\right),$$

$$\mathfrak{f}(\omega,\varphi(\omega),\zeta(\omega)) = \frac{1}{99}\left(\frac{\omega\zeta(\omega)}{3} + \frac{\omega\varphi(\omega)}{2} + \frac{5}{6}\right),$$

$$\mathfrak{g}(\omega,\varphi(\omega),\zeta(\omega)) = \frac{1}{98}\left(\frac{\zeta(\omega)}{5} + \omega\varphi(\omega) + 6\right),$$

$$|\mathfrak{f}(\omega,\varphi,\zeta)| \leq \frac{2}{97}, |\mathfrak{g}(\omega,\varphi,\zeta)| \leq \frac{1}{87},$$

$$|\mathfrak{h}_1(\omega,\varphi,\zeta) - \mathfrak{h}_1(\omega,\hat{\varphi},\hat{\zeta})| \leq \frac{1}{99}\{|\varphi - \hat{\varphi}| + |\zeta - \hat{\zeta}|\},$$

$$|\mathfrak{h}_2(\omega,\varphi,\zeta) - \mathfrak{h}_2(\omega,\hat{\varphi},\hat{\zeta})| \leq \frac{1}{98}\{|\varphi - \hat{\varphi}| + |\zeta - \hat{\zeta}|\}.$$

Moreover, we have

$$\begin{aligned} \mathcal{L}_1 &= 1.183791995, \mathcal{L}_2 = 1.1193470177, \\ \partial_\mathfrak{f} &= 0.02061855676, \partial_\mathfrak{g} = 0.0114942528, \\ \delta_i &= 0.01010101, \varepsilon_i = 0.010200816, \end{aligned} \quad (30)$$

as $i = 1,2$. *We substitute values in Equation* (12), *and we obtain*

$$2(\partial_\mathfrak{f}\mathcal{L}_1(\delta_1 + \delta_2) + \partial_\mathfrak{g}\mathcal{L}_2(\varepsilon_1 + \varepsilon_2)) \approx 0.0014651668 < 1.$$

Based on the computations mentioned above, all conditions of Theorem 4 are satisfied. Therefore, the BVP given by (29) guaranteed a unique solution on $[\xi,\mathcal{T}]$ (Table 1 and Figure 1).

Table 1. The impact of fractional order (v) on the condition $\mathcal{P}$ given by (12).

$\mathcal{T}$	$v = 0.15$	$v = 0.30$	$v = 0.45$	$v = 0.60$	$v = 0.75$	$v = 0.90$
			$\mathcal{P}$			
0.3	0.00169289	0.00164105	0.00156982	0.00148344	0.00138603	0.00128146
1.3	0.00338579	0.00364173	0.00386534	0.00405286	0.00420167	0.00431029
2.3	0.00507868	0.00580513	0.00654797	0.00729616	0.00803837	0.00876327
4.3	0.00677158	0.0080815	0.00951759	0.0110728	0.0127371	0.014498
5.3	0.00677158	0.0104457	0.0127207	0.0153029	0.0182023	0.0214241
6.3	0.0101574	0.0128824	0.016123	0.0199337	0.0243678	0.029476
7.3	0.0118503	0.015381	0.0197005	0.0249265	0.0311839	0.0386034

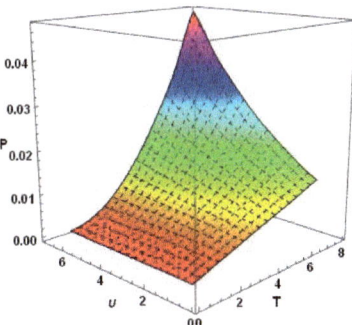

Figure 1. The impact of fractional order (v) on the condition $\mathcal{P}$ given by (12) is represented graphically. Based on the $\mathcal{P}$ value given by (12) and the conditions $\mathcal{A}_1$ and $\mathcal{A}_2$, the graph shown above describes the behavior of the solution of problem (29) for different values of $v \in (0, 1)$. It is noted that as $\mathcal{T}$ increases, the value of $\mathcal{P}$ increases as well and, with an increase in time, the condition $\mathcal{P}$ increases gradually for all values of $v \in (0, 1)$, and the $\mathcal{P}$ is clearly less than 1, satisfying the condition obtained in Theorem 4. An important observation to be made is that when order (v) is small, the value of $\mathcal{P}$ decreases with increasing time. As the order (v) increases, this trend changes with the value of $\mathcal{P}$ increasing with time. The figure describes the behavior of the solution.

6. Conclusions

In previous works, researchers investigated the existence and uniqueness of linear fractional differential equations involving ψ-Caputo. The legacy of this work lies in verifying the existence and uniqueness of solutions to a coupled system of ψ-Caputo hybrid fractional differential equations with Dirichlet boundary conditions. Our major findings are demonstrated using the Banach fixed point theorem and the alternative of Leray–Schauder. The stability of the solutions involved in the Hyers–Ulam type was investigated. We provide an example to demonstrate the study results. ψ-fractional calculus has its own prominence. For example, some researchers showed that by considering different ψs, a particular natural phenomenon can be remodeled with more accuracy. For replacing the fractional calculus by ordinary calculus, see [34]. In future studies, researchers can verify the existence, uniqueness and stability of the solutions for the system of equations given by Equation (1) using the ψ-Hilfer fractional derivative or any other derivatives such as the fractional Katugambula derivative. In addition, this system can be used in practical applications of the subject by taking our results as proven facts.

Author Contributions: Funding acquisition, M.A.; Investigation, K.A.; Methodology, M.A. and M.M.; Project administration, M.A.; Software, M.M.; Supervision, M.S.; Writing—original draft, M.A. and M.M.; Writing—review & editing, K.A., M.S. and M.M. The authors equally conceived of the study, participated in its design and coordination, drafted the manuscript, participated in the sequence alignment. All authors have read and agreed to the published version of the manuscript.

Funding: This work was supported by the Deanship of Scientific Research, Vice Presidency for Graduate Studies and Scientific Research, King Faisal University, Saudi Arabia (Project No. GRANT293).

Institutional Review Board Statement: Not serviceable.

Informed Consent Statement: Not serviceable.

Data Availability Statement: Not applicable.

Acknowledgments: The authors, therefore, acknowledge technical and financial support of DSR at KFU.

Conflicts of Interest: The authors declare no conflict of interest.

References

1. Kilbas, A.A.; Srivastava, H.M.; Trujillo, J.J. *Theory and Applications of Fractional Differential Equations*; Elsevier: Amsterdam, The Netherlands, 2006; Volume 204.
2. Podlubny, I. *Fractional Differential Equations: An Introduction to Fractional Derivatives, Fractional Differential Equations, to Methods of Their Solution and Some of Their Applications*; Elsevier: Amsterdam, The Netherlands, 1998.
3. Burton, T.A. A Fixed-Point Theorem of Krasnoselskii. *Appl. Math. Lett.* **1998**, *11*, 85–88. [CrossRef]
4. Smart, D.R. *Fixed Point Theorems*; Cambridge University Press: Cambridge, UK, 1980; Volume 66.
5. Manigandan, M.; Muthaiah, S.; Nandhagopal, T.; Vadivel, R.; Unyong, B.; Gunasekaran, N. Existence results for coupled system of nonlinear differential equations and inclusions involving sequential derivatives of fractional order. *AIMS Math.* **2022**, *7*, 723755. [CrossRef]
6. Sitho, S.; Ntouyas, S.K.; Samadi, A.; Tariboon, J. Boundary value problems for ψ-Hilfer type sequential fractional differential equations and inclusions with integral multi-point boundary conditions. *Mathematics* **2021**, *9*, 1001. [CrossRef]
7. Baleanu, D.; Jassim, H.K. Approximate solutions of the damped wave equation and dissipative wave equation in fractal strings. *Fractal Fract.* **2019**, *3*, 26. [CrossRef]
8. Baleanu, D.; Jassim, H.K. A modification fractional homotopy perturbation method for solving Helmholtz and coupled Helmholtz equations on Cantor sets. *Fractal Fract.* **2019**, *3*, 30. [CrossRef]
9. Baleanu, D.; Jassim, H.K.; Al Qurashi, M. Solving Helmholtz equation with local fractional derivative operators. *Fractal Fract.* **2019**, *3*, 43. [CrossRef]
10. Singh, J.; Jassim, H.K.; Kumar, D. An efficient computational technique for local fractional Fokker Planck equation. *Phys. A Stat. Mech. Appl.* **2020**, *555*, 124525. [CrossRef]
11. Baleanu, D.; Jassim, H.K. Exact solution of two-dimensional fractional partial differential equations. *Fractal Fract.* **2020**, *4*, 21. [CrossRef]
12. Awadalla, M.; Yameni Noupoue, Y.Y.; Asbeh, K.A. ψ-Caputo Logistic Population Growth Model. *J. Math.* **2021**, *2021*, 8634280.
13. Awadalla, M.; Noupoue, Y.Y.Y.; Abuasbeh, K. Population Growth Modeling via Rayleigh-Caputo Fractional Derivative. *J. Stat. Appl. Probab.* **2021**, *10*, 11–16.
14. Almeida, R. Variational problems involving a Caputo-type fractional derivative. *J. Optim. Theory Appl.* **2017**, *174*, 276–294. [CrossRef]
15. Awadalla, M.; Yameni, Y.Y. Modeling exponential growth and exponential decay real phenomena by ψ-Caputo fractional derivative. *J. Adv. Math. Comput. Sci.* **2018**, *28*, 1–13. [CrossRef]
16. Boutiara, A.; Abdo, M.S.; Benbachir, M. Existence results for ψ-Caputo fractional neutral functional integro-differential equations with finite delay. *Turk. J. Math.* **2020**, *44*, 2380–2401. [CrossRef]
17. Abdo, M.S.; Panchal, S.K.; Hussien, H.S. Fractional integro-differential equations with nonlocal conditions and *psi*–Hilfer fractional derivative. *Math. Model. Anal.* **2020**, *24*, 564–584. [CrossRef]
18. Almalahi, M.A.; Panchal, S.K. Some existence and stability results for ψ-Hilfer fractional implicit differential equation with periodic conditions. *J. Math. Anal. Model.* **2020**, *1*, 15. [CrossRef]
19. Subramanian, M.; Manigandan, M.; Tunç, C.; Gopal, T.N.; Alzabut, J. On system of nonlinear coupled differential equations and inclusions involving Caputo-type sequential derivatives of fractional order. *J. Taibah Univ. Sci.* **2022**, *16*, 1–23. [CrossRef]
20. Muthaiah, S.; Murugesan, M.; Thangaraj, N.G. Existence of solutions for nonlocal boundary value problem of Hadamard fractional differential equations. *Adv. Theory Nonlinear Anal. Appl.* **2019**, *3*, 162–173. [CrossRef]
21. Awadalla, M. Some Existence Results for a System of Nonlinear Sequential Fractional Differential Equations with Coupled Nonseparated Boundary Conditions. *Complexity* **2022**, *2022*, 8992894. [CrossRef]
22. Jiang, D.; Bai, C. On coupled Gronwall inequalities involving a ψ-fractional integral operator with its applications. *AIMS Math.* **2020**, *7*, 7728–7741. [CrossRef]
23. Boutiara, A.; Etemad, S.; Hussain, A.; Rezapour, S. The generalized U-H and U-H stability and existence analysis of a coupled hybrid system of integro-differential IVPs involving ψ-Caputo fractional operators. *Adv. Differ. Equ.* **2020**, *2021*, 95. [CrossRef]
24. Samadi, A.; Ntouyas, S.K.; Tariboon, J. Nonlocal coupled hybrid fractional system of mixed fractional derivatives via an extension of Darbo's theorem. *AIMS Math.* **2021**, *6*, 3915–3926. [CrossRef]
25. Ji, D.; Ge, W. A nonlocal boundary value problems for hybrid ψ-Caputo fractional integro-differential equations. *AIMS Math.* **2020**, *5*, 7175–7190. [CrossRef]
26. Shammakh, W.; Selvam, A.G.M.; Dhakshinamoorthy, V.; Alzabut, J. A Study of Generalized Hybrid Discrete Pantograph Equation via Hilfer Fractional Operator. *Fractal Fract.* **2022**, *6*, 152. [CrossRef]
27. Rus, I.A. Ulam stabilities of ordinary differential equations in a Banach space. *Carpath. J. Math.* **2010**, *26*, 103–107.
28. Almalahi, M.A.; Abdo, M.S.; Panchal, S.K. Existence and Ulam–Hyers stability results of a coupled system of ψ-Hilfer sequential fractional differential equations. *Results Appl. Math.* **2021**, *10*, 100142. [CrossRef]
29. Abdo, M.S.; Thabet, S.; Ahmad, B. The existence and Ulam–Hyers stability results for ψ-Hilfer fractional integrodifferential equations. *J. Pseudo-Differ. Oper. Appl.* **2020**, *11*, 1757–1780. [CrossRef]
30. Abbas, M.I. Four-point boundary value problems for a coupled system of fractional differential equations with ψ-Caputo fractional derivatives. *arXiv* **2020**, arXiv:2007.10325.

31. Aydin, M.; Mahmudov, N.I.; Aktuğlu, H.; Baytunç, E.; Atamert, M.S. On a study of the representation of solutions of a ψ-Caputo fractional differential equations with a single delay. *Electron. Res. Arch.* **2022**, *30*, 1016–1034. [CrossRef]
32. Derbazi, C.; Baitiche, Z.; Benchohra, M.; Graef, J.R. Extremal solutions to a coupled system of nonlinear fractional differential equations with Caputo fractional derivatives. *J. Math. Appl.* **2021**, *44*, 19–34. [CrossRef]
33. BAİTİCHE, Z.; DERBAZİ, C.; BENCHOHRA, M. ψ-Caputo fractional differential equations with multi-point boundary conditions by Topological Degree Theory. *Results Nonlinear Anal.* **2020**, *3*, 167–178.
34. Almeida, R. A Caputo fractional derivative of a function with respect to another function. *Commun. Nonlinear Sci. Numer. Simul.* **2017**, *44*, 460–481. [CrossRef]

Article

Existence of Solutions for Coupled Higher-Order Fractional Integro-Differential Equations with Nonlocal Integral and Multi-Point Boundary Conditions Depending on Lower-Order Fractional Derivatives and Integrals

Muthaiah Subramanian [1,†], Jehad Alzabut [2,3,†], Mohamed I. Abbas [4,†], Chatthai Thaiprayoon [5,6,*,†] and Weerawat Sudsutad [7,†]

1. Department of Mathematics, KPR Institute of Engineering and Technology, Coimbatore 641407, India; subramanianmcbe@gmail.com
2. Deparment of Mathematics and Sciences, Prince Sultan University, Riyadh 11586, Saudi Arabia; jalzabut@psu.edu.sa or jehad.alzabut@ostimteknik.edu.tr
3. Department of Industrial Engineering, OSTİM Technical University, 06374 Ankara, Turkey
4. Department of Mathematics and Computer Science, Faculty of Science, Alexandria University, Alexandria 21511, Egypt; miabbas@alexu.edu.eg
5. Research Group of Theoretical and Computation in Applied Science, Department of Mathematics, Faculty of Science, Burapha University, Chonburi 20131, Thailand
6. Center of Excellence in Mathematics, CHE, Sri Ayutthaya Road, Bangkok 10400, Thailand
7. Department of Statistics, Faculty of Science, Ramkhamhaeng University, Bangkok 10240, Thailand; weerawat.s@rumail.ru.ac.th
* Correspondence: chatthai@go.buu.ac.th
† These authors contributed equally to this work.

Abstract: In this article, we investigate the existence and uniqueness of solutions for a nonlinear coupled system of Liouville–Caputo type fractional integro-differential equations supplemented with non-local discrete and integral boundary conditions. The nonlinearity relies both on the unknown functions and their fractional derivatives and integrals in the lower order. The consequence of existence is obtained utilizing the alternative of Leray–Schauder, while the result of uniqueness is based on the concept of Banach contraction mapping. We introduced the concept of unification in the present work with varying parameters of the multi-point and classical integral boundary conditions. With the help of examples, the main results are well demonstrated.

Keywords: coupled system; integro-differential equations; Caputo derivatives; multi-point; integral boundary conditions; fixed point theorems

MSC: 26A33; 34A08; 34B15

1. Introduction

In the mathematical modeling of many real-world problems, the study of coupled systems of fractional orders of differential equations (FDEs) has gained significant attention; for example, chaotic system synchronization [1,2], anomalous diffusion [3], ecological models [4], etc. We refer to some papers for some recent results on coupled systems with FDEs [5–13]. The use of fractional calculus methods is quite prominent in the mathematical modeling of various processes and phenomena. The main reason is that fractional operators, unlike integer operators, are non-local and able to trace the past effects of the phenomena involved; see [14–19] for examples and details. Some researchers have addressed the problem of fractional boundary value problems (BVPs), and a significant trend can be seen in the recent literature; for example, see [20–37] and the references cited therein. A few authors have recently started investigating coupled fractional BVPs. Ahmad et al. [38] discussed the solvability of the following coupled FDEs with integral boundary conditions:

$$\begin{cases} {}^C\mathcal{D}^q x(t) = f(t, x(t), y(t)), \\ {}^C\mathcal{D}^p y(t) = h(t, x(t), y(t)), \\ x'(0) = \alpha \int_0^\xi x'(s)ds, \ x(1) = \beta \int_0^1 g(x'(s))ds, \\ y'(0) = \alpha_1 \int_0^\theta y'(s)ds, \ y(1) = \beta_1 \int_0^1 g(y'(s))ds, \\ t \in [0,1], \ 1 < q, p \leq 2, \ 0 \leq \xi, \theta \leq 1, \end{cases}$$

where ${}^C\mathcal{D}^q$, ${}^C\mathcal{D}^p$ denote the Caputo fractional derivatives (CFDs) of order q, p, f, $h \colon [0,1] \times \mathbb{R} \times \mathbb{R} \to \mathbb{R}$ are given continuous functions, and α, β, α_1, β_1 are real constants. The FDEs with integral and ordinary-fractional flux boundary conditions

$$\begin{cases} {}^C\mathcal{D}^\alpha x(t) = f(t, x(t), y(t)), \\ {}^C\mathcal{D}^\beta y(t) = h(t, x(t), y(t)), \\ x(0) + x(1) = a \int_0^1 x(s)ds, \ x'(0) = b\, {}^C\mathcal{D}^\gamma x(1), \\ y(0) + y(1) = a_1 \int_0^1 y(s)ds, \ y'(0) = b_1\, {}^C\mathcal{D}^\delta y(1), \\ t \in [0,1], \ 1 < \alpha, \beta \leq 2, \ 0 < \gamma, \delta \leq 1, \end{cases}$$

were discussed in [39], where ${}^C\mathcal{D}^\alpha$, ${}^C\mathcal{D}^\beta$, ${}^C\mathcal{D}^\gamma$, ${}^C\mathcal{D}^\delta$ denote the CFDs of order α, β, γ, δ, f, $h \colon [0,1] \times \mathbb{R}^2 \to \mathbb{R}$, are given continuous functions, and a, b, a_1, b_1 are real constants. Ahmad et al. analyzed in [40] the existence results for coupled system of FDEs:

$$\begin{cases} \mathcal{D}^\alpha u(t) = f(t, v(t), \mathcal{D}^p v(t)), \\ \mathcal{D}^\beta v(t) = g(t, u(t), \mathcal{D}^q u(t)), \\ u(0) = 0, \ u(1) = \gamma u(\eta), \\ v(0) = 0, \ v(1) = \gamma v(\eta), \\ 0 < t < 1, \ 1 < \alpha, \beta < 2, \ 0 < \eta < 1, \end{cases}$$

where $\mathcal{D}^\alpha$, $\mathcal{D}^\beta$, $\mathcal{D}^p$, $\mathcal{D}^q$ denote the Riemann–Liouville fractional derivatives of order α, β, p, q, f, $g \colon [0,1] \times \mathbb{R}^2 \to \mathbb{R}$ are given continuous functions, and γ is the real constant. Agarwal et al. [41] analyzed the results with discrete and integral boundary conditions of the existence of coupled fractional-order systems. In fractional BVP involving the Caputo derivatives, Subramanian et al. [42] studied coupled non-local slit-strip conditions.

In this article, we are investigating the existence of solutions for nonlinear coupled Caputo fractional integro-differential equations,

$$\begin{cases} {}^C\mathcal{D}^\varrho u(\tau) = f(\tau, u(\tau), v(\tau), {}^C\mathcal{D}^{\varsigma_1} v(\tau), \mathcal{I}^\zeta v(\tau)), \ \tau \in [0,T] := \mathcal{U}, \\ {}^C\mathcal{D}^\varsigma v(\tau) = g(\tau, u(\tau), {}^C\mathcal{D}^{\varrho_1} u(\tau), \mathcal{I}^\xi u(\tau), v(\tau)), \ \tau \in [0,T] := \mathcal{U}, \end{cases} \quad (1)$$

supplemented by nonlocal integral and multi-point boundary conditions,

$$\begin{cases} u(0) = \psi_1(v), \ u'(0) = \epsilon_1 \int_0^{\nu_1} v'(\theta)d\theta, \ u''(0) = 0, \cdots, u^{n-2}(0) = 0, \\ u(T) = \lambda_1 \int_0^{\delta_1} v(\theta)d\theta + \mu_1 \sum_{j=1}^{k-2} \omega_j v(\vartheta_j), \\ v(0) = \psi_2(u), \ v'(0) = \epsilon_2 \int_0^{\nu_2} u'(\theta)d\theta, \ v''(0) = 0, \cdots, v^{n-2}(0) = 0, \\ v(T) = \lambda_2 \int_0^{\delta_2} u(\theta)d\theta + \mu_2 \sum_{j=1}^{k-2} \omega_j u(\varphi_j), \end{cases} \quad (2)$$

where ${}^C\mathcal{D}^\varrho$, ${}^C\mathcal{D}^\varsigma$, ${}^C\mathcal{D}^{\varrho_1}$, ${}^C\mathcal{D}^{\varsigma_1}$ are the Caputo fractional derivatives of order $n-1 < \varrho, \varsigma < n$, $0 < \varrho_1, \varsigma_1 < 1$, $\mathcal{I}^\zeta$, $\mathcal{I}^\xi$ are the Riemann–Liouville fractional integrals of order $\zeta, \xi > 0$, f, $g \colon \mathcal{U} \times \mathbb{R}^4 \to \mathbb{R}$, $\psi_1, \psi_2 \colon \mathcal{C}(\mathcal{U}, \mathbb{R}) \to \mathbb{R}$ are given continuous functions, $0 < \nu_1 < \nu_2 < \delta_1 <$

$\delta_2 < \vartheta_1 < \varphi_1 < \cdots < \vartheta_{n-2} < \varphi_{n-2} < T$, and $\epsilon_i, \lambda_i, \mu_i$ $(i = 1, 2), \varpi_j, \omega_j$ $(j = 1, 2, \ldots, k-2)$ are positive real constants.

The rest of the article is assembled appropriately. In Section 2, we retrieve those concepts for a good reference and prove an auxiliary lemma, which provides the basis for solving the problem. Section 3 presents the primary outcomes, while Sections 4–6 provide examples, some important observations, and closing remarks, respectively.

2. Preliminaries

Firstly, we remember some fundamental fractional calculus definitions.

Definition 1. *The fractional integral of order α with the lower limit zero for a function $\mathfrak{f}$ is defined as*

$$I^\varrho \mathfrak{f}(\tau) = \frac{1}{\Gamma(\varrho)} \int_0^\tau \frac{\mathfrak{f}(s)}{(\tau-s)^{1-\varrho}} ds, \tau > 0, \varrho > 0, \qquad (3)$$

provided that the right-hand side is point-wise defined on $[0.\infty)$, where $\Gamma(\cdot)$ is the gamma function, which is defined by $\Gamma(\varrho) = \int_0^\infty \tau^{\varrho-1} e^{-\tau} d\tau$.

Definition 2. *The Riemann–Liouville fractional derivative of order $\varrho > 0$, $n-1 < \varrho < n, n \in \mathbb{N}$ is defined as*

$$D_{0+}^\varrho \mathfrak{f}(\tau) = \frac{1}{\Gamma(n-\varrho)} \left(\frac{d}{d\tau}\right)^n \int_0^\tau (\tau-s)^{n-\varrho-1} \mathfrak{f}(s) ds, \tau > 0, \qquad (4)$$

where the function $\mathfrak{f}$ has an absolutely continuous derivative up to order $(n-1)$.

Definition 3. *The Caputo derivative of order $\varrho \in [n-1, n)$ for a function $\mathfrak{f}: [0, \infty) \to (\mathbb{R})$ can be written as*

$$^C D_{0+}^\varrho \mathfrak{f}(\tau) = D_{0+}^\varrho \left(\mathfrak{f}(\tau) - \sum_{k=0}^{n-1} \frac{\tau^k}{k!} \mathfrak{f}^{(k)}(0)\right), \tau > 0, n-1 < \varrho < n. \qquad (5)$$

Note that the Caputo fractional derivative of order $\varrho \in [n-1, n)$ exists almost everywhere on $[0, \infty)$ if $\mathfrak{f} \in \mathcal{AC}^n([0, \infty), (\mathbb{R}))$.

Remark 1. *If $\mathfrak{f} \in \mathcal{C}^n[0, \infty)$, then*

$$^C D_{0+}^\varrho \hat{\mathfrak{f}}(\tau) = \frac{1}{\Gamma(n-\varrho)} \int_0^\tau \frac{\mathfrak{f}^{(n)}(s)}{(\tau-s)^{\varrho+1-n}} ds = I^{n-\varrho} \mathfrak{f}^{(n)}(\tau), \tau > 0, n-1 < \varrho < n.$$

Lemma 1. *For any $\hat{\mathfrak{f}}, \hat{g} \in C[0, T]$, the solution of the linear system of FDEs*

$$\begin{cases} {}^C \mathcal{D}^\varrho u(\tau) = \hat{\mathfrak{f}}(\tau), & \tau \in \mathcal{U}, \\ {}^C \mathcal{D}^\varsigma v(\tau) = \hat{g}(\tau), & \tau \in \mathcal{U}, \end{cases} \qquad (6)$$

supplemented with the boundary conditions (2) is equivalent to the system of integral equations

$$u(\tau) = \frac{1}{\Gamma(\varrho)} \int_0^\tau (\tau-\theta)^{\varrho-1} \hat{\mathfrak{f}}(\theta) d\theta + \psi_1(v)[1 + \kappa_1 \Lambda_4(\tau) - \Lambda_3(\tau)] + \psi_2(u)[\kappa_2 \Lambda_3(\tau) - \Lambda_4(\tau)]$$

$$+ \frac{\Lambda_2(\tau)\epsilon_2}{\Gamma(\varrho-1)} \int_0^{\nu_2} \left(\int_0^\theta (\theta-\sigma)^{\varrho-2} \hat{\mathfrak{f}}(\sigma) d\sigma\right) d\theta + \frac{\Lambda_1(\tau)\epsilon_1}{\Gamma(\varsigma-1)} \int_0^{\nu_1} \left(\int_0^\theta (\theta-\sigma)^{\varsigma-2} \hat{g}(\sigma) d\sigma\right) d\theta$$

$$+ \Lambda_4(\tau) \left[\frac{\lambda_2}{\Gamma(\varrho)} \int_0^{\delta_2} \left(\int_0^\theta (\theta-\sigma)^{\varrho-1} \hat{\mathfrak{f}}(\sigma) d\sigma\right) d\theta + \mu_2 \sum_{j=1}^{k-2} \frac{\omega_j}{\Gamma(\varrho)} \int_0^{\varphi_j} (\varphi_j - \theta)^{\varrho-1} \hat{\mathfrak{f}}(\theta) d\theta\right.$$

$$\left. - \frac{1}{\Gamma(\varsigma)} \int_0^T (T-\theta)^{\varsigma-1} \hat{g}(\theta) d\theta\right] + \Lambda_3(\tau) \left[\frac{\lambda_1}{\Gamma(\varsigma)} \int_0^{\delta_1} \left(\int_0^\theta (\theta-\sigma)^{\varsigma-1} \hat{g}(\sigma) d\sigma\right) d\theta\right.$$

$$+\mu_1 \sum_{j=1}^{k-2} \frac{\varpi_j}{\Gamma(\varsigma)} \int_0^{\vartheta_j} (\vartheta_j - \theta)^{\varsigma-1} \hat{g}(\theta) d\theta - \frac{1}{\Gamma(\varrho)} \int_0^T (T-\theta)^{\varrho-1} \hat{f}(\theta) d\theta \Bigg], \tag{7}$$

and

$$\begin{aligned}
v(\tau) &= \frac{1}{\Gamma(\varsigma)} \int_0^\tau (\tau - \theta)^{\varsigma-1} \hat{g}(\theta) d\theta + \psi_2(u)[1 + \kappa_2 \Lambda_7(\tau) - \Lambda_8(\tau)] + \psi_1(v)[\kappa_1 \Lambda_8(\tau) - \Lambda_7(\tau)] \\
&+ \frac{\Lambda_5(\tau)\epsilon_1}{\Gamma(\varsigma-1)} \int_0^{\nu_1} \left(\int_0^\theta (\theta - \sigma)^{\varsigma-2} \hat{g}(\sigma) d\sigma \right) d\theta + \frac{\Lambda_6(\tau)\epsilon_2}{\Gamma(\varrho-1)} \int_0^{\nu_2} \left(\int_0^\theta (\theta - \sigma)^{\varrho-2} \hat{f}(\sigma) d\sigma \right) d\theta \\
&+ \Lambda_7(\tau) \Bigg[\frac{\lambda_1}{\Gamma(\varsigma)} \int_0^{\delta_1} \left(\int_0^\theta (\theta - \sigma)^{\varsigma-1} \hat{g}(\sigma) d\sigma \right) d\theta + \mu_1 \sum_{j=1}^{k-2} \frac{\varpi_j}{\Gamma(\varsigma)} \int_0^{\vartheta_j} (\vartheta_j - \theta)^{\varsigma-1} \hat{g}(\theta) d\theta \\
&- \frac{1}{\Gamma(\varrho)} \int_0^T (T-\theta)^{\varrho-1} \hat{f}(\theta) d\theta \Bigg] + \Lambda_8(\tau) \Bigg[\frac{\lambda_2}{\Gamma(\varrho)} \int_0^{\delta_2} \left(\int_0^\theta (\theta - \sigma)^{\varrho-1} \hat{f}(\sigma) d\sigma \right) d\theta \\
&+ \mu_2 \sum_{j=1}^{k-2} \frac{\omega_j}{\Gamma(\varrho)} \int_0^{\varphi_j} (\varphi_j - \theta)^{\varrho-1} \hat{f}(\theta) d\theta - \frac{1}{\Gamma(\varsigma)} \int_0^T (T-\theta)^{\varsigma-1} \hat{g}(\theta) d\theta \Bigg],
\end{aligned} \tag{8}$$

where

$$\xi_1 = \frac{\lambda_1 \delta_1^2}{2} + \mu_1 \sum_{j=1}^{k-2} \varpi_j \vartheta_j, \; \xi_2 = \frac{\lambda_1 \delta_1^n}{n} + \mu_1 \sum_{j=1}^{k-2} \varpi_j \vartheta_j^{n-1}, \; \xi_3 = \frac{\lambda_2 \delta_2^2}{2} + \mu_2 \sum_{j=1}^{k-2} \omega_j \varphi_j, \; \xi_4 = \frac{\lambda_2 \delta_2^n}{n} + \mu_2 \sum_{j=1}^{k-2} \omega_j \varphi_j^{n-1}, \tag{9}$$

$$\hat{\gamma}_1 = 1 - \nu_1 \nu_2 \epsilon_1 \epsilon_2, \; \hat{\gamma}_2 = T^2 - \xi_1 \xi_3, \; \hat{\gamma}_3 = T^n - \xi_1 \xi_4, \; \hat{\gamma}_4 = T^{n-1} \xi_3 - \xi_4 T, \; \hat{\gamma}_5 = \xi_1 T^{n-1} - T\xi_2, \; \hat{\gamma}_6 = T^n - \xi_2 \xi_3, \tag{10}$$

$$v_1 = \hat{\gamma}_2 \nu_1 \nu_2^{n-1} \epsilon_1 \epsilon_2 + \hat{\gamma}_1 \hat{\gamma}_3, \; v_2 = \hat{\gamma}_2 \nu_2^{n-1} \epsilon_2 + \hat{\gamma}_1 \hat{\gamma}_4, \; v_3 = \hat{\gamma}_2 \nu_1^{n-1} \epsilon_1 + \hat{\gamma}_1 \hat{\gamma}_5, \; v_4 = \hat{\gamma}_2 \nu_1^{n-1} \nu_2 \epsilon_1 \epsilon_2 + \hat{\gamma}_1 \hat{\gamma}_6,$$

$$v = v_2 v_3 - v_1 v_4 \neq 0, \tag{11}$$

$$\eta_1 = 1 + \frac{(\nu_1 \nu_2^{n-1} \epsilon_2 \beta_1 - \nu_1^{n-1} \beta_5) \epsilon_1}{v}, \; \eta_2 = \epsilon_1 \nu_1 + \frac{(\nu_1 \nu_2^{n-1} \epsilon_2 \beta_2 - \nu_1^{n-1} \beta_6) \epsilon_1}{v}, \; \eta_3 = \frac{(\nu_1 \nu_2^{n-1} \epsilon_2 \beta_3 - \nu_1^{n-1} \beta_7) \epsilon_1}{v},$$

$$\eta_4 = \frac{(\nu_1 \nu_2^{n-1} \epsilon_2 \beta_4 - \nu_1^{n-1} \beta_8) \epsilon_1}{v}, \; \eta_5 = \epsilon_2 \nu_2 + \frac{(\nu_2^{n-1} \beta_1 - \epsilon_1 \nu_1^{n-1} \nu_2 \beta_5) \epsilon_2}{v}, \; \eta_6 = 1 + \frac{(\nu_2^{n-1} \beta_2 - \epsilon_1 \nu_1^{n-1} \nu_2 \beta_6) \epsilon_2}{v},$$

$$\eta_7 = \frac{(\nu_2^{n-1} \beta_3 - \epsilon_1 \nu_1^{n-1} \nu_2 \beta_7) \epsilon_2}{v}, \; \eta_8 = \frac{(\nu_2^{n-1} \beta_4 - \epsilon_1 \nu_1^{n-1} \nu_2 \beta_8) \epsilon_2}{v}, \tag{12}$$

$$\beta_1 = \hat{\gamma}_2(v_4 - v_3 \epsilon_2 \nu_2), \; \beta_2 = (v_4 \epsilon_1 \nu_1 - v_3)\hat{\gamma}_2, \; \beta_3 = (v_3 \xi_3 - v_4 T)\hat{\gamma}_1, \; \beta_4 = \hat{\gamma}_1(v_3 T - v_4 \xi_1),$$

$$\beta_5 = (v_2 - v_1 \epsilon_2 \nu_2)\hat{\gamma}_2, \; \beta_6 = (v_2 \epsilon_1 \nu_1 - v_1)\hat{\gamma}_2, \; \beta_7 = (v_1 \xi_3 - v_2 T)\hat{\gamma}_1, \; \beta_8 = \hat{\gamma}_1(v_1 T - v_2 \xi_1), \tag{13}$$

$$\kappa_1 = \lambda_2 \delta_2 + \mu_2 \sum_{j=1}^{k-2} \omega_j, \; \kappa_2 = \lambda_1 \delta_1 + \mu_1 \sum_{j=1}^{k-2} \varpi_j, \tag{14}$$

$$\Lambda_1(\tau) = \frac{\tau \eta_1}{\hat{\gamma}_1} + \frac{\tau^{n-1} \beta_1}{v}, \; \Lambda_2(\tau) = \frac{\tau \eta_2}{\hat{\gamma}_1} + \frac{\tau^{n-1} \beta_2}{v}, \; \Lambda_3(\tau) = \frac{\tau \eta_3}{\hat{\gamma}_1} + \frac{\tau^{n-1} \beta_3}{v}, \; \Lambda_4(\tau) = \frac{\tau \eta_4}{\hat{\gamma}_1} + \frac{\tau^{n-1} \beta_4}{v},$$

$$\Lambda_5(\tau) = \frac{\tau \eta_5}{\hat{\gamma}_1} - \frac{\tau^{n-1} \beta_5}{v}, \; \Lambda_6(\tau) = \frac{\tau \eta_6}{\hat{\gamma}_1} - \frac{\tau^{n-1} \beta_6}{v}, \; \Lambda_7(\tau) = \frac{\tau \eta_7}{\hat{\gamma}_1} - \frac{\tau^{n-1} \beta_7}{v}, \; \Lambda_8(\tau) = \frac{\tau \eta_8}{\hat{\gamma}_1} - \frac{\tau^{n-1} \beta_8}{v}. \tag{15}$$

Proof. Solving the FDEs (6) in a standard manner, we get

$$y(\tau) = \int_0^\tau \frac{(\tau-\theta)^{\varrho-1}}{\Gamma(\varrho)} \hat{f}(\theta) d\theta + a_0 + a_1 \tau + \cdots + a_{n-1} \tau^{n-1}, \tag{16}$$

$$z(\tau) = \int_0^\tau \frac{(\tau-\theta)^{\varsigma-1}}{\Gamma(\varsigma)} \hat{g}(\theta) d\theta + b_0 + b_1 \tau + \cdots + b_{n-1} \tau^{n-1}, \tag{17}$$

where $a_i, b_i \in \mathbb{R}, i = 0, 1, 2, \cdots, n-1$, are arbitrary constants. Using the boundary conditions (2) in (16) and (17) together with notations (9)–(15), we obtain $a_0 = \phi_1(z), b_0 = \phi_2(y)$, and

$$a_1 - b_1 \epsilon_1 \nu_1 - b_{n-1} \epsilon_1 \nu_1^{n-1} = \frac{\epsilon_1}{\Gamma(\varsigma-1)} \int_0^{\nu_1} \left(\int_0^\theta (\theta-\sigma)^{\varsigma-2} \hat{g}(\sigma) d\sigma \right) d\theta, \tag{18}$$

$$b_1 - a_1\nu_2\epsilon_2 - a_{n-1}\epsilon_2\nu_2^{n-1} = \frac{\epsilon_2}{\Gamma(\varrho-1)}\int_0^{\nu_2}\left(\int_0^\theta (\theta-\sigma)^{\varrho-2}\hat{f}(\sigma)d\sigma\right)d\theta, \qquad (19)$$

$$a_1 T + a_{n-1}T^{n-1} - b_1\xi_1 - b_{n-1}\xi_2 = \frac{\lambda_1}{\Gamma(\varsigma)}\int_0^{\delta_1}\left(\int_0^\theta (\theta-\sigma)^{\varsigma-1}\hat{g}(\sigma)d\sigma\right)d\theta$$

$$+ \mu_1 \sum_{j=1}^{k-2}\frac{\varpi_j}{\Gamma(\varsigma)}\int_0^{\vartheta_j}(\vartheta_j-\theta)^{\varsigma-1}\hat{g}(\theta)d\theta$$

$$- \frac{1}{\Gamma(\varrho)}\int_0^T (T-\theta)^{\varrho-1}\hat{f}(\theta)d\theta$$

$$+ \kappa_2\phi_2(y) - \phi_1(z), \qquad (20)$$

$$b_1 T + b_{n-1}T^{n-1} - a_1\xi_3 - a_{n-1}\xi_4 = \frac{\lambda_2}{\Gamma(\varrho)}\int_0^{\delta_2}\left(\int_0^\theta (\theta-\sigma)^{\varrho-1}\hat{f}(\sigma)d\sigma\right)d\theta$$

$$+ \mu_2 \sum_{j=1}^{k-2}\frac{\varpi_j}{\Gamma(\varrho)}\int_0^{\varphi_j}(\varphi_j-\theta)^{\varrho-1}\hat{f}(\theta)d\theta$$

$$- \frac{1}{\Gamma(\varsigma)}\int_0^T (T-\theta)^{\varsigma-1}\hat{g}(\theta)d\theta$$

$$+ \kappa_1\phi_1(z) - \phi_2(y). \qquad (21)$$

Solving the system (18)–(21) for a_1, a_{n-1}, b_1 and b_{n-1}, we get

$$a_1 = \frac{1}{\hat{\gamma}_1}\left[\frac{\eta_1\epsilon_1}{\Gamma(\varsigma-1)}\int_0^{\nu_1}\left(\int_0^\theta (\theta-\sigma)^{\varsigma-2}\hat{g}(\sigma)d\sigma\right)d\theta\right.$$

$$+ \frac{\eta_2\epsilon_2}{\Gamma(\varrho-1)}\int_0^{\nu_2}\left(\int_0^\theta (\theta-\sigma)^{\varrho-2}\hat{f}(\sigma)d\sigma\right)d\theta$$

$$+ \eta_3\left(\frac{\lambda_1}{\Gamma(\varsigma)}\int_0^{\delta_1}\left(\int_0^\theta (\theta-\sigma)^{\varsigma-1}\hat{g}(\sigma)d\sigma\right)d\theta\right.$$

$$+ \mu_1 \sum_{j=1}^{k-2}\frac{\varpi_j}{\Gamma(\varsigma)}\int_0^{\vartheta_j}(\vartheta_j-\theta)^{\varsigma-1}\hat{g}(\theta)d\theta - \frac{1}{\Gamma(\varrho)}\int_0^T (T-\theta)^{\varrho-1}\hat{f}(\theta)d\theta$$

$$\left.+ \kappa_2\phi_2(y) - \phi_1(z)\right) + \eta_4\left(\frac{\lambda_2}{\Gamma(\varrho)}\int_0^{\delta_2}\left(\int_0^\theta (\theta-\sigma)^{\varrho-1}\hat{f}(\sigma)d\sigma\right)d\theta\right.$$

$$+ \mu_2 \sum_{j=1}^{k-2}\frac{\varpi_j}{\Gamma(\varrho)}\int_0^{\varphi_j}(\varphi_j-\theta)^{\varrho-1}\hat{f}(\theta)d\theta - \frac{1}{\Gamma(\varsigma)}\int_0^T (T-\theta)^{\varsigma-1}\hat{g}(\theta)d\theta$$

$$\left.\left.+ \kappa_1\phi_1(z) - \phi_2(y)\right)\right],$$

$$b_1 = \frac{1}{\hat{\gamma}_1}\left[\frac{\eta_5\epsilon_1}{\Gamma(\varsigma-1)}\int_0^{\nu_1}\left(\int_0^\theta (\theta-\sigma)^{\varsigma-2}\hat{g}(\sigma)d\sigma\right)d\theta\right.$$

$$+ \frac{\eta_6\epsilon_2}{\Gamma(\varrho-1)}\int_0^{\nu_2}\left(\int_0^\theta (\theta-\sigma)^{\varrho-2}\hat{f}(\sigma)d\sigma\right)d\theta$$

$$+ \eta_7\left(\frac{\lambda_1}{\Gamma(\varsigma)}\int_0^{\delta_1}\left(\int_0^\theta (\theta-\sigma)^{\varsigma-1}\hat{g}(\sigma)d\sigma\right)d\theta\right.$$

$$+ \mu_1 \sum_{j=1}^{k-2}\frac{\varpi_j}{\Gamma(\varsigma)}\int_0^{\vartheta_j}(\vartheta_j-\theta)^{\varsigma-1}\hat{g}(\theta)d\theta - \frac{1}{\Gamma(\varrho)}\int_0^T (T-\theta)^{\varrho-1}\hat{f}(\theta)d\theta$$

$$
\begin{aligned}
&\quad + \kappa_2\phi_2(y) - \phi_1(z)\Big) + \eta_8\left(\frac{\lambda_2}{\Gamma(\varrho)}\int_0^{\delta_2}\left(\int_0^\theta (\theta-\sigma)^{\varrho-1}\hat{f}(\sigma)d\sigma\right)d\theta\right.\\
&\quad + \mu_2\sum_{j=1}^{k-2}\frac{\omega_j}{\Gamma(\varrho)}\int_0^{\varphi_j}(\varphi_j-\theta)^{\varrho-1}\hat{f}(\theta)d\theta - \frac{1}{\Gamma(\varsigma)}\int_0^T(T-\theta)^{\varsigma-1}\hat{g}(\theta)d\theta\\
&\quad \left.+ \kappa_1\phi_1(z) - \phi_2(y)\Big)\right],
\end{aligned}
$$

$$
\begin{aligned}
a_{n-1} = \frac{1}{v}\Bigg[&\frac{\beta_1\epsilon_1}{\Gamma(\varsigma-1)}\int_0^{v_1}\left(\int_0^\theta (\theta-\sigma)^{\varsigma-2}\hat{g}(\sigma)d\sigma\right)d\theta\\
&+ \frac{\beta_2\epsilon_2}{\Gamma(\varrho-1)}\int_0^{v_2}\left(\int_0^\theta (\theta-\sigma)^{\varrho-2}\hat{f}(\sigma)d\sigma\right)d\theta\\
&+ \beta_3\left(\frac{\lambda_1}{\Gamma(\varsigma)}\int_0^{\delta_1}\left(\int_0^\theta (\theta-\sigma)^{\varsigma-1}\hat{g}(\sigma)d\sigma\right)d\theta\right.\\
&+ \mu_1\sum_{j=1}^{k-2}\frac{\varpi_j}{\Gamma(\varsigma)}\int_0^{\vartheta_j}(\vartheta_j-\theta)^{\varsigma-1}\hat{g}(\theta)d\theta - \frac{1}{\Gamma(\varrho)}\int_0^T(T-\theta)^{\varrho-1}\hat{f}(\theta)d\theta\\
&+ \kappa_2\phi_2(y) - \phi_1(z)\Big) + \beta_4\left(\frac{\lambda_2}{\Gamma(\varrho)}\int_0^{\delta_2}\left(\int_0^\theta (\theta-\sigma)^{\varrho-1}\hat{f}(\sigma)d\sigma\right)d\theta\right.\\
&+ \mu_2\sum_{j=1}^{k-2}\frac{\omega_j}{\Gamma(\varrho)}\int_0^{\varphi_j}(\varphi_j-\theta)^{\varrho-1}\hat{f}(\theta)d\theta - \frac{1}{\Gamma(\varsigma)}\int_0^T(T-\theta)^{\varsigma-1}\hat{g}(\theta)d\theta\\
&\left.+ \kappa_1\phi_1(z) - \phi_2(y)\Big)\right],
\end{aligned}
$$

$$
\begin{aligned}
b_{n-1} = \frac{-1}{v}\Bigg[&\frac{\beta_5\epsilon_1}{\Gamma(\varsigma-1)}\int_0^{v_1}\left(\int_0^\theta (\theta-\sigma)^{\varsigma-2}\hat{g}(\sigma)d\sigma\right)d\theta\\
&+ \frac{\beta_6\epsilon_2}{\Gamma(\varrho-1)}\int_0^{v_2}\left(\int_0^\theta (\theta-\sigma)^{\varrho-2}\hat{f}(\sigma)d\sigma\right)d\theta\\
&+ \beta_7\left(\frac{\lambda_1}{\Gamma(\varsigma)}\int_0^{\delta_1}\left(\int_0^\theta (\theta-\sigma)^{\varsigma-1}\hat{g}(\sigma)d\sigma\right)d\theta\right.\\
&+ \mu_1\sum_{j=1}^{k-2}\frac{\varpi_j}{\Gamma(\varsigma)}\int_0^{\vartheta_j}(\vartheta_j-\theta)^{\varsigma-1}\hat{g}(\theta)d\theta - \frac{1}{\Gamma(\varrho)}\int_0^T(T-\theta)^{\varrho-1}\hat{f}(\theta)d\theta\\
&+ \kappa_2\phi_2(y) - \phi_1(z)\Big) + \beta_8\left(\frac{\lambda_2}{\Gamma(\varrho)}\int_0^{\delta_2}\left(\int_0^\theta (\theta-\sigma)^{\varrho-1}\hat{f}(\sigma)d\sigma\right)d\theta\right.\\
&+ \mu_2\sum_{j=1}^{k-2}\frac{\omega_j}{\Gamma(\varrho)}\int_0^{\varphi_j}(\varphi_j-\theta)^{\varrho-1}\hat{f}(\theta)d\theta - \frac{1}{\Gamma(\varsigma)}\int_0^T(T-\theta)^{\varsigma-1}\hat{g}(\theta)d\theta\\
&\left.+ \kappa_1\phi_1(z) - \phi_2(y)\Big)\right],
\end{aligned}
$$

where $\hat{\gamma}_1$, v, η_i and β_i $i = 1, 2, \cdots, 8$, are given by (10)–(13) respectively. Substituting the values of a_0, a_1, a_{n-1}, b_0, b_1 and b_{n-1}, in (16) and (17), we obtain the solutions (7) and (8). □

3. Existence and Uniqueness Results

We define space $\mathcal{G} = \{u | u \in C(\mathcal{U}, \mathbb{R}), {}^C\mathcal{D}^{\varrho_1}u \in C(\mathcal{U}, \mathbb{R})\}$ equipped with norm $\|u\|_{\mathcal{G}} = \|u\| + \|{}^C\mathcal{D}^{\varrho_1}u\| = \sup_{\tau \in \mathcal{U}}|u(\tau)| + \sup_{\tau \in \mathcal{U}}|{}^C\mathcal{D}^{\varrho_1}u(\tau)|$. Furthermore, $\mathcal{H} = \{v | v \in C(\mathcal{U}, \mathbb{R}), {}^C\mathcal{D}^{\varsigma_1}v \in C(\mathcal{U}, \mathbb{R})\}$ equipped with norm $\|v\|_{\mathcal{H}} = \|v\| + \|{}^C\mathcal{D}^{\varsigma_1}v\| = \sup_{\tau \in \mathcal{U}}|v(\tau)| + \sup_{\tau \in \mathcal{U}}|{}^C\mathcal{D}^{\varsigma_1}v(\tau)|$. Obviously $(\mathcal{G}, \|\cdot\|_{\mathcal{G}})$ and $(\mathcal{H}, \|\cdot\|_{\mathcal{H}})$ are Banach spaces, and thus the product space $(\mathcal{G} \times \mathcal{H}, \|\cdot\|_{\mathcal{G} \times \mathcal{H}})$ is a Banach space with norm $\|(u,v)\|_{\mathcal{G} \times \mathcal{H}} = \|u\|_{\mathcal{G}} + \|v\|_{\mathcal{H}}$ for $(u,v) \in \mathcal{G} \times \mathcal{H}$.

Using Lemma 1, we consider an operator $\Pi : \mathcal{G} \times \mathcal{H} \to \mathcal{G} \times \mathcal{H}$ as

$$\Pi(u,v)(\tau) = (\Pi_1(u,v)(\tau), \Pi_2(u,v)(\tau)), \tag{22}$$

where

$$\begin{aligned}\Pi_1(u,v)(\tau) &= \frac{1}{\Gamma(\varrho)}\int_0^\tau (\tau-\theta)^{\varrho-1}\widehat{S}_u(\theta)d\theta + \psi_1(v)[1+\kappa_1\Lambda_4(\tau)-\Lambda_3(\tau)] + \psi_2(u)[\kappa_2\Lambda_3(\tau)-\Lambda_4(\tau)] \\ &+ \frac{\Lambda_2(\tau)\epsilon_2}{\Gamma(\varrho-1)}\int_0^{\nu_2}\left(\int_0^\theta (\theta-\sigma)^{\varrho-2}\widehat{S}_u(\sigma)d\sigma\right)d\theta + \frac{\Lambda_1(\tau)\epsilon_1}{\Gamma(\varsigma-1)}\int_0^{\nu_1}\left(\int_0^\theta (\theta-\sigma)^{\varsigma-2}\widetilde{S}_v(\sigma)d\sigma\right)d\theta \\ &+ \Lambda_4(\tau)\bigg[\frac{\lambda_2}{\Gamma(\varrho)}\int_0^{\delta_2}\left(\int_0^\theta (\theta-\sigma)^{\varrho-1}\widehat{S}_u(\sigma)d\sigma\right)d\theta + \mu_2\sum_{j=1}^{k-2}\frac{\omega_j}{\Gamma(\varrho)}\int_0^{\varphi_j}(\varphi_j-\theta)^{\varrho-1}\widehat{S}_u(\theta)d\theta \\ &- \frac{1}{\Gamma(\varsigma)}\int_0^T (T-\theta)^{\varsigma-1}\widetilde{S}_v(\theta)d\theta\bigg] + \Lambda_3(\tau)\bigg[\frac{\lambda_1}{\Gamma(\varsigma)}\int_0^{\delta_1}\left(\int_0^\theta (\theta-\sigma)^{\varsigma-1}\widetilde{S}_v(\sigma)d\sigma\right)d\theta \\ &+ \mu_1\sum_{j=1}^{k-2}\frac{\omega_j}{\Gamma(\varsigma)}\int_0^{\vartheta_j}(\vartheta_j-\theta)^{\varsigma-1}\widetilde{S}_v(\theta)d\theta - \frac{1}{\Gamma(\varrho)}\int_0^T (T-\theta)^{\varrho-1}\widehat{S}_u(\theta)d\theta\bigg],\end{aligned} \tag{23}$$

and

$$\begin{aligned}\Pi_2(u,v)(\tau) &= \frac{1}{\Gamma(\varsigma)}\int_0^\tau (\tau-\theta)^{\varsigma-1}\widetilde{S}_v(\theta)d\theta + \psi_2(u)[1+\kappa_2\Lambda_7(\tau)-\Lambda_8(\tau)] + \psi_1(v)[\kappa_1\Lambda_8(\tau)-\Lambda_7(\tau)] \\ &+ \frac{\Lambda_5(\tau)\epsilon_1}{\Gamma(\varsigma-1)}\int_0^{\nu_1}\left(\int_0^\theta (\theta-\sigma)^{\varsigma-2}\widetilde{S}_v(\sigma)d\sigma\right)d\theta + \frac{\Lambda_6(\tau)\epsilon_2}{\Gamma(\varrho-1)}\int_0^{\nu_2}\left(\int_0^\theta (\theta-\sigma)^{\varrho-2}\widehat{S}_u(\sigma)d\sigma\right)d\theta \\ &+ \Lambda_7(\tau)\bigg[\frac{\lambda_1}{\Gamma(\varsigma)}\int_0^{\delta_1}\left(\int_0^\theta (\theta-\sigma)^{\varsigma-1}\widetilde{S}_v(\sigma)d\sigma\right)d\theta + \mu_1\sum_{j=1}^{k-2}\frac{\omega_j}{\Gamma(\varsigma)}\int_0^{\vartheta_j}(\vartheta_j-\theta)^{\varsigma-1}\widetilde{S}_v(\theta)d\theta \\ &- \frac{1}{\Gamma(\varrho)}\int_0^T (T-\theta)^{\varrho-1}\widehat{S}_u(\theta)d\theta\bigg] + \Lambda_8(\tau)\bigg[\frac{\lambda_2}{\Gamma(\varrho)}\int_0^{\delta_2}\left(\int_0^\theta (\theta-\sigma)^{\varrho-1}\widehat{S}_u(\sigma)d\sigma\right)d\theta \\ &+ \mu_2\sum_{j=1}^{k-2}\frac{\omega_j}{\Gamma(\varrho)}\int_0^{\varphi_j}(\varphi_j-\theta)^{\varrho-1}\widehat{S}_u(\theta)d\theta - \frac{1}{\Gamma(\varsigma)}\int_0^T (T-\theta)^{\varsigma-1}\widetilde{S}_v(\theta)d\theta\bigg].\end{aligned} \tag{24}$$

where

$$\begin{aligned}\widehat{S}_u(\tau) &= f(\tau, u(\tau), v(\tau), {}^C\mathcal{D}^{\varsigma_1}v(\tau), \mathcal{I}^\xi v(\tau)), \ \tau \in \mathcal{U}, \\ \widetilde{S}_v(\tau) &= g(\tau, u(\tau), {}^C\mathcal{D}^{\varrho_1}u(\tau), \mathcal{I}^\xi u(\tau), v(\tau)), \ \tau \in \mathcal{U},\end{aligned}$$

and Λ_i ($i = 1, 2, \cdots, 8$) are given by (15). Suitable for computation, we represent

$$\Delta_1 = \frac{1}{\Gamma(\varrho+1)}\left[T^\varrho(1+\overline{\Lambda}_3) + \overline{\Lambda}_2\epsilon_2\nu_2^\varrho + \overline{\Lambda}_4\left(\lambda_2\frac{\delta_2^{\varrho+1}}{(\varrho+1)} + \mu_2\sum_{j=1}^{k-2}\omega_j\varphi_j^\varrho\right)\right], \tag{25}$$

$$\Delta_2 = \frac{1}{\Gamma(\varsigma+1)}\left[T^\varsigma\overline{\Lambda}_4 + \overline{\Lambda}_1\epsilon_1\nu_1^\varsigma + \overline{\Lambda}_3\left(\lambda_1\frac{\delta_1^{\varsigma+1}}{(\varsigma+1)} + \mu_1\sum_{j=1}^{k-2}\omega_j\vartheta_j^\varsigma\right)\right], \tag{26}$$

$$\Delta_3 = \frac{1}{\Gamma(\varrho+1)}\left[T^\varrho \overline{\Lambda}_7 + \overline{\Lambda}_6 \epsilon_2 \nu_2^\varrho + \overline{\Lambda}_8\left(\lambda_2 \frac{\delta_2^{\varrho+1}}{(\varrho+1)} + \mu_2 \sum_{j=1}^{k-2}\omega_j \varphi_j^\varrho\right)\right], \qquad (27)$$

$$\Delta_4 = \frac{1}{\Gamma(\varsigma+1)}\left[T^\varsigma(1+\overline{\Lambda}_8) + \overline{\Lambda}_5 \epsilon_1 \nu_1^\varsigma + \overline{\Lambda}_7\left(\lambda_1 \frac{\delta_1^{\varsigma+1}}{(\varsigma+1)} + \mu_1 \sum_{j=1}^{k-2}\omega_j \vartheta_j^\varsigma\right)\right], \qquad (28)$$

$$\widehat{\Delta}_1 = \frac{1}{\Gamma(\varrho+1)}\left[\varrho T^{\varrho-1} + \overline{\Lambda}_3' T^\varrho + \overline{\Lambda}_2' \epsilon_2 \nu_2^\varrho + \overline{\Lambda}_4'\left(\lambda_2 \frac{\delta_2^{\varrho+1}}{(\varrho+1)} + \mu_2 \sum_{j=1}^{k-2}\omega_j \varphi_j^\varrho\right)\right], \qquad (29)$$

$$\widehat{\Delta}_2 = \frac{1}{\Gamma(\varsigma+1)}\left[T^\varsigma \overline{\Lambda}_4' + \overline{\Lambda}_1' \epsilon_1 \nu_1^\varsigma + \overline{\Lambda}_3'\left(\lambda_1 \frac{\delta_1^{\varsigma+1}}{(\varsigma+1)} + \mu_1 \sum_{j=1}^{k-2}\omega_j \vartheta_j^\varsigma\right)\right], \qquad (30)$$

$$\widehat{\Delta}_3 = \frac{1}{\Gamma(\varrho+1)}\left[T^\varrho \overline{\Lambda}_7' + \overline{\Lambda}_6' \epsilon_2 \nu_2^\varrho + \overline{\Lambda}_8'\left(\lambda_2 \frac{\delta_2^{\varrho+1}}{(\varrho+1)} + \mu_2 \sum_{j=1}^{k-2}\omega_j \varphi_j^\varrho\right)\right], \qquad (31)$$

$$\widehat{\Delta}_4 = \frac{1}{\Gamma(\varsigma+1)}\left[\varsigma T^{\varsigma-1} + \overline{\Lambda}_8' T^\varsigma + \overline{\Lambda}_5' \epsilon_1 \nu_1^\varsigma + \overline{\Lambda}_7'\left(\lambda_1 \frac{\delta_1^{\varsigma+1}}{(\varsigma+1)} + \mu_1 \sum_{j=1}^{k-2}\omega_j \vartheta_j^\varsigma\right)\right], \qquad (32)$$

$$\Phi_1 = \left(\Delta_1 + \frac{T^{1-\varrho_1}}{\Gamma(2-\varrho_1)}\widehat{\Delta}_1 + \Delta_3 + \frac{T^{1-\varsigma_1}}{\Gamma(2-\varsigma_1)}\widehat{\Delta}_3\right)r_0 + \left(\Delta_2 + \frac{T^{1-\varrho_1}}{\Gamma(2-\varrho_1)}\widehat{\Delta}_2 + \Delta_4 + \frac{T^{1-\varsigma_1}}{\Gamma(2-\varsigma_1)}\widehat{\Delta}_4\right)s_0, \qquad (33)$$

$$\Phi_2 = \left(\Delta_1 + \frac{T^{1-\varrho_1}}{\Gamma(2-\varrho_1)}\widehat{\Delta}_1 + \Delta_3 + \frac{T^{1-\varsigma_1}}{\Gamma(2-\varsigma_1)}\widehat{\Delta}_3\right)r_1$$
$$+ \left(\Delta_2 + \frac{T^{1-\varrho_1}}{\Gamma(2-\varrho_1)}\widehat{\Delta}_2 + \Delta_4 + \frac{T^{1-\varsigma_1}}{\Gamma(2-\varsigma_1)}\widehat{\Delta}_4\right)\left(\max\{s_1, s_2\} + \frac{s_3 T^\zeta}{\Gamma(\zeta+1)}\right)$$
$$+ \left\{\kappa_2 \overline{\Lambda}_3 + \overline{\Lambda}_4 + \frac{T^{1-\varrho_1}(\kappa_2 \overline{\Lambda}_3' + \overline{\Lambda}_4')}{\Gamma(2-\varrho_1)} + 1 + \kappa_2 \overline{\Lambda}_7 + \overline{\Lambda}_8 + \frac{T^{1-\varsigma_1}(\kappa_2 \overline{\Lambda}_7' + \overline{\Lambda}_8')}{\Gamma(2-\varsigma_1)}\right\}\mathcal{W}_2, \qquad (34)$$

$$\Phi_3 = \left(\Delta_1 + \frac{T^{1-\varrho_1}}{\Gamma(2-\varrho_1)}\widehat{\Delta}_1 + \Delta_3 + \frac{T^{1-\varsigma_1}}{\Gamma(2-\varsigma_1)}\widehat{\Delta}_3\right)\left(\max\{r_2, r_3\} + \frac{r_4 T^\xi}{\Gamma(\xi+1)}\right)$$
$$+ \left(\Delta_2 + \frac{T^{1-\varrho_1}}{\Gamma(2-\varrho_1)}\widehat{\Delta}_2 + \Delta_4 + \frac{T^{1-\varsigma_1}}{\Gamma(2-\varsigma_1)}\widehat{\Delta}_4\right)s_4$$
$$+ \left\{1 + \kappa_1 \overline{\Lambda}_4 + \overline{\Lambda}_3 + \frac{T^{1-\varrho_1}(\kappa_1 \overline{\Lambda}_4' + \overline{\Lambda}_3')}{\Gamma(2-\varrho_1)} + \kappa_1 \overline{\Lambda}_8 + \overline{\Lambda}_7 + \frac{T^{1-\varsigma_1}(\kappa_1 \overline{\Lambda}_8' + \overline{\Lambda}_7')}{\Gamma(2-\varsigma_1)}\right\}\mathcal{W}_1, \qquad (35)$$

$$\Psi_1 = \Delta_1 \iota_1 \mathcal{V}_1 + \Delta_2 \iota_2 \mathcal{V}_2 + (1+\kappa_1 \overline{\Lambda}_4 + \overline{\Lambda}_3)\mathcal{V}_1 + (\kappa_2 \overline{\Lambda}_3 + \overline{\Lambda}_4)\mathcal{V}_2, \qquad (36)$$

$$\Psi_2 = \widehat{\Delta}_1 \iota_1 \mathcal{V}_1 + \widehat{\Delta}_2 \iota_2 \mathcal{V}_2 + (\kappa_1 \overline{\Lambda}_4' + \overline{\Lambda}_3')\mathcal{V}_1 + (\kappa_2 \overline{\Lambda}_3' + \overline{\Lambda}_4')\mathcal{V}_2, \qquad (37)$$

$$\Psi_3 = \Delta_4 \iota_2 \mathcal{V}_2 + \Delta_3 \iota_1 \mathcal{V}_1 + (1 + \kappa_2 \overline{\Lambda}_7 + \overline{\Lambda}_8)\mathcal{V}_2 + (\kappa_1 \overline{\Lambda}_8 + \overline{\Lambda}_7)\mathcal{V}_1, \qquad (38)$$

$$\Psi_4 = \widehat{\Delta}_4 \iota_2 \mathcal{V}_2 + \widehat{\Delta}_3 \iota_1 \mathcal{V}_1 + (\kappa_2 \overline{\Lambda}_7' + \overline{\Lambda}_8')\mathcal{V}_2 + (\kappa_1 \overline{\Lambda}_8' + \overline{\Lambda}_7')\mathcal{V}_1, \qquad (39)$$

$$\mathcal{P}_1 = \Delta_1 \mathcal{T}_1 + \Delta_2 \mathcal{T}_2, \quad \mathcal{P}_2 = \widehat{\Delta}_1 \mathcal{T}_1 + \widehat{\Delta}_2 \mathcal{T}_2, \quad \mathcal{P}_3 = \Delta_4 \mathcal{T}_2 + \Delta_3 \mathcal{T}_1, \quad \mathcal{P}_4 = \widehat{\Delta}_4 \mathcal{T}_2 + \widehat{\Delta}_3 \mathcal{T}_1, \qquad (40)$$

$$\overline{\mathcal{P}} = \mathcal{P}_1 + \frac{T^{1-\varrho_1}}{\Gamma(2-\varrho_1)}\mathcal{P}_2, \quad \widehat{\mathcal{P}} = \mathcal{P}_3 + \frac{T^{1-\varsigma_1}}{\Gamma(2-\varsigma_1)}\mathcal{P}_4, \qquad (41)$$

$$\Psi = \Psi_1 + \frac{T^{1-\varrho_1}}{\Gamma(2-\varrho_1)}\Psi_2, \quad \widehat{\Psi} = \Psi_3 + \frac{T^{1-\varsigma_1}}{\Gamma(2-\varsigma_1)}\Psi_4, \qquad (42)$$

$$\mathcal{T}_1 = \sup_{\tau \in \mathcal{U}} f(\tau, 0, 0, 0, 0) < \infty, \quad \mathcal{T}_2 = \sup_{\tau \in \mathcal{U}} g(\tau, 0, 0, 0, 0) < \infty,$$

$$\iota_1 = 1 + \frac{T^\xi}{\Gamma(\xi+1)}, \quad \iota_2 = 1 + \frac{T^\zeta}{\Gamma(\zeta+1)}, \qquad (43)$$

where $\overline{\Lambda}_i = \max\limits_{\tau \in \mathcal{H}} |\Lambda_i(\tau)|$ and $\overline{\Lambda}'_i = \max\limits_{\tau \in \mathcal{H}} |\Lambda'_i(\tau)|$ $i = 1, 2, \cdots, 8$. We need the following assumptions in the forthcoming analysis: $f, g : \mathcal{U} \times \mathbb{R}^4 \to \mathbb{R}$ and $\psi_1, \psi_2 : \mathcal{C}(\mathcal{U}, \mathbb{R}) \to \mathbb{R}$ are continuous functions $\psi_1(0) = \psi_2(0) = 0$.

($\mathcal{F}_1$) There exist positive constants r_i and $s_i \geq 0$, $r_0 > 0$, $s_0 > 0$, $\forall w_i \in \mathbb{R}, i = 1, 2, 3, 4$.

$$|f(\tau, w_1, w_2, w_3, w_4)| \leq r_0 + r_1|w_1| + r_2|w_2| + r_3|w_3| + r_4|w_4|,$$
$$|g(\tau, w_1, w_2, w_3, w_4)| \leq s_0 + s_1|w_1| + s_2|w_2| + s_3|w_3| + s_4|w_4|.$$

($\mathcal{F}_2$) There exists positive constants $\mathcal{W}_1, \mathcal{W}_2 > 0$,

$$|\psi_1(v)| \leq \mathcal{W}_1\|v\|, \quad |\psi_2(u)| \leq \mathcal{W}_2\|u\|, \forall u, v \in \mathcal{C}(\mathcal{U}, \mathbb{R}).$$

($\mathcal{F}_3$) There exist positive constants $\mathcal{V}_i, i = 1, 2, \forall \tau \in \mathcal{U}$ and $r_i, s_i \in \mathbb{R}(i = 1, 2, 3, 4)$, we have

$$|f(\tau, r_1, r_2, r_3, r_4) - f(\tau, s_1, s_2, s_3, s_4)| \leq \mathcal{V}_1\Big(|r_1 - s_1| + |r_2 - s_2| + |r_3 - s_3| + |r_4 - s_4|\Big),$$
$$|g(\tau, r_1, r_2, r_3, r_4) - g(\tau, s_1, s_2, s_3, s_4)| \leq \mathcal{V}_2\Big(|r_1 - s_1| + |r_2 - s_2| + |r_3 - s_3| + |r_4 - s_4|\Big).$$

($\mathcal{F}_4$) There exist positive constants $\mathcal{V}_i$ ($i = 1, 2$) such that

$$|\psi_1(r_1) - \psi_1(r_2)| \leq \mathcal{V}_1\|r_1 - r_2\|, \quad |\psi_2(r_1) - \psi_2(r_2)| \leq \mathcal{V}_2\|r_1 - r_2\|,$$

$\forall r_1, r_2 \in \mathbb{R}$.

Theorem 1. *Assume that* ($\mathcal{F}_1$) *and* ($\mathcal{F}_2$) *hold. Further, if* $\hat{\Phi} = \min\{\Phi_2, \Phi_3\} < 1$, *then the problem* (1) *and* (2) *has at least one solution on* $\mathcal{U}$.

Proof. In the first step, we show that operator $\Pi : \mathcal{G} \times \mathcal{H} \to \mathcal{G} \times \mathcal{H}$ is completely continuous. Operator Π is continuous by the continuity of f, g, ψ_1, ψ_2 functions. Let $\Omega \subset \mathcal{G} \times \mathcal{H}$ be bounded. Then, $\exists$ positive constants $\mathcal{L}_f$ and $\mathcal{L}_g$ such that

$$|\widehat{S}_u(\tau)| = |f(\tau, u(\tau), v(\tau), {}^C\mathcal{D}^{\varsigma_1}v(\tau), \mathcal{I}^{\xi}v(\tau))| \leq \mathcal{L}_f$$
$$|\widetilde{S}_v(\tau)| = |g(\tau, u(\tau), v(\tau), {}^C\mathcal{D}^{\varrho_1}u(\tau), \mathcal{I}^{\xi}u(\tau), v(\tau))| \leq \mathcal{L}_g,$$

$\forall (u, v) \in \Omega$, and constants $\mathcal{L}_{\psi_1}, \mathcal{L}_{\psi_2} > 0$ such that $|\psi_1(v)| \leq \mathcal{L}_{\psi_1}, |\psi_2(u)| \leq \mathcal{L}_{\psi_2}, \forall u, v \in \mathcal{C}(\mathcal{U}, \mathbb{R})$. Then, for any $(u, v) \in \Omega$, we have

$$\begin{aligned}|\Pi_1(u,v)(\tau)| &\leq \frac{1}{\Gamma(\varrho)}\int_0^\tau (\tau-\theta)^{\varrho-1}|\widehat{S}_u(\theta)|d\theta + |\psi_1(v)|[1 + \kappa_1|\Lambda_4(\tau)| + |\Lambda_3(\tau)|] + |\psi_2(u)|[\kappa_2|\Lambda_3(\tau)| + |\Lambda_4(\tau)|]\\
&\quad + \frac{|\Lambda_2(\tau)|\epsilon_2}{\Gamma(\varrho-1)}\int_0^{\nu_2}\left(\int_0^\theta (\theta-\sigma)^{\varrho-2}|\widehat{S}_u(\sigma)d\sigma\right)d\theta + \frac{|\Lambda_1(\tau)|\epsilon_1}{\Gamma(\varsigma-1)}\int_0^{\nu_1}\left(\int_0^\theta (\theta-\sigma)^{\varsigma-2}|\widetilde{S}_v(\sigma)d\sigma\right)d\theta\\
&\quad + |\Lambda_4(\tau)|\left[\frac{\lambda_2}{\Gamma(\varrho)}\int_0^{\delta_2}\left(\int_0^\theta (\theta-\sigma)^{\varrho-1}|\widehat{S}_u(\sigma)d\sigma\right)d\theta + \mu_2\sum_{j=1}^{k-2}\frac{\omega_j}{\Gamma(\varrho)}\int_0^{\varphi_j}(\varphi_j - \theta)^{\varrho-1}|\widehat{S}_u(\theta)|d\theta\right.\\
&\quad \left.+ \frac{1}{\Gamma(\varsigma)}\int_0^T (T-\theta)^{\varsigma-1}|\widetilde{S}_v(\theta)|d\theta\right] + |\Lambda_3(\tau)|\left[\frac{\lambda_1}{\Gamma(\varsigma)}\int_0^{\delta_1}\left(\int_0^\theta (\theta-\sigma)^{\varsigma-1}|\widetilde{S}_v(\sigma)d\sigma\right)d\theta\right.\\
&\quad \left.+ \mu_1\sum_{j=1}^{k-2}\frac{\omega_j}{\Gamma(\varsigma)}\int_0^{\vartheta_j}(\vartheta_j - \theta)^{\varsigma-1}|\widetilde{S}_v(\theta)|d\theta + \frac{1}{\Gamma(\varrho)}\int_0^T (T-\theta)^{\varrho-1}|\widehat{S}_u(\theta)|d\theta\right]\\
&\leq \Delta_1\mathcal{L}_f + \Delta_2\mathcal{L}_g + [1 + \kappa_1\overline{\Lambda_4} + \overline{\Lambda_3}]\mathcal{L}_{\psi_1} + [\kappa_2\overline{\Lambda_3} + \overline{\Lambda_4}]\mathcal{L}_{\psi_2}.\end{aligned}$$

Likewise, we get $|\Pi'_1(u,v)(\tau)| \leq \hat{\Delta}_1 \mathcal{L}_f + \hat{\Delta}_2 \mathcal{L}_g + [\kappa_1 \overline{\Lambda'_4} + \overline{\Lambda'_3}]\mathcal{L}_{\psi_1} + [\kappa_2 \overline{\Lambda'_3} + \overline{\Lambda'_4}]\mathcal{L}_{\psi_2}$, which implies that $|{}^C\mathcal{D}^{\varrho_1}\Pi_1(u,v)(\tau)| \leq \frac{T^{1-\varrho_1}}{\Gamma(2-\varrho_1)}(\hat{\Delta}_1 \mathcal{L}_f + \hat{\Delta}_2 \mathcal{L}_g + [\kappa_1 \overline{\Lambda'_4} + \overline{\Lambda'_3}]\mathcal{L}_{\psi_1} + [\kappa_2 \overline{\Lambda'_3} + \overline{\Lambda'_4}]\mathcal{L}_{\psi_2})$. Thus, we have

$$\|\Pi_1(u,v)\|_{\mathcal{G}} \leq \Delta_1 \mathcal{L}_f + \Delta_2 \mathcal{L}_g + [1 + \kappa_1 \overline{\Lambda_4} + \overline{\Lambda_3}]\mathcal{L}_{\psi_1} + [\kappa_2 \overline{\Lambda_3} + \overline{\Lambda_4}]\mathcal{L}_{\psi_2}$$
$$+ \frac{T^{1-\varrho_1}}{\Gamma(2-\varrho_1)}(\hat{\Delta}_1 \mathcal{L}_f + \hat{\Delta}_2 \mathcal{L}_g + [\kappa_1 \overline{\Lambda'_4} + \overline{\Lambda'_3}]\mathcal{L}_{\psi_1} + [\kappa_2 \overline{\Lambda'_3} + \overline{\Lambda'_4}]\mathcal{L}_{\psi_2}). \tag{44}$$

We obtain that, equivalently, $|\Pi_2(u,v)(\tau)| \leq \Delta_4 \mathcal{L}_g + \Delta_3 \mathcal{L}_f + [1 + \kappa_2 \overline{\Lambda_7} + \overline{\Lambda_8}]\mathcal{L}_{\psi_2} + [\kappa_1 \overline{\Lambda_8} + \overline{\Lambda_7}]\mathcal{L}_{\psi_1}$, and $|\Pi'_2(u,v)(\tau)| \leq \hat{\Delta}_4 \mathcal{L}_g + \hat{\Delta}_3 \mathcal{L}_f + [\kappa_2 \overline{\Lambda'_7} + \overline{\Lambda'_8}]\mathcal{L}_{\psi_2} + [\kappa_1 \overline{\Lambda'_8} + \overline{\Lambda'_7}]\mathcal{L}_{\psi_1}$, which implies that $|{}^C\mathcal{D}^{\varsigma_1}\Pi_2(u,v)(\tau)| \leq \frac{T^{1-\varsigma_1}}{\Gamma(2-\varsigma_1)}(\hat{\Delta}_4 \mathcal{L}_g + \hat{\Delta}_3 \mathcal{L}_f + [\kappa_2 \overline{\Lambda'_7} + \overline{\Lambda'_8}]\mathcal{L}_{\psi_2} + [\kappa_1 \overline{\Lambda'_8} + \overline{\Lambda'_7}]\mathcal{L}_{\psi_1})$. Thus, we have

$$\|\Pi_2(u,v)\|_{\mathcal{H}} \leq \Delta_4 \mathcal{L}_g + \Delta_3 \mathcal{L}_f + [1 + \kappa_2 \overline{\Lambda_7} + \overline{\Lambda_8}]\mathcal{L}_{\psi_2} + [\kappa_1 \overline{\Lambda_8} + \overline{\Lambda_7}]\mathcal{L}_{\psi_1}$$
$$+ \frac{T^{1-\varsigma_1}}{\Gamma(2-\varsigma_1)}(\hat{\Delta}_4 \mathcal{L}_g + \hat{\Delta}_3 \mathcal{L}_f + [\kappa_2 \overline{\Lambda'_7} + \overline{\Lambda'_8}]\mathcal{L}_{\psi_2} + [\kappa_1 \overline{\Lambda'_8} + \overline{\Lambda'_7}]\mathcal{L}_{\psi_1}). \tag{45}$$

Thus, Π is uniformly bounded by (44) and (45). Operator Π must be shown to be equicontinuous.

For $\tau_1, \tau_2 \in \mathcal{U}$ with $\tau_1 < \tau_2$, we have

$$|\Pi_1(u,v)(\tau_2) - \Pi_1(u,v)(\tau_1)|$$
$$\leq \frac{\mathcal{L}_f}{\Gamma(\varrho+1)}[(\tau_2 - \tau_1)^\varrho + (\tau_2^\varrho - \tau_1^\varrho)] + |\psi_1(v)|\Big[\kappa_1(|\Lambda_4(\tau_2) - \Lambda_4(\tau_1)|) + (|\Lambda_3(\tau_2) - \Lambda_3(\tau_1)|)\Big]$$
$$+ |\psi_2(u)|\Big[\kappa_2(|\Lambda_3(\tau_2) - \Lambda_3(\tau_1)|) + (|\Lambda_4(\tau_2) - \Lambda_4(\tau_1)|)\Big] + \frac{(|\Lambda_2(\tau_2) - \Lambda_2(\tau_1)|)\epsilon_2 \nu_2^\varrho \mathcal{L}_f}{\Gamma(\varrho+1)}$$
$$+ \frac{(|\Lambda_1(\tau_2) - \Lambda_1(\tau_1)|)\epsilon_1 \nu_1^\varsigma \mathcal{L}_g}{\Gamma(\varsigma+1)} + (|\Lambda_4(\tau_2) - \Lambda_4(\tau_1)|)\Bigg[\frac{\lambda_2 \delta_2^{\varrho+1} \mathcal{L}_f}{\Gamma(\varrho+2)} + \mu_2 \sum_{j=1}^{k-2} \frac{\omega_j (\varphi_j)^\varrho \mathcal{L}_f}{\Gamma(\varrho+1)} + \frac{T^\varsigma \mathcal{L}_g}{\Gamma(\varsigma+1)}\Bigg]$$
$$+ (\Lambda_3(\tau_2) - \Lambda_3(\tau_1))\Bigg[\frac{\lambda_1 \delta_1^{\varsigma+1} \mathcal{L}_g}{\Gamma(\varsigma+2)} + \mu_1 \sum_{j=1}^{k-2} \frac{\omega_j \vartheta_j^\varsigma \mathcal{L}_g}{\Gamma(\varsigma+1)} + \frac{T^\varrho \mathcal{L}_f}{\Gamma(\varrho+1)}\Bigg],$$

and

$$|\Pi'_1(u,v)(\tau_2) - \Pi'_1(u,v)(\tau_1)|$$
$$\leq \Bigg|\int_0^{\tau_1} \frac{[(\tau_2-\theta)^{\varrho-2} - (\tau_1-\theta)^{\varrho-2}]}{\Gamma(\varrho-1)} \times f(\theta, u(\theta), v(\theta), {}^C\mathcal{D}^{\varsigma_1}v(\theta), \mathcal{I}^{\tilde{\varsigma}}v(\theta))d\theta\Bigg|$$
$$+ \Bigg|\int_{\tau_1}^{\tau_2} \frac{(\tau_2-\theta)^{\varrho-2}}{\Gamma(\varrho-1)} f(\theta, u(\theta), v(\theta), {}^C\mathcal{D}^{\varsigma_1}v(\theta), \mathcal{I}^{\tilde{\varsigma}}v(\theta))d\theta\Bigg| + |\psi_1(v)|\Big[\kappa_1(|\Lambda'_4(\tau_2) - \Lambda'_4(\tau_1)|) + (|\Lambda'_3(\tau_2) - \Lambda'_3(\tau_1)|)\Big]$$
$$+ |\psi_2(u)|\Big[\kappa_2(|\Lambda'_3(\tau_2) - \Lambda'_3(\tau_1)|) + (|\Lambda'_4(\tau_2) - \Lambda'_4(\tau_1)|)\Big] + \frac{(|\Lambda'_2(\tau_2) - \Lambda'_2(\tau_1)|)\epsilon_2 \nu_2^\varrho \mathcal{L}_f}{\Gamma(\varrho+1)}$$
$$+ \frac{(|\Lambda'_1(\tau_2) - \Lambda'_1(\tau_1)|)\epsilon_1 \nu_1^\varsigma \mathcal{L}_g}{\Gamma(\varsigma+1)} + (|\Lambda'_4(\tau_2) - \Lambda'_4(\tau_1)|)\Bigg[\frac{\lambda_2 \delta_2^{\varrho+1} \mathcal{L}_f}{\Gamma(\varrho+2)} + \mu_2 \sum_{j=1}^{k-2} \frac{\omega_j (\varphi_j)^\varrho \mathcal{L}_f}{\Gamma(\varrho+1)} + \frac{T^\varsigma \mathcal{L}_g}{\Gamma(\varsigma+1)}\Bigg]$$
$$+ (|\Lambda'_3(\tau_2) - \Lambda'_3(\tau_1)|)\Bigg[\frac{\lambda_1 \delta_1^{\varsigma+1} \mathcal{L}_g}{\Gamma(\varsigma+2)} + \mu_1 \sum_{j=1}^{k-2} \frac{\omega_j \vartheta_j^\varsigma \mathcal{L}_g}{\Gamma(\varsigma+1)} + \frac{T^\varrho \mathcal{L}_f}{\Gamma(\varrho+1)}\Bigg].$$

Thus, we have

$$
\begin{aligned}
&|{}^C\mathcal{D}^{\varrho_1}\Pi_1(u,v)(\tau_2) - {}^C\mathcal{D}^{\varrho_1}\Pi_1(u,v)(\tau_1)| \\
&\leq \frac{T^{1-\varrho_1}}{\Gamma(2-\varrho_1)}\left\{\frac{\mathcal{L}_f}{\Gamma(\varrho)}[(\tau_2-\tau_1)^{\varrho-1}+(\tau_2^{\varrho-1}-\tau_1^{\varrho-1})] + |\psi_1(v)|\left[\kappa_1(|\Lambda_4'(\tau_2)-\Lambda_4'(\tau_1)|)+(|\Lambda_3'(\tau_2)-\Lambda_3'(\tau_1)|)\right]\right. \\
&+|\psi_2(u)|\left[\kappa_2(|\Lambda_3'(\tau_2)-\Lambda_3'(\tau_1)|)+(|\Lambda_4'(\tau_2)-\Lambda_4'(\tau_1)|)\right] + \frac{(|\Lambda_2'(\tau_2)-\Lambda_2'(\tau_1)|)\epsilon_2 \nu_2^\varrho \mathcal{L}_f}{\Gamma(\varrho+1)} \\
&+\frac{(|\Lambda_1'(\tau_2)-\Lambda_1'(\tau_1)|)\epsilon_1 \nu_1^\varsigma \mathcal{L}_g}{\Gamma(\varsigma+1)} + (|\Lambda_4'(\tau_2)-\Lambda_4'(\tau_1)|)\left[\frac{\lambda_2 \delta_2^{\varrho+1}\mathcal{L}_f}{\Gamma(\varrho+2)} + \mu_2 \sum_{j=1}^{k-2}\frac{\omega_j(\varphi_j)^\varrho \mathcal{L}_f}{\Gamma(\varrho+1)} + \frac{T^\varsigma \mathcal{L}_g}{\Gamma(\varsigma+1)}\right] \\
&\left.+(|\Lambda_3'(\tau_2)-\Lambda_3'(\tau_1)|)\left[\frac{\lambda_1 \delta_1^{\varsigma+1}\mathcal{L}_g}{\Gamma(\varsigma+2)} + \mu_1 \sum_{j=1}^{k-2}\frac{\omega_j \vartheta_j^\varsigma \mathcal{L}_g}{\Gamma(\varsigma+1)} + \frac{T^\varrho \mathcal{L}_f}{\Gamma(\varrho+1)}\right]\right\}.
\end{aligned}
$$

Thus, we obtain $\|\Pi_1(u,v)(\tau_2) - \Pi_1(u,v)(\tau_1)\|_{\mathcal{G}} \to 0$ independent of u and v as $\tau_2 \to \tau_1$. According to the above, we get

$$
\begin{aligned}
&|\Pi_2(u,v)(\tau_2) - \Pi_2(u,v)(\tau_1)| \\
&\leq \frac{\mathcal{L}_g}{\Gamma(\varsigma+1)}[(\tau_2-\tau_1)^\varsigma + (\tau_2^\varsigma - \tau_1^\varsigma)] + |\psi_2(u)|\left[\kappa_2(|\Lambda_7(\tau_2)-\Lambda_7(\tau_1)|)+(|\Lambda_8(\tau_2)-\Lambda_8(\tau_1)|)\right] \\
&+|\psi_1(v)|\left[\kappa_1(|\Lambda_8(\tau_2)-\Lambda_8(\tau_1)|)+(|\Lambda_7(\tau_2)-\Lambda_7(\tau_1)|)\right] + \frac{(|\Lambda_5(\tau_2)-\Lambda_5(\tau_1)|)\epsilon_1 \nu_1^\varsigma \mathcal{L}_g}{\Gamma(\varsigma+1)} \\
&+\frac{(|\Lambda_6(\tau_2)-\Lambda_6(\tau_1)|)\epsilon_2 \nu_2^\varrho \mathcal{L}_f}{\Gamma(\varrho+1)} + (|\Lambda_7(\tau_2)-\Lambda_7(\tau_1)|)\left[\frac{\lambda_1 \delta_1^{\varsigma+1}\mathcal{L}_g}{\Gamma(\varsigma+2)} + \mu_1 \sum_{j=1}^{k-2}\frac{\omega_j \vartheta_j^\varsigma \mathcal{L}_g}{\Gamma(\varsigma+1)} + \frac{T^\varrho \mathcal{L}_f}{\Gamma(\varrho+1)}\right] \\
&+(|\Lambda_8(\tau_2)-\Lambda_8(\tau_1)|)\left[\frac{\lambda_2 \delta_2^{\varrho+1}\mathcal{L}_f}{\Gamma(\varrho+2)} + \mu_2 \sum_{j=1}^{k-2}\frac{\omega_j(\varphi_j)^\varrho \mathcal{L}_f}{\Gamma(\varrho+1)} + \frac{T^\varsigma \mathcal{L}_g}{\Gamma(\varsigma+1)}\right],
\end{aligned}
$$

and

$$
\begin{aligned}
&|\Pi_2'(u,v)(\tau_2) - \Pi_2'(u,v)(\tau_1)| \\
&\leq \left|\int_0^{\tau_1} \frac{[(\tau_2-\theta)^{\varsigma-2}-(\tau_1-\theta)^{\varsigma-2}]}{\Gamma(\varsigma-1)} \times g(\theta, u(\theta), {}^C\mathcal{D}^{\varrho_1}u(\theta), \mathcal{I}^\zeta u(\theta), v(\theta))d\theta\right| \\
&+\left|\int_{\tau_1}^{\tau_2} \frac{(\tau_2-\theta)^{\varsigma-2}}{\Gamma(\varsigma-1)} g(\theta, u(\theta), {}^C\mathcal{D}^{\varrho_1}u(\theta), \mathcal{I}^\zeta u(\theta), v(\theta))d\theta\right| + |\psi_2(u)|\left[\kappa_2(|\Lambda_7'(\tau_2)-\Lambda_7'(\tau_1)|)+(|\Lambda_8'(\tau_2)-\Lambda_8'(\tau_1)|)\right] \\
&+|\psi_1(v)|\left[\kappa_1(|\Lambda_8'(\tau_2)-\Lambda_8'(\tau_1)|)+(|\Lambda_7'(\tau_2)-\Lambda_7'(\tau_1)|)\right] + \frac{(|\Lambda_5'(\tau_2)-\Lambda_5'(\tau_1)|)\epsilon_1 \nu_1^\varsigma \mathcal{L}_g}{\Gamma(\varsigma+1)} \\
&+\frac{(|\Lambda_6'(\tau_2)-\Lambda_6'(\tau_1)|)\epsilon_2 \nu_2^\varrho \mathcal{L}_f}{\Gamma(\varrho+1)} + (|\Lambda_7'(\tau_2)-\Lambda_7'(\tau_1)|)\left[\frac{\lambda_1 \delta_1^{\varsigma+1}\mathcal{L}_g}{\Gamma(\varsigma+2)} + \mu_1 \sum_{j=1}^{k-2}\frac{\omega_j \vartheta_j^\varsigma \mathcal{L}_g}{\Gamma(\varsigma+1)} + \frac{T^\varrho \mathcal{L}_f}{\Gamma(\varrho+1)}\right] \\
&+(|\Lambda_8'(\tau_2)-\Lambda_8'(\tau_1)|)\left[\frac{\lambda_2 \delta_2^{\varrho+1}\mathcal{L}_f}{\Gamma(\varrho+2)} + \mu_2 \sum_{j=1}^{k-2}\frac{\omega_j(\varphi_j)^\varrho \mathcal{L}_f}{\Gamma(\varrho+1)} + \frac{T^\varsigma \mathcal{L}_g}{\Gamma(\varsigma+1)}\right].
\end{aligned}
$$

Consequently, we have

$$|{}^C\mathcal{D}^{\varsigma_1}\Pi_2(u,v)(\tau_2) - {}^C\mathcal{D}^{\varsigma_1}\Pi_2(u,v)(\tau_1)|$$
$$\leq \frac{T^{1-\varsigma_1}}{\Gamma(2-\varsigma_1)}\left\{\frac{\mathcal{L}_g}{\Gamma(\varsigma+1)}[(\tau_2-\tau_1)^\varsigma + (\tau_2^\varsigma - \tau_1^\varsigma)] + |\psi_2(u)|\left[\kappa_2(|\Lambda_7'(\tau_2) - \Lambda_7'(\tau_1)|) + (|\Lambda_8'(\tau_2) - \Lambda_8'(\tau_1)|)\right]\right.$$
$$+ |\psi_1(v)|\left[\kappa_1(|\Lambda_8'(\tau_2) - \Lambda_8'(\tau_1)|) + (|\Lambda_7'(\tau_2) - \Lambda_7'(\tau_1)|)\right] + \frac{(|\Lambda_5'(\tau_2) - \Lambda_5'(\tau_1)|)\epsilon_1 v_1^\varsigma \mathcal{L}_g}{\Gamma(\varsigma+1)}$$
$$+ \frac{(|\Lambda_6'(\tau_2) - \Lambda_6'(\tau_1)|)\epsilon_2 v_2^\varrho \mathcal{L}_f}{\Gamma(\varrho+1)} + (|\Lambda_7'(\tau_2) - \Lambda_7'(\tau_1)|)\left[\frac{\lambda_1\delta_1^{\varsigma+1}\mathcal{L}_g}{\Gamma(\varsigma+2)} + \mu_1\sum_{j=1}^{k-2}\frac{\omega_j\vartheta_j^\varsigma\mathcal{L}_g}{\Gamma(\varsigma+1)} + \frac{T^\varrho\mathcal{L}_f}{\Gamma(\varrho+1)}\right]$$
$$+ (|\Lambda_8'(\tau_2) - \Lambda_8'(\tau_1)|)\left[\frac{\lambda_2\delta_2^{\varrho+1}\mathcal{L}_f}{\Gamma(\varrho+2)} + \mu_2\sum_{j=1}^{k-2}\frac{\omega_j(\varphi_j)^\varrho\mathcal{L}_f}{\Gamma(\varrho+1)} + \frac{T^\varsigma\mathcal{L}_g}{\Gamma(\varsigma+1)}\right]\right\},$$

which means that $\|\Pi_2(u,v)(\tau_2) - \Pi_2(u,v)(\tau_1)\|_\mathcal{H} \to 0$ independent of u and v as $\tau_2 \to \tau_1$. Hence, the operator $\Pi(u,v)$ is equicontinuous, and thus it is completely continuous by Lemma (see Lemma 1.2 [15]). Next, we demonstrate that the set $\Phi = \{(u,v) \in \mathcal{G} \times \mathcal{H} | (u,v) = \eta\Pi(u,v), 0 < \eta < 1\}$ is bounded. Let $(u,v) \in \Phi$; then, $(u,v) = \eta\Pi(u,v)$, and for any $\tau \in \mathcal{U}$, we have $u(\tau) = \eta\Pi_1(u,v)(\tau), v(\tau) = \eta\Pi_2(u,v)(\tau)$. Thus,

$$|u(\tau)|_\mathcal{G} \leq \Delta_1\left(r_0 + r_1\|u\|_\mathcal{G} + \left(\max\{r_2,r_3\} + \frac{r_4 T^\xi}{\Gamma(\xi+1)}\right)\|v\|_\mathcal{H}\right)$$
$$+ \Delta_2\left(s_0 + \left(\max\{s_1,s_2\} + \frac{s_3 T^\zeta}{\Gamma(\zeta+1)}\right)\|u\|_\mathcal{G} + s_4\|v\|_\mathcal{H}\right)$$
$$+ \left(1 + \kappa_1|\overline{\Lambda}_4| + |\overline{\Lambda}_3|\right)\mathcal{W}_1\|v\|_\mathcal{H} + \left(\kappa_2|\overline{\Lambda}_3| + |\overline{\Lambda}_4|\right)\mathcal{W}_2\|u\|_\mathcal{G},$$

$$|u'(\tau)| \leq \widehat{\Delta}_1\left(r_0 + r_1\|u\|_\mathcal{G} + \left(\max\{r_2,r_3\} + \frac{r_4 T^\xi}{\Gamma(\xi+1)}\right)\|v\|_\mathcal{H}\right)$$
$$+ \widehat{\Delta}_2\left(s_0 + \left(\max\{s_1,s_2\} + \frac{s_3 T^\zeta}{\Gamma(\zeta+1)}\right)\|u\|_\mathcal{G} + s_4\|v\|_\mathcal{H}\right)$$
$$+ \left(\kappa_1|\overline{\Lambda}_4'| + |\overline{\Lambda}_3'|\right)\mathcal{W}_1\|v\|_\mathcal{H} + \left(\kappa_2|\overline{\Lambda}_3'| + |\overline{\Lambda}_4'|\right)\mathcal{W}_2\|u\|_\mathcal{G},$$

$$|{}^C\mathcal{D}^{\varrho_1}u(\tau)| \leq \frac{T^{1-\varrho_1}}{\Gamma(2-\varrho_1)}\left\{\widehat{\Delta}_1\left(r_0 + r_1\|u\|_\mathcal{G} + \left(\max\{r_2,r_3\} + \frac{r_4 T^\xi}{\Gamma(\xi+1)}\right)\|v\|_\mathcal{H}\right)\right.$$
$$+ \widehat{\Delta}_2\left(s_0 + \left(\max\{s_1,s_2\} + \frac{s_3 T^\zeta}{\Gamma(\zeta+1)}\right)\|u\|_\mathcal{G} + s_4\|v\|_\mathcal{H}\right)$$
$$\left. + \left(\kappa_1|\overline{\Lambda}_4'| + |\overline{\Lambda}_3'|\right)\mathcal{W}_1\|v\|_\mathcal{H} + \left(\kappa_2|\overline{\Lambda}_3'| + |\overline{\Lambda}_4'|\right)\mathcal{W}_2\|u\|_\mathcal{G}\right\}.$$

Hence, we have

$$\|u\| \leq \Delta_1\left(r_0 + r_1\|u\|_{\mathcal{G}} + \left(\max\{r_2, r_3\} + \frac{r_4 T^{\xi}}{\Gamma(\xi+1)}\right)\|v\|_{\mathcal{H}}\right)$$

$$+\Delta_2\left(s_0 + \left(\max\{s_1, s_2\} + \frac{s_3 T^{\zeta}}{\Gamma(\zeta+1)}\right)\|u\|_{\mathcal{G}} + s_4\|v\|_{\mathcal{H}}\right)$$

$$+\left(1 + \kappa_1|\overline{\Lambda}_4| + |\overline{\Lambda}_3|\right)\mathcal{W}_1\|v\|_{\mathcal{H}} + \left(\kappa_2|\overline{\Lambda}_3| + |\overline{\Lambda}_4|\right)\mathcal{W}_2\|u\|_{\mathcal{G}}$$

$$+\frac{T^{1-\varrho_1}}{\Gamma(2-\varrho_1)}\left\{\widehat{\Delta}_1\left(r_0 + r_1\|u\|_{\mathcal{G}} + \left(\max\{r_2, r_3\} + \frac{r_4 T^{\xi}}{\Gamma(\xi+1)}\right)\|v\|_{\mathcal{H}}\right)\right. \quad (46)$$

$$+\widehat{\Delta}_2\left(s_0 + \left(\max\{s_1, s_2\} + \frac{s_3 T^{\zeta}}{\Gamma(\zeta+1)}\right)\|u\|_{\mathcal{G}} + s_4\|v\|_{\mathcal{H}}\right)$$

$$\left. +\left(\kappa_1|\overline{\Lambda}_4'| + |\overline{\Lambda}_3'|\right)\mathcal{W}_1\|v\|_{\mathcal{H}} + \left(\kappa_2|\overline{\Lambda}_3'| + |\overline{\Lambda}_4'|\right)\mathcal{W}_2\|u\|_{\mathcal{G}}\right\}.$$

According to the above, we get

$$\|v\| \leq \Delta_4\left(s_0 + \left(\max\{s_1, s_2\} + \frac{s_3 T^{\zeta}}{\Gamma(\zeta+1)}\right)\|u\|_{\mathcal{G}} + s_4\|v\|_{\mathcal{H}}\right)$$

$$+\Delta_3\left(r_0 + r_1\|u\|_{\mathcal{G}} + \left(\max\{r_2, r_3\} + \frac{r_4 T^{\xi}}{\Gamma(\xi+1)}\right)\|v\|_{\mathcal{H}}\right)$$

$$+\left(1 + \kappa_2|\overline{\Lambda}_7| + |\overline{\Lambda}_8|\right)\mathcal{W}_2\|u\|_{\mathcal{G}} + \left(\kappa_1|\overline{\Lambda}_8| + |\overline{\Lambda}_7|\right)\mathcal{W}_1\|v\|_{\mathcal{H}}$$

$$+\frac{T^{1-\varsigma_1}}{\Gamma(2-\varsigma_1)}\left\{\widehat{\Delta}_4\left(s_0 + \left(\max\{s_1, s_2\} + \frac{s_3 T^{\zeta}}{\Gamma(\zeta+1)}\right)\|u\|_{\mathcal{G}} + s_4\|v\|_{\mathcal{H}}\right)\right. \quad (47)$$

$$+\widehat{\Delta}_3\left(r_0 + r_1\|u\|_{\mathcal{G}} + \left(\max\{r_2, r_3\} + \frac{r_4 T^{\xi}}{\Gamma(\xi+1)}\right)\|v\|_{\mathcal{H}}\right)$$

$$\left. +\left(\kappa_2|\overline{\Lambda}_7'| + |\overline{\Lambda}_8'|\right)\mathcal{W}_2\|u\|_{\mathcal{G}} + \left(\kappa_1|\overline{\Lambda}_8'| + |\overline{\Lambda}_7'|\right)\mathcal{W}_1\|v\|_{\mathcal{H}}\right\}.$$

Using the above inequalities in combination with the notations (46) and (47), we deduce the result below. $\|u\| + \|v\| \leq \Phi_1 + \min\{\Phi_2, \Phi_3\}\|(u, v)\|_{\mathcal{G} \times \mathcal{H}}$, which leads to $\|(u, v)\|_{\mathcal{G} \times \mathcal{H}} \leq \frac{\Phi_1}{1 - \min\{\Phi_2, \Phi_3\}}$. This concludes that the set $\min\{\Phi_2, \Phi_3\}$ is bounded. Therefore, operator Π has at least one fixed point by Theorem (see Theorem 1.9 [15]), which means the system (1)–(2) has at least one solutions on $\mathcal{U}$. □

Theorem 2. *Assume that* $(\mathcal{F}_3)$ *and* $(\mathcal{F}_4)$ *holds. Additionally, if*

$$\Psi + \widehat{\Psi} < 1, \quad (48)$$

where $\Psi, \widehat{\Psi}$ *are defined by (42), then on* $\mathcal{U}$ *there is a unique solution to the problems (1) and (2).*

Proof. Let us fix this $\widehat{\varepsilon} \geq \max\left\{\frac{\overline{\mathcal{P}} + \widehat{\mathcal{P}}}{1 - (\Psi + \widehat{\Psi})}\right\}$, where $\Psi, \widehat{\Psi}$ and $\overline{\mathcal{P}}, \widehat{\mathcal{P}}$ are respectively given by (41) and (42), and show that $\Pi B_{\widehat{\varepsilon}} \subset B_{\widehat{\varepsilon}}$, where the operator Π is given by (22) and $B_{\widehat{\varepsilon}} = \{(u, v) \in \mathcal{G} \times \mathcal{H} : \|(u, v)\| \leq \widehat{\varepsilon}\}$. For $(u, v) \in B_{\widehat{\varepsilon}}, \tau \in \mathcal{H}$, we have

$$|\widehat{S}_u(\tau)| = |f(\tau, u(\tau), v(\tau), {}^C\mathcal{D}^{\varsigma_1}v(\tau), \mathcal{I}^{\xi}v(\tau))| \leq \mathcal{V}_1\iota_1\Big(\|(u, v)\|_{\mathcal{G} \times \mathcal{H}}\Big) + \mathcal{T}_1 \leq \mathcal{V}_1\iota_1\widehat{\varepsilon} + \mathcal{T}_1,$$

$$|\widehat{S}_v(\tau)| = |g(\tau, u(\tau), {}^C\mathcal{D}^{\varrho_1}u(\tau), \mathcal{I}^{\zeta}u(\tau), v(\tau))| \leq \mathcal{V}_2\iota_2\Big(\|(u, v)\|_{\mathcal{G} \times \mathcal{H}}\Big) + \mathcal{T}_2 \leq \mathcal{V}_2\iota_2\widehat{\varepsilon} + \mathcal{T}_2,$$

$$|\psi_1(v)| \leq \mathcal{V}_1\widehat{\varepsilon}, \ |\psi_2(u)| \leq \mathcal{V}_2\widehat{\varepsilon},$$

which lead to
$$|\Pi_1(u,v)(\tau)| \leq \Psi_1 \widehat{\varepsilon} + \mathcal{P}_1,$$
where Ψ_1 and $\mathcal{P}_1$ are given by (36) and (40). With the above notes, we get
$$|\Pi_1'(u,v)(\tau)| \leq \Psi_2 \widehat{\varepsilon} + \mathcal{P}_2,$$
which means that
$$|{}^C\mathcal{D}^{\varrho_1} \Pi_1(u,v)(\tau)| \leq \frac{T^{1-\varrho_1}}{\Gamma(2-\varrho_1)}\left(\Psi_2 \widehat{\varepsilon} + \mathcal{P}_2\right).$$
Thus, we get
$$\|\Pi_1(u,v)\|_{\mathcal{G}} \leq \left(\Psi_1 + \frac{T^{1-\varrho_1}}{\Gamma(2-\varrho_1)}\Psi_2\right)\widehat{\varepsilon} + \left(\mathcal{P}_1 + \frac{T^{1-\varrho_1}}{\Gamma(2-\varrho_1)}\mathcal{P}_2\right). \qquad (49)$$
Similarly, we get
$$|\Pi_2(u,v)(\tau)| \leq \Psi_3 \widehat{\varepsilon} + \mathcal{P}_3,$$
where Ψ_3 and $\mathcal{P}_3$ are given by (38) and (40). With the above notes, we get
$$|\Pi_2'(u,v)(\tau)| \leq \Psi_4 \widehat{\varepsilon} + \mathcal{P}_4,$$
which means that
$$|{}^C\mathcal{D}^{\varsigma_1} \Pi_2(u,v)(\tau)| \leq \frac{T^{1-\varsigma_1}}{\Gamma(2-\varsigma_1)}\left(\Psi_4 \widehat{\varepsilon} + \mathcal{P}_4\right).$$
Hence, we have
$$\|\Pi_2(u,v)\|_{\mathcal{H}} \leq \left(\Psi_3 + \frac{T^{1-\varsigma_1}}{\Gamma(2-\varsigma_1)}\Psi_4\right)\widehat{\varepsilon} + \left(\mathcal{P}_3 + \frac{T^{1-\varsigma_1}}{\Gamma(2-\varsigma_1)}\mathcal{P}_4\right). \qquad (50)$$

So, (49) and (50) follow $\|\Pi(u,v)\|_{\mathcal{G}\times\mathcal{H}} \leq \widehat{\varepsilon}$, and thus, $\Pi \mathcal{B}_{\widehat{\varepsilon}} \subset \mathcal{B}_{\widehat{\varepsilon}}$.

Now, for $(u_1, v_1), (u_2, v_2) \in \mathcal{G} \times \mathcal{H}$ and any $\tau \in \mathcal{U}$, we have
$$|\Pi_1(u_1,v_1)(\tau) - \Pi_1(u_2,v_2)(\tau)| \leq \Psi_1(\|u_1 - u_2\|_{\mathcal{G}} + \|v_1 - v_2\|_{\mathcal{H}}).$$
Next, we find that
$$|\Pi_1'(u_1,v_1)(\tau) - \Pi_1'(u_2,v_2)(\tau)| \leq \Psi_2(\|u_1 - u_2\|_{\mathcal{G}} + \|v_1 - v_2\|_{\mathcal{H}}).$$
Thus, we have
$$|{}^C\mathcal{D}^{\varrho_1}\Pi_1(u_1,v_1)(\tau) - {}^C\mathcal{D}^{\varrho_1}\Pi_1(u_2,v_2)(\tau)| \leq \frac{T^{1-\varrho_1}}{\Gamma(2-\varrho_1)}\left(\Psi_2(\|u_1 - u_2\|_{\mathcal{G}} + \|v_1 - v_2\|_{\mathcal{H}})\right),$$
Hence, we get
$$\|\Pi_1(u_1,v_1) - \Pi_1(u_2,v_2)\|_{\mathcal{G}} \leq \left(\Psi_1 + \frac{T^{1-\varrho_1}}{\Gamma(2-\varrho_1)}\Psi_2\right)(\|u_1 - u_2\|_{\mathcal{G}} + \|v_1 - v_2\|_{\mathcal{H}}). \qquad (51)$$
Similarly, we have
$$\|\Pi_2(u_1,v_1) - \Pi_2(u_2,v_2)\|_{\mathcal{H}} \leq \left(\Psi_3 + \frac{T^{1-\varsigma_1}}{\Gamma(2-\varsigma_1)}\Psi_4\right)(\|u_1 - u_2\|_{\mathcal{G}} + \|v_1 - v_2\|_{\mathcal{H}}). \qquad (52)$$
So, (51) and (52) follow
$$\|\Pi(u_1,v_1) - \Pi(u_2,v_2)\|_{\mathcal{G}\times\mathcal{H}}$$
$$\leq \left(\Psi_1 + \frac{T^{1-\varrho_1}}{\Gamma(2-\varrho_1)}\Psi_2 + \Psi_3 + \frac{T^{1-\varsigma_1}}{\Gamma(2-\varsigma_1)}\Psi_4\right)(\|u_1 - u_2\|_{\mathcal{G}} + \|v_1 - v_2\|_{\mathcal{H}}).$$

It follows that, in view of the condition (48), the operator Π is a contraction. Thus, by Theorem (see Theorem 1.2.2 [14]), the system (1) and (2) has a unique solution on $\mathcal{U}$. □

4. Examples

Example 1. *Consider the system of Caputo type FIDEs given by*

$$\begin{cases} {}^C\mathcal{D}^{\frac{68}{25}}u(\tau) = f(\tau, u(\tau), v(\tau), {}^C\mathcal{D}^{\frac{44}{25}}v(\tau), \mathcal{I}^{\frac{46}{25}}v(\tau)), \\ {}^C\mathcal{D}^{\frac{62}{25}}v(\tau) = g(\tau, u(\tau), {}^C\mathcal{D}^{\frac{73}{50}}u(\tau), \mathcal{I}^{\frac{39}{25}}u(\tau), v(\tau)), \end{cases} \quad (53)$$

subject to the boundary conditions

$$\begin{cases} u(0) = \psi_1(v), u'(0) = \epsilon_1 \int_0^{\nu_1} v'(\theta)d\theta, \; u(T) = \lambda_1 \int_0^{\delta_1} v(\theta)d\theta + \mu_1 \sum_{j=1}^{k-2} \varpi_j v(\vartheta_j), \\ v(0) = \psi_2(u), v'(0) = \epsilon_2 \int_0^{\nu_2} u'(\theta)d\theta, \; v(T) = \lambda_2 \int_0^{\delta_2} u(\theta)d\theta + \mu_2 \sum_{j=1}^{k-2} \omega_j u(\varphi_j). \end{cases} \quad (54)$$

Here, $\varrho = \frac{68}{25}, \varsigma = \frac{62}{25}, \varrho_1 = \frac{73}{50}, \varsigma_1 = \frac{44}{25}, \xi = \frac{46}{25}, \zeta = \frac{39}{25}, T = 1, \delta_1 = \frac{1}{8}, \delta_2 = \frac{37}{200}, \vartheta_1 = \frac{37}{250}, \vartheta_2 = \frac{79}{500}, \vartheta_3 = \frac{47}{250}, \vartheta_4 = \frac{11}{50}, \varphi_1 = \frac{113}{500}, \varphi_2 = \frac{59}{250}, \varphi_3 = \frac{6}{25}, \varphi_4 = \frac{49}{200}, \varpi_1 = \frac{1}{160}, \varpi_2 = \frac{58}{625}, \varpi_3 = \frac{29}{400}, \varpi_4 = \frac{21}{250}, \omega_1 = \frac{17}{200}, \omega_2 = \frac{12}{125}, \omega_3 = \frac{19}{250}, \omega_4 = \frac{7}{125}, \lambda_1 = \frac{1}{80}, \lambda_2 = \frac{7}{200}, \mu_1 = \frac{9}{400}, \mu_2 = \frac{23}{500}, \epsilon_1 = \frac{11}{400}, \epsilon_2 = \frac{19}{500}, \nu_1 = \frac{53}{200}, \nu_2 = \frac{133}{500}.$ We consider the functions,

$$|f(\tau, u_1, u_2, u_3, u_4)| \leq \frac{1}{20(\tau^2+1)} + \frac{1}{70(2+\tau)^2}\left(2u_2 + \frac{|u_1|}{1+|u_1|}\right) + \frac{\sin u_3}{700} + \frac{\arctan u_4}{140(3+\tau)},$$

$$|g(\tau, u_1, u_2, u_3, u_4)| \leq \frac{1}{(\tau^4+1)2} + \frac{1}{150(1+\tau^2)}\left(\frac{u_2}{3} + 3u_1\right) + \frac{\cos u_3}{800} + \frac{|u_4|}{400(1+|u_4|)},$$

$$|\psi_1(v)| \leq \frac{1}{110}\|v\|, \quad |\psi_2(u)| \leq \frac{1}{600}\|u\|.$$

Clearly

$$|f(\tau, u_1, u_2, u_3, u_4)| \leq \frac{1}{20} + \frac{1}{140}|u_1| + \frac{1}{70}|u_2| + \frac{1}{700}|u_3| + \frac{1}{420}|u_4|,$$

$$|g(\tau, u_1, u_2, u_3, u_4)| \leq \frac{1}{2} + \frac{1}{50}|u_1| + \frac{1}{450}|u_2| + \frac{1}{800}|u_3| + \frac{1}{400}|u_4|,$$

$$|\psi_1(v)| \leq \frac{1}{110}\|v\|, \quad |\psi_2(u)| \leq \frac{1}{600}\|u\|.$$

With the given data, we find that $r_0 = \frac{1}{20}, r_1 = \frac{1}{140}, r_2 = \frac{1}{70}, r_3 = \frac{1}{700}, r_4 = \frac{1}{420}, s_0 = \frac{1}{2}, s_1 = \frac{1}{50}, s_2 = \frac{1}{450}, s_3 = \frac{1}{800}, s_4 = \frac{1}{400}, \Delta_1 = 0.46845200402823617, \Delta_2 = 0.0007227881649342847, \Delta_3 = 0.0011251030301272463, \Delta_4 = 0.6151822290610394, \widehat{\Delta}_1 = 0.8713184743902467, \widehat{\Delta}_2 = 0.0014641295646385377, \widehat{\Delta}_3 = 0.00186307333192, \widehat{\Delta}_4 = 1.0704190784503973$, we find that $\widehat{\Phi} = \min\{\Phi_1, \Phi_2\} < 1$. Thus, the assumption of Theorem 1 holds and the problem (53) and (54) has at least one solution on $[0, 1]$.

Example 2. *We consider the functions*

$$|f(\tau, u_1, u_2, u_3, u_4)| \leq \frac{1}{9\sqrt{\tau^2+64}}\left(\frac{3}{\tau+1} + \cos(u_1+u_2) + \frac{|u_3|}{|u_3|+1} + \arctan u_4\right),$$

$$|g(\tau, u_1, u_2, u_3, u_4)| \leq \frac{1}{24\sqrt{36+\tau^2}}\left(\frac{\tau^2}{\tau+2} + \left(u_2 + \frac{|u_1|}{1+|u_1|}\right) + \sin u_3 + |u_4|\right),$$

$$|\psi_1(v)| \leq \frac{1}{110}\|v\|, \quad |\psi_2(u)| \leq \frac{1}{60}\|u\|.$$

Using the given data, it is found that $\mathcal{V}_1 = \frac{1}{72}, \mathcal{V}_2 = \frac{1}{144}, \mathcal{V}_1 = \frac{1}{110}, \mathcal{V}_2 = \frac{1}{60}$, $\Delta_1 = 0.46845200402823617, \Delta_2 = 0.0007227881649342847, \Delta_3 = 0.0011251030301272463, \Delta_4 = 0.6151822290610394, \widehat{\Delta}_1 = 0.8713184743902467, \widehat{\Delta}_2 = 0.0014641295646385377,$

$\hat{\Delta}_3 = 0.00186307333192$, $\hat{\Delta}_4 = 1.0704190784503973$, with $\Psi_1 + \frac{T^{1-\varrho_1}}{\Gamma(2-\varrho_1)}\Psi_2 \approx 0.0514018187$ 3251667, and $\Psi_3 + \frac{T^{1-\varsigma_1}}{\Gamma(2-\varsigma_1)}\Psi_4 \approx 0.05324949686716335$; hence, the Theorem 2 is satisfied, and here the problem (53)–(54) has a unique solution on $[0, 1]$.

5. A Variant of a Problem

Note that the boundary conditions (1) include the strips of different lengths when modifying the strips in boundary conditions to the same lengths (1); then, the problem reduces to the form

$$\begin{cases} u(0) = \psi_1(v), \ u'(0) = \epsilon_1 \int_0^v v'(\theta)d\theta, \ u''(0) = 0, \cdots, u^{n-2}(0) = 0, \\ u(T) = \lambda_1 \int_0^\delta v(\theta)d\theta + \mu_1 \sum_{j=1}^{k-2} \omega_j v(\vartheta_j), \\ v(0) = \psi_2(u), \ v'(0) = \epsilon_2 \int_0^v u'(\theta)d\theta, \ v''(0) = 0, \cdots, v^{n-2}(0) = 0, \\ v(T) = \lambda_2 \int_0^\delta u(\theta)d\theta + \mu_2 \sum_{j=1}^{k-2} \omega_j u(\vartheta_j). \end{cases} \quad (55)$$

Concerning the problem (1) with (55) instead of (2), we obtained the operator $\hat{\Pi}: \mathcal{G} \times \mathcal{H} \to \mathcal{G} \times \mathcal{H}$ defined by

$$\hat{\Pi}(u,v)(\tau) = (\hat{\Pi}_1(u,v)(\tau), \hat{\Pi}_2(u,v)(\tau)),$$

where

$$\begin{aligned}
\hat{\Pi}_1(u,v)(\tau) &= \frac{1}{\Gamma(\varrho)}\int_0^\tau (\tau-\theta)^{\varrho-1}\hat{\mathcal{Q}}_u(\theta)d\theta + \psi_1(v)[1+\kappa_1\Lambda_4(\tau)-\Lambda_3(\tau)] + \psi_2(u)[\kappa_2\Lambda_3(\tau)-\Lambda_4(\tau)] \\
&+ \frac{\Lambda_2(\tau)\epsilon_2}{\Gamma(\varrho-1)}\int_0^v\left(\int_0^\theta (\theta-\sigma)^{\varrho-2}\hat{\mathcal{Q}}_u(\sigma)d\sigma\right)d\theta + \frac{\Lambda_1(\tau)\epsilon_1}{\Gamma(\varsigma-1)}\int_0^v\left(\int_0^\theta (\theta-\sigma)^{\varsigma-2}\check{\mathcal{Q}}_v(\sigma)d\sigma\right)d\theta \\
&+ \Lambda_4(\tau)\left[\frac{\lambda_2}{\Gamma(\varrho)}\int_0^\delta\left(\int_0^\theta (\theta-\sigma)^{\varrho-1}\hat{\mathcal{Q}}_u(\sigma)d\sigma\right)d\theta + \mu_2\sum_{j=1}^{k-2}\frac{\omega_j}{\Gamma(\varrho)}\int_0^{\vartheta_j}(\vartheta_j-\theta)^{\varrho-1}\hat{\mathcal{Q}}_u(\theta)d\theta\right. \\
&\left. -\frac{1}{\Gamma(\varsigma)}\int_0^T (T-\theta)^{\varsigma-1}\check{\mathcal{Q}}_v(\theta)d\theta\right] + \Lambda_3(\tau)\left[\frac{\lambda_1}{\Gamma(\varsigma)}\int_0^\delta\left(\int_0^\theta (\theta-\sigma)^{\varsigma-1}\check{\mathcal{Q}}_v(\sigma)d\sigma\right)d\theta\right. \\
&\left. +\mu_1\sum_{j=1}^{k-2}\frac{\omega_j}{\Gamma(\varsigma)}\int_0^{\vartheta_j}(\vartheta_j-\theta)^{\varsigma-1}\check{\mathcal{Q}}_v(\theta)d\theta - \frac{1}{\Gamma(\varrho)}\int_0^T (T-\theta)^{\varrho-1}\hat{\mathcal{Q}}_u(\theta)d\theta\right],
\end{aligned} \quad (56)$$

and

$$\begin{aligned}
\hat{\Pi}_2(u,v)(\tau) &= \frac{1}{\Gamma(\varsigma)}\int_0^\tau (\tau-\theta)^{\varsigma-1}\check{\mathcal{Q}}_v(\theta)d\theta + \psi_2(u)[1+\kappa_2\Lambda_7(\tau)-\Lambda_8(\tau)] + \psi_1(v)[\kappa_1\Lambda_8(\tau)-\Lambda_7(\tau)] \\
&+ \frac{\Lambda_5(\tau)\epsilon_1}{\Gamma(\varsigma-1)}\int_0^v\left(\int_0^\theta (\theta-\sigma)^{\varsigma-2}\check{\mathcal{Q}}_v(\sigma)d\sigma\right)d\theta + \frac{\Lambda_6(\tau)\epsilon_2}{\Gamma(\varrho-1)}\int_0^v\left(\int_0^\theta (\theta-\sigma)^{\varrho-2}\hat{\mathcal{Q}}_u(\sigma)d\sigma\right)d\theta \\
&+ \Lambda_7(\tau)\left[\frac{\lambda_1}{\Gamma(\varsigma)}\int_0^\delta\left(\int_0^\theta (\theta-\sigma)^{\varsigma-1}\check{\mathcal{Q}}_v(\sigma)d\sigma\right)d\theta + \mu_1\sum_{j=1}^{k-2}\frac{\omega_j}{\Gamma(\varsigma)}\int_0^{\vartheta_j}(\vartheta_j-\theta)^{\varsigma-1}\check{\mathcal{Q}}_v(\theta)d\theta\right. \\
&\left. -\frac{1}{\Gamma(\varrho)}\int_0^T (T-\theta)^{\varrho-1}\hat{\mathcal{Q}}_u(\theta)d\theta\right] + \Lambda_8(\tau)\left[\frac{\lambda_2}{\Gamma(\varrho)}\int_0^\delta\left(\int_0^\theta (\theta-\sigma)^{\varrho-1}\hat{\mathcal{Q}}_u(\sigma)d\sigma\right)d\theta\right. \\
&\left. +\mu_2\sum_{j=1}^{k-2}\frac{\omega_j}{\Gamma(\varrho)}\int_0^{\vartheta_j}(\vartheta_j-\theta)^{\varrho-1}\hat{\mathcal{Q}}_u(\theta)d\theta - \frac{1}{\Gamma(\varsigma)}\int_0^T (T-\theta)^{\varsigma-1}\check{\mathcal{Q}}_v(\theta)d\theta\right].
\end{aligned} \quad (57)$$

where

$$\begin{aligned}
\hat{\mathcal{Q}}_u(\tau) &= f(\tau, u(\tau), v(\tau), {}^C\mathcal{D}^{\varsigma_1}v(\tau), \mathcal{I}^\zeta v(\tau)), \ \tau \in \mathcal{U}, \\
\check{\mathcal{Q}}_v(\tau) &= g(\tau, u(\tau), {}^C\mathcal{D}^{\varrho_1}u(\tau), \mathcal{I}^\zeta u(\tau), v(\tau)), \ \tau \in \mathcal{U}.
\end{aligned}$$

and

$$\xi_1 = \frac{\lambda_1 \delta^2}{2} + \mu_1 \sum_{j=1}^{k-2} \omega_j \vartheta_j, \quad \xi_2 = \frac{\lambda_1 \delta^n}{n} + \mu_1 \sum_{j=1}^{k-2} \omega_j \vartheta_j^{n-1}, \quad \xi_3 = \frac{\lambda_2 \delta^2}{2} + \mu_2 \sum_{j=1}^{k-2} \omega_j \vartheta_j, \quad \xi_4 = \frac{\lambda_2 \delta^n}{n} + \mu_2 \sum_{j=1}^{k-2} \omega_j \vartheta_j^{n-1},$$

$$\hat{\gamma}_1 = 1 - v^2 \epsilon_1 \epsilon_2, \quad \hat{\gamma}_2 = T^2 - \xi_1 \xi_3, \quad \hat{\gamma}_3 = T^n - \xi_1 \xi_4, \quad \hat{\gamma}_4 = T^{n-1} \xi_3 - \xi_4 T, \quad \hat{\gamma}_5 = \xi_1 T^{n-1} - T \xi_2, \quad \hat{\gamma}_6 = T^n - \xi_2 \xi_3,$$

$$v_1 = \hat{\gamma}_2 v^n \epsilon_1 \epsilon_2 + \hat{\gamma}_1 \hat{\gamma}_3, \quad v_2 = \hat{\gamma}_2 v^{n-1} \epsilon_2 + \hat{\gamma}_1 \hat{\gamma}_4, \quad v_3 = \hat{\gamma}_2 v^{n-1} \epsilon_1 + \hat{\gamma}_1 \hat{\gamma}_5, \quad v_4 = \hat{\gamma}_2 v^n \epsilon_1 \epsilon_2 + \hat{\gamma}_1 \hat{\gamma}_6, \quad v = v_2 v_3 - v_1 v_4 \neq 0,$$

$$\eta_1 = 1 + \frac{(v^n \epsilon_2 \beta_1 - v^{n-1} \beta_5) \epsilon_1}{v}, \quad \eta_2 = \epsilon_1 v + \frac{(v^n \epsilon_2 \beta_2 - v^{n-1} \beta_6) \epsilon_1}{v}, \quad \eta_3 = \frac{(v^n \epsilon_2 \beta_3 - v^{n-1} \beta_7) \epsilon_1}{v},$$

$$\eta_4 = \frac{(v^n \epsilon_2 \beta_4 - v^{n-1} \beta_8) \epsilon_1}{v}, \quad \eta_5 = \epsilon_2 v + \frac{(v^{n-1} \beta_1 - \epsilon_1 v^n \beta_5) \epsilon_2}{v}, \quad \eta_6 = 1 + \frac{(v^{n-1} \beta_2 - \epsilon_1 v^n \beta_6) \epsilon_2}{v},$$

$$\eta_7 = \frac{(v^{n-1} \beta_3 - \epsilon_1 v^n \beta_7) \epsilon_2}{v}, \quad \eta_8 = \frac{(v^{n-1} \beta_4 - \epsilon_1 v^n \beta_8) \epsilon_2}{v},$$

$$\beta_1 = \hat{\gamma}_2 (v_4 - v_3 \epsilon_2 v), \quad \beta_2 = (v_4 \epsilon_1 v - v_3) \hat{\gamma}_2, \quad \beta_3 = (v_3 \xi_3 - v_4 T) \hat{\gamma}_1, \quad \beta_4 = \hat{\gamma}_1 (v_3 T - v_4 \xi_1),$$

$$\beta_5 = (v_2 - v_1 \epsilon_2 v) \hat{\gamma}_2, \quad \beta_6 = (v_2 \epsilon_1 v - v_1) \hat{\gamma}_2, \quad \beta_7 = (v_1 \xi_3 - v_2 T) \hat{\gamma}_1, \quad \beta_8 = \hat{\gamma}_1 (v_1 T - v_2 \xi_1),$$

$$\kappa_1 = \lambda_2 \delta + \mu_2 \sum_{j=1}^{k-2} \omega_j, \quad \kappa_2 = \lambda_1 \delta + \mu_1 \sum_{j=1}^{k-2} \omega_j,$$

$$\Lambda_1(\tau) = \frac{\tau \eta_1}{\hat{\gamma}_1} + \frac{\tau^{n-1} \beta_1}{v}, \quad \Lambda_2(\tau) = \frac{\tau \eta_2}{\hat{\gamma}_1} + \frac{\tau^{n-1} \beta_2}{v}, \quad \Lambda_3(\tau) = \frac{\tau \eta_3}{\hat{\gamma}_1} + \frac{\tau^{n-1} \beta_3}{v}, \quad \Lambda_4(\tau) = \frac{\tau \eta_4}{\hat{\gamma}_1} + \frac{\tau^{n-1} \beta_4}{v},$$

$$\Lambda_5(\tau) = \frac{\tau \eta_5}{\hat{\gamma}_1} - \frac{\tau^{n-1} \beta_5}{v}, \quad \Lambda_6(\tau) = \frac{\tau \eta_6}{\hat{\gamma}_1} - \frac{\tau^{n-1} \beta_6}{v}, \quad \Lambda_7(\tau) = \frac{\tau \eta_7}{\hat{\gamma}_1} - \frac{\tau^{n-1} \beta_7}{v}, \quad \Lambda_8(\tau) = \frac{\tau \eta_8}{\hat{\gamma}_1} - \frac{\tau^{n-1} \beta_8}{v}.$$

6. Discussion

For Caputo form FIDEs, we examined the consequences of existence and uniqueness supplemented by non-local multi-point and integral boundary conditions by Leray–Schauder's alternative and Banach's fixed-point theorem. By fixing the parameters (ϵ_1, ϵ_2, λ_1, λ_2, μ_1, μ_2) involved in the problem (1) and (2), our results correspond to certain specific problems. Suppose that taking $\lambda_1 = \lambda_2 = \mu_1 = \mu_2 = 0$ in the results provided, we are given the problems (1) with the form

$$\begin{cases} u(0) = \psi_1(v), \ u'(0) = \epsilon_1 \int_0^{v_1} v'(\theta) d\theta, \ u''(0) = 0, \cdots, u^{n-2}(0) = 0, \ u(T) = 0, \\ v(0) = \psi_2(u), \ v'(0) = \epsilon_2 \int_0^{v_2} u'(\theta) d\theta, \ v''(0) = 0, \cdots, v^{n-2}(0) = 0, \ v(T) = 0, \end{cases}$$

while the results are

$$\begin{cases} u(0) = \psi_1(v), \ u'(0) = 0, \cdots, u^{n-2}(0) = 0, \ u(T) = \lambda_1 \int_0^{\delta_1} v(\theta) d\theta + \mu_1 \sum_{j=1}^{k-2} \omega_j v(\vartheta_j), \\ v(0) = \psi_2(u), \ v'(0) = 0, \cdots, v^{n-2}(0) = 0 \ v(T) = \lambda_2 \int_0^{\delta_2} u(\theta) d\theta + \mu_2 \sum_{j=1}^{k-2} \omega_j u(\varphi_j), \end{cases}$$

followed by $\epsilon_1 = \epsilon_2 = 0$. Using the methods used in the previous section, we can solve the above-related problems (1) and (2).

Author Contributions: Conceptualization, M.S., J.A. and M.I.A.; methodology and validation, M.S., J.A. and M.I.A.; investigation and formal analysis, C.T., J.A. and W.S.; resources, M.S.; data curation, M.I.A.; writing—original draft preparation, M.S. and J.A.; writing—review and editing, C.T. and W.S.; funding acquisition, C.T. and J.A. All authors have read and agreed to the published version of the manuscript.

Funding: This work was financially supported by the Faculty of Science, Burapha University, Thailand (Grant no. SC06/2564).

Institutional Review Board Statement: Not applicable.

Informed Consent Statement: Not applicable.

Data Availability Statement: Not applicable.

Acknowledgments: Alzabut is thankful and grateful to Prince Sultan University and OSTİM Technical University for their endless support. C. Thaiprayoon would like to gratefully acknowledge Burapha University and the Center of Excellence in Mathematics (CEM), CHE, Sri Ayutthaya Rd., Bangkok, 10400, Thailand, for supporting this research.

Conflicts of Interest: The authors have stated that they have no competing interest.

References

1. Faieghi, M.; Kuntanapreeda, S.; Delavari, H.; Baleanu, D. LMI-based stabilization of a class of fractional-order chaotic systems. *Nonlinear Dyn.* **2013**, *72*, 301–309. [CrossRef]
2. Ge, Z.M.; Ou, C.Y. Chaos synchronization of fractional order modified Duffing systems with parameters excited by a chaotic signal. *Chaos Solitons Fractals* **2008**, *35*, 705–717. [CrossRef]
3. Sokolov, I.M.; Klafter, J.; Blumen, A. Fractional kinetics. *Phys. Today* **2002**, *55*, 48–54. [CrossRef]
4. Javidi, M.; Ahmad, B. Dynamic analysis of time fractional order phytoplankton–toxic phytoplankton–zooplankton system. *Ecol. Model.* **2015**, *318*, 8–18. [CrossRef]
5. Jiang, C.; Zada, A.; Şenel, M.T.; Li, T. Synchronization of bidirectional N-coupled fractional-order chaotic systems with ring connection based on antisymmetric structure. *Adv. Differ. Equ.* **2019**, *2019*, 456. [CrossRef]
6. Wang, J.; Zada, A.; Waheed, H. Stability analysis of a coupled system of nonlinear implicit fractional anti-periodic boundary value problem. *Math. Methods Appl. Sci.* **2019**, *42*, 6706–6732. [CrossRef]
7. Ali, Z.; Zada, A.; Shah, K. On Ulam's stability for a coupled systems of nonlinear implicit fractional differential equations. *Bull. Malays. Math. Sci. Soc.* **2019**, *42*, 2681–2699. [CrossRef]
8. Shah, K.; Khan, R.A.; Baleanu, D. Study of implicit type coupled system of non-integer order differential equations with antiperiodic boundary conditions. *Math. Methods Appl. Sci.* **2019**, *42*, 2033–2042.
9. Ali, A.; Shah, K.; Jarad, F.; Gupta, V.; Abdeljawad, T. Existence and stability analysis to a coupled system of implicit type impulsive boundary value problems of fractional-order differential equations. *Adv. Differ. Equ.* **2019**, *2019*, 101. [CrossRef]
10. Subramanian, M.; Kumar, A.R.V.; Gopal, T.N. A writ large analysis of complex order coupled differential equations in the ourse of coupled non-local multi-point boundary conditions. *Adv. Stud. Contemp. Math.* **2019**, *29*, 505–520.
11. Muthaiah, S.; Baleanu, D.; Thangaraj, N.G. Existence and Hyers-Ulam type stability results for nonlinear coupled system of Caputo-Hadamard type fractional differential equations. *AIMS Math.* **2020**, *6*, 168. [CrossRef]
12. Subramanian, M.; Zada, A. Existence and uniqueness of solutions for coupled systems of Liouville-Caputo type fractional integrodifferential equations with Erdélyi-Kober integral conditions. *Int. J. Nonlinear Sci. Numer. Simul.* **2020**, *22*, 543–557. [CrossRef]
13. Matar, M.M.; Amra, I.A.; Alzabut, J. Existence of solutions for tripled system of fractional differential equations involving cyclic permutation boundary conditions. *Bound. Value Probl.* **2020**, *2020*, 140. [CrossRef]
14. Smart, D.R. *Fixed Point Theorems*; Cambridge University Press: London, UK, 1980; Volume 66.
15. Yong, Z.; Jinrong, W.; Lu, Z. *Basic Theory of Fractional Differential Equations*; World Scientific: Singapore, 2016.
16. Granas, A.; Dugundji, J. *Fixed Point Theory*; Springer: Berlin/Heidelberg, Germany, 2013.
17. Kilbas, A.A.A.; Srivastava, H.M.; Trujillo, J.J. *Theory and Applications of Fractional Differential Equations*, Elsevier: Amsterdam, The Netherlands, 2006; Volume 204.
18. Machado, J.T.; Kiryakova, V.; Mainardi, F. Recent history of fractional calculus. *Commun. Nonlinear Sci. Numer. Simul.* **2011**, *16*, 1140–1153. [CrossRef]
19. Valério, D.; Machado, J.T.; Kiryakova, V. Some pioneers of the applications of fractional calculus. *Fract. Calc. Appl. Anal.* **2014**, *17*, 552–578. [CrossRef]
20. Subramanian, M.; Kumar, A.R.V.; Gopal, T.N. Analysis of fractional boundary value problem with non-local integral strip boundary conditions. *Nonlinear Stud.* **2019**, *26*, 445–454.
21. Subramanian, M.; Kumar, A.R.V.; Gopal, T.N. Analysis of fractional boundary value problem with non local flux multi-point conditions on a Caputo fractional differential equation. *Mathematica* **2019**, *64*, 511–527. [CrossRef]
22. Muthaiah, S.; Murugesan, M.; Thangaraj, N.G. Fractional Differential Equations Involving Hadamard Fractional Derivatives with Nonlocal Multi-point Boundary Conditions. *Discontinuity Nonlinearity Complex.* **2020**, *9*, 421–431.
23. Muthaiah, S.; Muthu, S.; Murugesan, M.; Thangaraj, N.G. On generalized Caputo fractional differential equations and inclusions with non-local generalized fractional integral boundary conditions. *Malaya J. Mat.* **2020**, *8*, 1099–1109.
24. Muthaiah, S.; Murugesan, M.; Thangaraj, N.G. Existence of Solutions for Nonlocal Boundary Value Problem of Hadamard Fractional Differential Equations. *Adv. Theory Nonlinear Anal. Its Appl.* **2020**, *3*, 162–173. [CrossRef]
25. Ali, Z.; Zada, A.; Shah, K. Existence and stability analysis of three point boundary value problem. *Int. J. Appl. Comput. Math.* **2017**, *3*, 651–664. [CrossRef]
26. Zada, A.; Rizwan, R.; Xu, J.; Fu, Z. On implicit impulsive Langevin equation involving mixed order derivatives. *Adv. Differ. Equ.* **2019**, *2019*, 489. [CrossRef]

27. Shah, K.; Ali, A.; Bushnaq, S. Hyers-Ulam stability analysis to implicit Cauchy problem of fractional differential equations with impulsive conditions. *Math. Methods Appl. Sci.* **2018**, *41*, 8329–8345. [CrossRef]
28. Subramanian, M.; Baleanu, D. Stability and Existence Analysis to a Coupled System of Caputo Type Fractional Differential Equations with Erdelyi-Kober Integral Boundary Conditions. *Appl. Math.* **2020**, *14*, 415–424.
29. Subramanian, M.; Kumar, A.R.V.; Gopal, T.N. A strategic view on the consequences of classical integral sub-strips and coupled nonlocal multi-point boundary conditions on a combined Caputo fractional differential equation. *Proc. Jangjeon Math. Soc.* **2019**, *22*, 437–453.
30. Muthaiah, S.; Baleanu, D. Existence of Solutions for Nonlinear Fractional Differential Equations and Inclusions Depending on Lower-Order Fractional Derivatives. *Axioms* **2020**, *9*, 44. [CrossRef]
31. Ahmad, B.; Nieto, J.J.; Alsaedi, A.; Aqlan, M.H. A coupled system of Caputo-type sequential fractional differential equations with coupled (periodic/anti-periodic type) boundary conditions. *Mediterr. J. Math.* **2017**, *14*, 227. [CrossRef]
32. Shah, K.; Wang, J.; Khalil, H.; Khan, R.A. Existence and numerical solutions of a coupled system of integral BVP for fractional differential equations. *Adv. Differ. Equ.* **2018**, *2018*, 149. [CrossRef]
33. Li, Y.; Shah, K.; Khan, R.A. Iterative technique for coupled integral boundary value problem of non-integer order differential equations. *Adv. Differ. Equ.* **2017**, *2017*, 251. [CrossRef]
34. Shah, K.; Khalil, H.; Khan, R.A. Upper and lower solutions to a coupled system of nonlinear fractional differential equations. *Prog. Fract. Differ. Appl.* **2015**, *1*, 010102. [CrossRef]
35. Subramanian, M.; Manigandan, M.; Tunç, C.; Gopal, T.; Alzabut, J. On system of nonlinear coupled differential equations and inclusions involving Caputo-type sequential derivatives of fractional order. *J. Taibah Univ. Sci.* **2022**, *16*, 1–23. [CrossRef]
36. Etemad, S.; Tellab, B.; Alzabut, J.; Rezapour, S.; Abbas, M.I. Approximate solutions and Hyers–Ulam stability for a system of the coupled fractional thermostat control model via the generalized differential transform. *Adv. Differ. Equ.* **2021**, *2021*, 428. [CrossRef]
37. Baghani, H.; Alzabut, J.; Farokhi-Ostad, J.; Nieto, J.J. Existence and uniqueness of solutions for a coupled system of sequential fractional differential equations with initial conditions. *J. Pseudo-Differ. Oper. Appl.* **2020**, *11*, 1731–1741. [CrossRef]
38. Ahmad, B.; Ntouyas, S.K.; Alsaedi, A. On solvability of a coupled system of fractional differential equations supplemented with a new kind of flux type integral boundary conditions. *J. Comput. Anal. Appl.* **2018**, *24*, 1304–1312.
39. Ahmad, B.; Ntouyas, S.K.; Alsaedi, A. Fractional differential equations with integral and ordinary-fractional flux boundary conditions. *J. Comput. Anal. Appl.* **2016**, *52*, 52–61.
40. Ahmad, B.; Nieto, J.J. Existence results for a coupled system of nonlinear fractional differential equations with three-point boundary conditions. *Comput. Math. Appl.* **2009**, *58*, 1838–1843. [CrossRef]
41. Agarwal, R.P.; Ahmad, B.; Garout, D.; Alsaedi, A. Existence results for coupled nonlinear fractional differential equations equipped with nonlocal coupled flux and multi-point boundary conditions. *Chaos Solitons Fractals* **2017**, *102*, 149–161. [CrossRef]
42. Subramanian, M.; Kumar, A.R.V.; Gopal, T.N. Influence of coupled nonlocal slit-strip conditions involving Caputo derivative in fractional boundary value problem. *Discontinuity Nonlinearity Complex.* **2019**, *8*, 429–445.

MDPI
St. Alban-Anlage 66
4052 Basel
Switzerland
Tel. +41 61 683 77 34
Fax +41 61 302 89 18
www.mdpi.com

Mathematics Editorial Office
E-mail: mathematics@mdpi.com
www.mdpi.com/journal/mathematics

www.ingramcontent.com/pod-product-compliance
Lightning Source LLC
LaVergne TN
LVHW070543100526
838202LV00012B/365